W9-BRV-962

ALSO BY SCOTT MILLER

*The President and the Assassin: McKinley, Terror, and
Empire at the Dawn of the American Century*

An American Spymaster and

the German Resistance in WWII

AGENT 110

SCOTT MILLER

SIMON & SCHUSTER

NEW YORK   LONDON   TORONTO   SYDNEY   NEW DELHI

Simon & Schuster
1230 Avenue of the Americas
New York, NY 10020

First Simon & Schuster hardcover edition March 2017

SIMON & SCHUSTER and colophon are registered trademarks of Simon & Schuster, Inc.

For information about special discounts for bulk purchases, please contact
Simon & Schuster Special Sales at 1-866-506-1949 or business@simonandschuster.com.

The Simon & Schuster Speakers Bureau can bring authors to your live event.
For more information or to book an event, contact the
Simon & Schuster Speakers Bureau at 1-866-248-3049
or visit our website at www.simonspeakers.com.

Interior design by Ruth Lee-Mui

Manufactured in the United States of America

10 9 8 7 6 5 4 3 2 1

Library of Congress Cataloging-in-Publication Data

Names: Miller, Scott, 1960– author.
Title: Agent 110 : Allen Dulles, American spymaster, and the
German underground in World War II / Scott Miller.
Other titles: Agent One Ten
Description: First Simon & Schuster hardcover edition. | New York : Simon
    & Schuster, 2017. | "Simon & Schuster nonfiction original hardcover"—
    Title page verso. | Includes bibliographical references and index.
Identifiers: LCCN 2016025790| ISBN 9781451693386 (hardcover : alkaline paper) |
    ISBN 9781451693393 (paperback : alkaline paper) | ISBN 9781451693409 (ebook)
Subjects: LCSH: Dulles, Allen, 1893–1969. | World War, 1939–1945—Secret service—United
    States. | World War, 1939–1945—Secret service—Switzerland. | Espionage, American—
    Germany—History—20th century. | Anti-Nazi movement—Germany. | Spies—United
    States—Biography. | Intelligence officers—United States—Biography. | United States. Office
    of Strategic Services—Biography. | Germany—Politics and government—1933–1945.
Classification: LCC D810.S8 D835 2017 | DDC 940.54/5673092—dc23
LC record available at https://lccn.loc.gov/2016025790

ISBN 978-1-4516-9338-6
ISBN 978-1-4516-9340-9 (ebook)

The OSS insignia is a registered trademark of The OSS Society, Inc., and is used with its permission.

To Karen

Contents

Preface

In the wee hours of July 21, 1944, Colonel Claus von Stauffenberg, a decorated veteran of the German army's North African campaigns with the looks of a matinée idol, was led out of army headquarters in Berlin. He and three other condemned officers were told to wait in a narrow courtyard illuminated by truck headlights as a firing squad was hastily assembled. His sleeve soaked with blood from a gunfight only minutes earlier, Stauffenberg watched as the first three men were shot and their bodies carried away. Positioning himself to face the riflemen, Stauffenberg shouted a final act of defiance, "Long live our sacred Germany!"

The executions were the start of what would become a massive bloodletting throughout Germany, Adolf Hitler's retribution for an attempt on his life in East Prussia only twelve hours earlier. That attack at the "Wolf's Lair," Hitler's heavily fortified command post, had initially seemed to succeed, as a powerful bomb had detonated only feet from the Führer as he reviewed maps and battle plans with trusted advisers. Several had been killed. Believing that Hitler was among them, Stauffenberg and scores of others had launched a bold coup attempt that afternoon that had virtually shut down Berlin. Yet Hitler, incredibly, had emerged badly shaken but very much alive.

I first learned of the details of that night when working in Frankfurt as a correspondent for *The Wall Street Journal*. On a visit to Berlin, a friend pointed out to me the scene of the executions at the old army headquarters.

The event seized my imagination, starting with the bravery of the men who had launched the plot. The odds of succeeding were slim, and the masterminds behind what is celebrated as Operation Valkyrie knew the grisly consequences of failure. Just as mesmerizing for me was how close they came to pulling it off. Were it not for small twists of fate, the conspirators would have changed the course of history.

Years later, I came across the seemingly unrelated figure of Allen Dulles. He is most famous for his service as the head of the US Central Intelligence Agency during the height of the Cold War. The failed Bay of Pigs invasion in Cuba and numerous US-sponsored coup attempts, from Iran to Indonesia, are part of his legacy from that era. Less known is Dulles's role during World War II in Switzerland, where he set up a station for the CIA's predecessor, the Office of Strategic Services (OSS).

Assigned the code number 110, Dulles made the station arguably the most valuable of America's intelligence-gathering outposts. He and his men organized commando raids, cultivated spies in the heart of Hitler's government, and rescued informants from the Gestapo. Dulles reveled in such operations and retold his exploits for years in books such as *Great True Spy Stories*. In the words of a British intelligence officer, Kenneth Strong, Dulles was "the last great Romantic of Intelligence," a man whose stock-in-trade consisted of "secrets and mysteries."

Running a spy ring, Dulles was party to numerous intriguing adventures, yet from my perspective, this didn't necessarily provide a cohesive story line. For some time I wrestled with finding a common thread that would tie his work together and add a larger element to the narrative. With the help of my editor, Alice Mayhew, I unearthed the story that became this book—that of the German resistance leaders and the American spy who worked with them.

Men and women in Germany had been trying to depose Hitler for years before Dulles arrived in Bern, Switzerland, in late 1942. They were a diverse bunch, some working alone, others in groups, each driven by his or her own reasons. Such was their determination and cunning that on several occasions Hitler had barely escaped plots against him. Dulles, a former diplomat and lawyer with numerous German business contacts, offered a fresh resource.

As my research progressed, I discovered layers to the basic narrative. The story of Dulles and the resistance foreshadowed the Cold War. Almost as important as unseating Hitler was the concern over the nature of the regime that would replace him. Would Germany align itself with the West, or would it fall into the orbit of the Soviet Union? This was a question that greatly troubled Dulles, and it informed much of his work. He once described the conspirators as "realistic enough to appreciate that the Germany which would survive Hitler would not be a military or a political power, but under the control of the victors. But which of the victors?"

As the war entered its final phase, and relations between the United States and the Soviet Union were already strained, a covert operation by Dulles to secure the surrender of all German forces in Italy precipitated the two powers' most open disagreement to that point. The Soviets perceived secret talks with SS general Karl Wolff as a trick to exclude them from the fruits of victory. Stalin reacted with venom. In the days before President Roosevelt died on April 12, 1945, the two Allied leaders exchanged a series of bitter messages over Dulles's negotiations that portended deeper troubles in the future.

Most important for me was the narrative and the characters that comprised it. Though the vast majority of those who plotted against Hitler did not survive, the ones who did left thoughtful records that allowed me to flesh out their personal stories. The German double agent Hans Bernd Gisevius, who became Dulles's main contact with one branch of the underground, displayed an arrogance that masked private worries about what he would accomplish in life. The well-born American Mary Bancroft, who worked for Dulles and had an affair with him, put great store in her intuition and the interesting people she encountered through his assignments. The clever Fritz Kolbe had no training in espionage, yet he managed to outwit Germany's most sophisticated security operatives and would grow ever more ambitious.

As with any work of nonfiction, deciding what to leave out and what to include was difficult. This story is not intended to be an exhaustive account of the years Dulles spent in Switzerland, or of every aspect of the German resistance. Ultimately, this book is about the plight of people caught up in extraordinary times. Many could simply have chosen to play it safe and sit out the war as comfortably as possible. Yet driven by moral outrage and, frankly, by thrill as well, they rose to challenge one of the most feared governments of the twentieth century.

SCOTT MILLER
Seattle

Time Line

APRIL 7, 1893—Allen Welsh Dulles is born in Watertown, New York.

JUNE 16, 1914—Dulles graduates from Princeton University.

SEPTEMBER 22, 1926—Dulles resigns from the US Foreign Service and soon joins the law firm Sullivan & Cromwell.

DECEMBER 7, 1941—Japan attacks Pearl Harbor in Honolulu, Hawaii.

DECEMBER 11, 1941—Germany declares war on the United States.

JUNE 13, 1942—President Franklin Roosevelt establishes the Office of Strategic Services (OSS).

NOVEMBER 2, 1942—Dulles leaves New York for his OSS assignment in Switzerland.

DECEMBER 1942—Dulles meets Mary Bancroft, an American who would help with intelligence work and with whom he would begin an affair.

JANUARY 1943—Dulles meets the Abwehr agent Hans Bernd Gisevius.

JANUARY 14–24, 1943—Prime Minister Winston Churchill and President Roosevelt meet in Casablanca, Morocco. Roosevelt says Germany must surrender unconditionally.

AUGUST 19, 1943—Dulles meets Fritz Kolbe. Code-named "George Wood," Kolbe would become one of the best human sources of information that the United States had about Nazi Germany.

FEBRUARY 4–11, 1944—Roosevelt, Churchill, and Joseph Stalin meet at Yalta, in the Crimea.

JULY 20, 1944—Colonel Claus von Stauffenberg leads a failed coup attempt against Adolf Hitler. Gisevius goes into hiding.

MARCH 8, 1945—Dulles meets SS general Karl Wolff in Zurich. Operation Sunrise talks begin.

APRIL 12, 1945—Roosevelt dies in Warm Springs, Georgia.

APRIL 29, 1945—Two German officers, part of Operation Sunrise, sign documents surrendering German troops in Italy.

APRIL 30, 1945—Hitler commits suicide in the Führerbunker in Berlin.

MAY 2, 1945—German forces in Italy surrender as agreed under Operation Sunrise.

MAY 7, 1945—German officers sign an unconditional surrender document in Reims, France, ending World War II in Europe.

SEPTEMBER 20, 1945—President Harry Truman signs an executive order disbanding the OSS.

DECEMBER 1945—Dulles formally leaves the OSS and returns to the United States.

FEBRUARY 1953—Dulles becomes director of the Central Intelligence Agency.

JANUARY 28, 1969—Dulles dies.

Principal Characters

AIREY, TERENCE—British army major general who met with Dulles on Operation Sunrise.

ALEXANDER, HAROLD—British field marshal, commander of Allied forces in the Mediterranean.

BANCROFT, MARY—American journalist who helped Dulles with his OSS work in Switzerland.

BECK, LUDWIG—German general and chief of the general staff. Resigned in 1938. Leader in the resistance thereafter.

BLUM, PAUL—OSS officer who joined Dulles in Bern in 1944.

BRUCE, DAVID—Head of the OSS's London station.

CANARIS, WILHELM—Chief of the Abwehr, the German military intelligence service. Protected and supported resistance leaders opposed to Hitler.

CIANO, GALEAZZO—Italian minister of foreign affairs, 1936–1943.

DANSEY, CLAUDE—Deputy head of the British Secret Intelligence Service (MI6) who despised Dulles and his operation in Switzerland.

DOLLMANN, EUGEN—SS colonel. Worked with Dulles on Operation Sunrise.

DONOVAN, WILLIAM—Head of the American spy service, the Office of Strategic Services.

DULLES, ALLEN—OSS station chief, Bern, Switzerland, 1942–1945. Code number 110.

DULLES, JOHN FOSTER—Older brother of Allen Dulles.

GISEVIUS, HANS BERND—Member of the Abwehr who opposed Hitler and worked with Dulles.

GOEBBELS, JOSEPH—Reichsminister of propaganda, 1933–1945.

GOERDELER, CARL FRIEDRICH—Member of the resistance; former mayor of Leipzig.

HARRIMAN, W. AVERELL—American ambassador to the Soviet Union.

HAUSMANN, MAX—Head of a private school in Switzerland who helped connect Dulles with SS officers during Operation Sunrise.

HIMMLER, HEINRICH—Reichsführer of the SS. Responsible for German security services and police forces, including the Gestapo.

HULL, CORDELL—US secretary of state, 1933–1944.

KALTENBRUNNER, ERNST—SS general and head of the Reich Main Security Office (RSHA), which incorporated numerous police and security services, such as the Gestapo and the Sicherheitsdienst (SD), the intelligence agency of the SS.

KENNAN, GEORGE F.—American diplomat and, late in the war, deputy head of mission, Moscow.

KEITEL, WILHELM—German field marshal who opposed Operation Sunrise.

KOLBE, FRITZ—Member of the German Foreign Ministry who supplied Dulles with secret Nazi documents. Code-named "George Wood."

LANGBEHN, CARL—Berlin attorney who opposed the Nazis. Arranged a meeting between Himmler and Popitz to discuss a coup.

LEMNITZER, LYMAN—US army general. Worked with Dulles on Operation Sunrise negotiation.

MAYER, GERALD—US Office of War Information officer. Helped Dulles get set up in Bern.

MENZIES, STEWART—Chief of MI6, 1939–1952.

MOLOTOV, VYACHESLAV—Soviet minister for foreign affairs, 1939–1949.

MOLTKE, HELMUTH JAMES GRAF VON—German aristocrat who worked in the Abwehr and helped found the Kreisau Circle resistance group.

MUSSOLINI, EDDA—Daughter of Italian prime minister Benito Mussolini and wife of Italian foreign minister (1936–1943) Galeazzo Ciano.

OSTER, HANS—German army officer who joined the Abwehr. A principal figure in plots to depose or murder Hitler.

PARILLI, LUIGI—Italian businessman who had connections with the SS.

PARRI, FERRUCCIO—Italian resistance fighter. Prime minister, 1945.

PHILBY, H. A. R. ("KIM")—MI6 agent who spied for the Soviets.

POPITZ, JOHANNES—German Finance Ministry official who met with Himmler in 1943 to discuss a coup.

RIBBENTROP, JOACHIM VON—Reichsminister for foreign affairs, 1938–1945.

SCHELLENBERG, WALTER—SS general in charge of foreign intelligence. Close confidant of Himmler.

SCHULTE, EDUARD—German industrialist who reported Nazi plans for mass murder of Jews. An important source for Dulles.

SCHULZE-GAEVERNITZ, GERO VON—German-American businessman living in Switzerland who worked with Dulles and the OSS in Bern.

STAUFFENBERG, CLAUS VON—German army officer who led the Valkyrie plot to kill Hitler on July 20, 1944.

TRESCKOW, HENNING VON—German army general who plotted to kill Hitler in March 1943. Also joined the July 20, 1944, plot to assassinate the Führer.

TROTT ZU SOLZ, ADAM VON—German diplomat and an important figure in the Kreisau Circle resistance group.

WAIBEL, MAX—Swiss intelligence officer who worked with Dulles.

WOLFF, KARL—SS general and commander of SS forces in Italy who contacted Dulles about surrendering German forces in the country.

ZIMMER, GUIDO—SS captain who participated in the first meetings about Operation Sunrise.

AGENT
110

CHAPTER

1

Portal on the Reich

At movie houses across America in 1942, newsreels depicted maps of Europe that showed territory occupied by Germany and its allies. Stretching across the screen, from the English Channel to the Soviet Union, the Nazi reach and terror seemed unstoppable. One small pocket, though, was carefully illustrated to show an area that did not belong to the Germans. Pointing through the projector's flickering light, parents might have noted to their children that the missing piece of the Third Reich was Switzerland, that country of soaring peaks, fields of cows, and alpine meadows, just as they may have seen in Shirley Temple's 1937 movie *Heidi*.

What few American parents knew was that Switzerland was home to a thriving community of spies. Secret agents—German, Hungarian, Japanese, British, American, Italian, Chinese, Polish, and Soviet—had been drawn to the country for years for its long-standing policy of neutrality and its geographic position at the heart of Europe. By day, secret agents plotted one another's political destruction. By night, at the Hotel Bellevue Palace, they laughed and drank at tables within easy earshot of each other. At the golf course, intelligence agents politely allowed their faster counterparts from enemy nations to play through. At fragrant bakeries, they patiently stood in the same lines for the morning's croissants.

Where so many spies congregated, so did their camp followers, scoundrels hoping to make a quick franc peddling information of suspect quality, resistance fighters, and women willing to trade their bodies to advance their cause. Everyone, or so it seemed, was a double agent trying to keep all the stories straight.

On a chilly Sunday in January 1943, an American with the physique of a lifelong tennis player strode through the quiet streets of the nation's financial capital, Zurich. Allen Dulles, a portrait of confidence, had been in Switzerland only a couple of months in the employ of the US government. To anyone who would ask, he would say he served as a special assistant to the American head of mission, Leland Harrison. The claim made sense for someone like him, a suitable way for a former diplomat to do his part for the war effort. Yet aiding the American minister was not the reason he had come to Switzerland. William Donovan, the head of the Office of Strategic Services (OSS), the fledgling American intelligence service, had assigned him to get a Swiss station up and running to spy on Nazi Germany.

At age forty-nine, Dulles was one of those rare individuals whose vintage only improved with the years. His hair, though slightly thinning, was still sufficient for a respectable part, and his mustache was full. A Wall Street lawyer and a member of a family that ranked among America's ruling class—two relatives had served as secretaries of state—he projected a worldliness that was unusual for an American. Maybe it was the blue eyes that twinkled behind round rimless glasses or the disarming pipe perched between his teeth, but Dulles could, when he wished, assume an engaging personality that made others take an instant liking.

Dulles was in Zurich to meet a man he had been warned to avoid, a German named Hans Bernd Gisevius. Like Dulles, Gisevius lived in Switzerland under false pretenses. Officially he carried the title of vice consul attached to the German mission in Zurich. Espionage circles knew that he was really an agent of the Abwehr, the intelligence arm of the German military. As a newcomer, Dulles was an obvious target for Germans like Gisevius who feasted on inexperienced spies. Yet exactly because he was new to town and eager to establish an intelligence network as quickly as possible, Dulles had kept an open mind. "Our countries were at war. A meeting between us was hardly according to protocol," Dulles later wrote. Checking with what few contacts he had been able to develop, Dulles concluded that if he kept his guard up, meeting the German spy was worth the risk.

Greeting Gisevius at an undisclosed location, Dulles was confronted with a solidly built, handsome man who was more than a little imposing. Standing some six feet four inches, he was known to his friends as "*Der Lange*" or "the tall one." At first blush, Gisevius exuded the air of an academic. With his round thick glasses, he had the look of a "learned professor of Latin or Greek." Yet he had spent virtually his entire career in German security and police services, including the Prussian Gestapo, and he bore the imprints of the profession. His manner was stiff, formal, and guarded, and he frequently came across as arrogant. One who knew him well attributed a "brutal" aspect to his appearance.

Gisevius had come to Dulles with a clear agenda. He explained that there were many brave souls in Germany who wanted to rid their country of Adolf Hitler and were ready to take action. All they needed was help from the Americans, which they hoped Dulles could arrange. They could kill or depose the Führer, but Gisevius and his friends needed to know whether Washington would negotiate a peace treaty with a new German government. Overthrowing their Fascist dictator without such assurances, he said, could lead to revolution and chaos.

Dulles dismissed Gisevius that night without any record that he offered the slightest encouragement. Gisevius would soon travel to Berlin to join fellow conspirators in a bold plot, while Dulles dove into what he considered more important projects.

•   •   •

Though Dulles didn't take Gisevius seriously that evening, much of what the German said rang true. Allied intelligence services knew there were pockets of resistance within Germany. In company canteens, noisy local beer halls, and even closed-door meeting rooms at the German army headquarters in Berlin, groups of men and women had gathered to plot against Hitler since the first of the eerie torchlight parades in 1933 that signaled the Nazis' rise to power. Their motivations were varied—religious leaders detested the Führer's merciless attacks on Jews; politicians, especially those on the left, hated his attitude toward the Communists; and army officers were terrified he would ruin the Wehrmacht. All feared that Hitler was leading their beloved country to ruin.

Some resistance members had been making their way to the West to issue warnings. In the late 1930s, several had traveled to Switzerland to open lines of communication with the British government. Others had turned to contacts in the British aristocracy. One, a Munich lawyer, Josef Müller, made contact with the British using Pope Pius XII as an intermediary. Still another, the German politician Carl Friedrich Goerdeler, had turned to Jakob Wallenberg, a member of the Swedish banking family, to reach out to Western capitals.

Yet Dulles had reason to be wary about Gisevius. In November 1939, the Abwehr had captured two British spies near the Dutch town of Venlo, after German agents had similarly approached them to work together. Although it was unlikely the Germans would try to kidnap Dulles himself—the Swiss took a dim view of such lawlessness—it was possible, even likely, that Gisevius's purpose was to worm his way into Dulles's confidence to gain information that could be used to break American codes or discover the identity of Allied agents.

Another reason for caution was the nature of Dulles's assignment. His superiors had made it clear before he left Washington that he was to lead psychological campaigns to demoralize the German people and troops, to learn what he could about Nazi secret weapons, and to deliver order of battle intelligence such as enemy troop strengths. Dulles also hoped to work with members of resistance movements, and he had access to money to help fund their operations. But engaging in high-level political negotiations exceeded his brief.

CHAPTER

2

"I Have Never Believed in Turning Back"

Dulles's journey to Switzerland had begun a little over a year before his meeting with Gisevius. On the afternoon of December 7, 1941, he was lounging at his town house on tree-lined East Sixty-First Street in New York City. He and his wife, Clover, had hosted a debutante ball for their daughter Joan at the Hampshire House on Central Park South the previous evening and were starting the day slowly. He looked forward to listening to a football game between the New York Giants and the rival Brooklyn Dodgers at the Polo Grounds. At about three in the afternoon, Dulles heard a report that the Japanese had just attacked the US Pacific Fleet at Pearl Harbor in Honolulu, Hawaii.

Around the same time, the public-address system in the stadium crackled with an announcement that William Donovan was to report to a telephone for an important call from Washington. President Roosevelt wanted Donovan, the head of a recently established espionage unit called the office of the Coordinator of Information (COI), in Washington immediately.

Donovan and Dulles were well acquainted. Once competing Wall Street lawyers, they shared an interest in international affairs and public service, played tennis together, and were members of the same clubs. Donovan had occasionally turned to Dulles for advice about getting his fledgling American spy agency up and running. When the United States formally entered the war a few days after Pearl Harbor, he persuaded Dulles to join the group.

For several months Dulles ran a COI station in New York, operating out of the former offices of a diamond merchant on the thirty-sixth floor of the International Building at Rockefeller Center. There he assembled a staff of men and women charged with learning all they could about Nazi Germany. Relations with important Germans living in the United States were established. Agents greeted ships arriving in New York from Europe to interview people who may have recently been in the Third Reich. Used clothing of German fashion was purchased to supply prospective American agents. A special maritime office was established at 42 Broadway, where foreign sailors were forced to submit to interviews to obtain information about ports such as Genoa, Marseilles, and Naples. In one report, Dulles's team collected information and maps about the latest conditions around the Sahara desert from a French engineer.

It was a period of learning on the job for Donovan's entire enterprise. Though George Washington had promoted covert operations during the Revolutionary War, intelligence gathering had become a lost art for Americans in the twentieth century. Protected from much of the rest of the world by two oceans, Americans were not supposed to care about the secrets of other countries. Spying was considered a dirty business—Henry Stimson, the secretary of state in the Hoover administration, famously remarked that "gentlemen don't read each other's mail." Even in the late 1930s, though the United States was cracking enemy codes, human sources of intelligence were limited to a few dozen ambassadors and military attachés. Pearl Harbor, where the US Navy had been caught asleep by the Japanese sneak attack, was a testament to how low American intelligence had sunk. The coming of war finally awakened the United States to the need for better intelligence gathering. In June 1942, the president broke up the COI and created the OSS. American espionage entered a new age of excitement and at times mind-boggling confusion.

With mild blue eyes, a "rather dumpy, corpulent figure," a soft voice, and ill-fitting clothes, Donovan ran the OSS with little thought to such basic tools as organizational charts or a chain of command. Ambitious staffers soon learned that the best way to land an assignment was simply to walk past Donovan's open office door when he looked up. Some training manuals were hastily published, prepared with help from the British, but staffers understood they would have to live by their wits and even came to embrace their reputation as "enthusiastic amateurs."

Donovan made good use of a secret budget to assemble a staff of academics, lawyers, journalists, movie directors, business leaders, and counterfeiters. The actor Sterling Hayden, dubbed "the Most Beautiful Man in the Movies," joined Donovan's team, as did a Major League Baseball player, the multilingual Moe Berg. Long before she would become a famous chef, Julia Child signed on with the OSS as a researcher.

Donovan established the OSS headquarters in a three-story granite building at Twenty-Fifth and E Streets atop Washington's Navy Hill, a structure the OSS shared for a time with caged animals the Public Health Service used for syphilis research. For a few weeks, Donovan and members of his team were subjected to noxious odors as the dead creatures were disposed of in a nearby incinerator.

Yet the OSS was a thrilling place to work. Agents were deployed to exotic locations around the world with generous bank accounts and little direct supervision. Thanks to the work of OSS inventors, many packed fascinating toys to help carry out their missions. Deep in the basement of OSS headquarters, a New England commercial chemist and inventor, Stanley Lovell, crafted gadgets for Donovan's field agents that were the stuff of James Bond. From his laboratories emerged miniature cameras tucked into matchbooks, explosives shaped like lumps of coal, and bombs made with

combustible powder that looked like flour and could be kneaded and baked
into bread.

Soon Donovan began to set up stations abroad, and few locales looked
as promising as Switzerland. "Switzerland is now, as it was in the last war, the
one most advantageous place for the obtaining of information concerning the
European Axis powers," Donovan wrote. As an initial step, he dispatched a
former Treasury Department official, Charles Dyar, to Bern in early 1942, his
cover that of financial attaché to the US mission. Dyar did a good job, but
Donovan soon concluded that "we need badly a man of a different type." What
the post really demanded was someone who could "mingle freely with intellectual and business circles in Switzerland in order to tap the constant and enormous flow of information that comes from Germany and Italy to these people."

Dulles didn't speak German well and likely would have heartily agreed
with Mark Twain's assessment of "the Awful German Language," but he had
many qualities that made him a solid candidate for the post. For starters, he
was well acquainted with Bern, widely considered the best city in which to
establish an OSS station. There he had first tasted life as a spy in 1918, when
he had been a young diplomat in the State Department. Settling into his post,
Dulles listened intently as the first secretary of the legation outlined his duties: "I guess the best thing for you to do is take charge of intelligence. Keep
your ears open. This place is swarming with spies." Given a helping hand by
friends in the Swiss secret service, Dulles quickly established communication links into Central Europe and the Balkans, tried to launch talks between
the White House and the Austrian emperor, and weeded out German agents
who applied at the mission for visas to the United States. "I cannot tell you
much about what I do," he wrote his father one night, "except that it has to
do with intelligence."

Dulles had also demonstrated that he possessed the right emotional
makeup for his stealth profession when he met and struck up a relationship
with a pretty young Czech woman who worked at the US mission. After
he was seen out with her a couple of times, he was approached by a British
agent who told him that his friend was not what she seemed. She had been
passing secret information to the Austrians, and her betrayal had led to the

arrest and execution of two Czech agents. That she was coerced to provide intelligence—the Austrians had threatened to harm her family back home— mattered not to the British.

A few evenings later, Dulles took the woman out to dinner and, as arranged, walked her home through the Old City. At a corner near the Nydegg Church, two men approached the couple and, as Dulles watched, silently bundled her away. "I never heard what happened to her," he said. "It was my first lesson in intelligence. Never be certain that someone is not betraying you, just because you like and trust them."

After his stint in Switzerland during World War I, Dulles had dabbled in espionage while stationed with the State Department in Constantinople, now Istanbul, in 1921. There he learned that an American naval vessel anchored in the Sea of Marmara could intercept shortwave radio traffic between Moscow and Communist outposts around the world, so he set up a system for eavesdropping on the communications. He collected so much information that he had to hire two Russian translators, running up a bill that made government bean counters back in Washington fume.

A few years later, practicing law in New York, Dulles occasionally attended a secretive group of leading Americans who had developed their own private espionage center, which they called "the ROOM." Founded by Vincent Astor and other New York elites in 1927, the society included bankers, a naturalist, an aviation expert, a national tennis champion, and Franklin Delano Roosevelt. Known only to a small number of people, the group met at an apartment at 34 East Sixty-Second Street, which had an unlisted telephone number and a mail drop. Though the primary purpose of the gatherings was for members to trade information that might be useful in their various business enterprises, many simply wanted to rub elbows with adventurers. The ROOM often invited such guest speakers as the British author and former intelligence agent W. Somerset Maugham and the arctic explorer and naval commander Richard Byrd.

All this experience wasn't the only reason Dulles may have won the Swiss posting—Donovan also likely wanted to get him out of his hair. Though the two enjoyed a good working relationship, Dulles never seemed to fully accept Donovan as his superior. The product of an established American Protestant family, compared with Donovan and his bootstrapping clan of Irish Catholic immigrants, Dulles hungered to be the one running things and making history. Once, visiting Donovan in his room at the Saint Regis Hotel in New York, Dulles found his boss's door open and papers spread all over the bed, apparently left there while Donovan was using the bathroom. Dulles scooped up the papers; phoning Donovan from the lobby, he asked about a memorandum that was among the documents. Silence filled the telephone line until Dulles began to laugh, a prank that Donovan didn't find funny.

By the autumn of 1942, Donovan had begun serious planning to send Dulles—assigned the code number 110 by rough alphabetical order—to Switzerland.

Getting to Switzerland during wartime was easier said than done. Dulles had to travel through Vichy France, a puppet state of Germany, to get there. For the time being, the Vichy government maintained diplomatic relations with the United States and allowed Americans to pass through its borders. But it would not do so for long. American troops, Dulles was warned, were planning an attack in North Africa as part of an Allied invasion. Once that happened, analysts in Washington figured that the Nazis would quickly occupy all of France and arrest any Americans they found on its soil.

Racing to get to Switzerland before the invasion, Dulles left New York in early November on a "flying boat" that could land on water. Among the plane's refueling stops were the Azores, roughly nine hundred miles west of the European coast. The islands were well positioned for such flights, but they were also a constant headache for flight crews, as planes were forced to maneuver on largely unprotected and rough waters. Indeed, bad weather passed over the islands just as Dulles arrived, making the seas too choppy for his plane to take off. Only after a couple of days of watching the skies and fretting over the looming American invasion in North Africa were Dulles and the other passengers finally allowed to board their plane for the last leg of the flight, to Lisbon. After a night at the sumptuous Hotel Avis, Dulles hurried to the Spanish coast, where he caught a train north to the small Catalan fishing village of Portbou.

Disembarking while customs officials checked paperwork, he joined a Swiss passenger for a quick meal. "While we were eating, another Swiss passenger ran up to our table somewhat breathlessly and told us the exciting news: The Americans and the British had landed in North Africa! I tried to appear surprised and unconcerned—I was not surprised, but I was deeply concerned."

Dulles now faced an anxious decision. He had an hour before the train to France departed and paced nervously around the station weighing his options. Should he keep going? Would they find him? How would Vichy authorities treat an American now that US forces had landed in North Africa? "It was one of the toughest decisions I ever had to make," he wrote, "but I have never believed in turning back where there is any chance of going forward." With considerable trepidation, Dulles boarded the train.

For a spy-in-waiting, Dulles got off to an oddly conspicuous start. Minutes after leaving Spain, his train came to a stop at the French border town of Cerbère, where crowds had gathered in the streets. News of the landings in Africa had spread fast, and many people had convinced themselves that their liberation from the Germans was imminent. "When the townspeople heard that an American had arrived, they seemed to feel I was the advance guard, that American troops were on the next boat, and the defeat of the Nazis was just around the corner." It didn't help that Dulles pulled out a bottle of cognac and passed it around.

Though Agent 110 was something of a star attraction in Cerbère, the authorities paid him little attention, and that evening he departed for Annemasse, an unremarkable French village that was the last stop before the safety of Switzerland.

Watching the French countryside pass outside his window during the night, Dulles was sure that the Nazis would take control of the border crossings by morning, if not sooner. The nearer he drew to the Swiss frontier, the edgier he felt. At each stop he made a point of disembarking and lingering on the station platform as long as possible in the belief that he might escape

German controls that way. Finally, by late morning, his train came to a stop. Switzerland was now almost in sight. A quick change of trains and he would be home free.

As he descended the stairs from his coach and began to move along the platform, Dulles noticed that a line had formed in front of a desk where French gendarmes were seated. Standing behind them, watching over each passenger, was a man in street clothes who Dulles concluded must have been an agent of the Gestapo.

Agent 110 shuffled forward with the other passengers, hoping that Vichy policy had not yet changed. Reaching the front, he was asked to present his papers, an American diplomatic passport with his real name.

Noting that the man standing before him was an American, the French policeman immediately handed Dulles's passport to the German agent and the two briefly conversed, the German writing something in a small notebook. The Frenchman asked Dulles to step aside.

The officer said that his men had just received orders to detain all Americans and Britons at the border. He must now make a telephone call. Dulles knew the following moments would decide his fate for years to come. He could be allowed to proceed to Switzerland and begin his work for the OSS, or be placed under arrest and led to a French prison, or worse. "If I were picked up by the Nazis in Vichy France the best I could hope for would be internment for the duration of the war." At least, Dulles congratulated himself, he wasn't transporting any secret documents.

The clock on the station wall showed the time was a little before noon.

Ever confident in his ability to charm, Dulles turned to the gendarme and launched into the "most impassioned and, I believe, most eloquent speech that I had ever made in French." Noting a long and happy history between the United States and France, Dulles argued that all his papers were in order, he held a valid visa, and there was no legal reason for him to be detained. French authorities, he continued, surely had more important things to do than worry about one wayward American. When that didn't work, Dulles let the policeman glimpse the contents of his wallet—a wad of large-denomination Swiss notes. Neither the speech nor the bribe worked.

It was a moment that tested Dulles's mettle. Throughout his life, he had relied on a natural affability to get himself through tense situations, yet that skill had now failed him. Glancing around the station, he assessed exit routes and thought of making a run for it. Perhaps he could lose himself among others on the platform and eventually sneak across the border. "It wouldn't have been easy," he concluded.

With a final tick, both hands on the clock now pointed straight up.

The Gestapo agent who was blocking Dulles's way may have represented a ruthless organization, but rules were rules, and twelve o'clock meant it was time for lunch. The German abruptly handed Dulles's documents back to the French officer and spun toward the station's exit.

The gendarme slid over to Dulles, passport in hand. France, he declared, was not a nation of collaborators. "Go ahead. You see our cooperation [with the Germans] is only symbolic." Dulles scrambled aboard the train with the last of the other passengers.

Passing into Switzerland, Dulles was confronted with a country that, though neutral, had been transformed by the war. For several years the Swiss lived in near-constant fear that the Germans would invade. On at least one occasion they had been so convinced that the Germans were coming that civilians in the northern cantons had packed up their belongings to flee south. With a population of four million, Switzerland had early on mobilized some 450,000 well-trained and well-equipped soldiers, a figure that would swell during the war. Troops ranging from white-bearded grandfathers to apple-cheeked teenagers strung concertina wire, installed tank traps, and dug machine-gun posts. Road signs across the country had been taken down to confuse possible invaders. Ski patrols, clad in white, kept watch from high in the Alps.

From their late teens, Swiss men joined military reserve units that gathered regularly for much of their lives, each man provided with a rifle that he kept at home. Their marksmanship, as much a national passion as skiing, was superb. Equipment, too, was first-rate, down to the iconic all-purpose knives that Swiss soldiers carried. Demolition experts placed charges in tunnels and viaducts that could be detonated to slow a German advance and render the country less valuable if it were conquered. There were even plans to destroy a dam and flood a valley to stop the Germans from invading.

Heavily dependent on trade for many of the basic ingredients of life, the Swiss were willing to deal with anybody who could pay in hard cash. Swiss factories produced some of the best precision equipment and parts in the world, which the Swiss were happy, even desperate, to sell. In business offices they could haggle over contracts with ruthless Teutons one minute and make plans for a display of Swiss watches at a Yankee trade show the next. Swiss banks accepted deposits from high-ranking Nazis, no questions asked.

Life in neutral Switzerland was oddly surreal. The war meant nightly blackouts, rationing, and shortages of food and fuel. Yet within sight of Germany and the most feared secret police in the world, Swiss citizens could sit in outdoor cafés and openly mock Hitler. Many, despite the country's long historical and linguistic ties to Germany, eagerly did so. At ski resorts and spas, the Swiss would laugh and sip hot chocolate, while a valley away, men, women, and children lived and died in wretched conditions.

Bern, Dulles's final destination, was built on a horseshoe-shaped ridge of sandstone surrounded by the Aare River flowing swiftly one hundred–odd feet below. Dating to the twelfth century, the Old City was a tangle of cobblestoned streets and gingerbread buildings. Medieval shopping arcades festooned with the Swiss flag—red with a white cross—led to the famous Zeitglockenturm, one of the city's ancient landmarks. Its tower piercing the skyline, the clock proclaimed each hour with a gilded, oversize figure of Chronos appearing to strike its bell. On clear days, the city's 120,000 or so inhabitants could view the magnificent peaks of the Bernese Alps in the distance.

Finally alighting at Bern's central station, Dulles cut through the Bahnhofplatz and headed for the American mission. He was ushered in and moments later was exchanging warm greetings with the head of mission, Leland Harrison.

Harrison, a product of Harvard and a career diplomat who had been in Switzerland since 1937, had known Dulles for decades. But before the two could chat about old times, the formalities of their meeting had to be observed—the sign and countersign required to prove that neither was an imposter. "Where did you have dinner your last night in Washington, D.C.?" Harrison asked. "At the Metropolitan Club," Dulles answered, the two so amused at playing the charade that their roaring laughter could be heard far down the hall.

CHAPTER

3

The "Eternal Plotter"

Compared with Dulles, Gisevius had traveled a more winding and dangerous road to their meeting in January 1943. An "eternal plotter" in the words of one colleague, Gisevius was lucky just to be alive.

The son of a Prussian high court judge and a lawyer by training, Gisevius was opinionated and outspoken. Early in his career he had thrown himself into the major conservative causes of 1920s Germany, and political articles he authored resulted in several libel charges, one brought by Chancellor Heinrich Brüning.

In 1933, Gisevius joined the State Secret Police of Prussia, known in German as the Gestapo. Ambitious and cunning, he aspired to a senior place in the organization but was eventually disillusioned. The Nazis had yet to fully exploit the Gestapo to suppress dissent and to arrest their opponents, but working there offered Gisevius a disturbing window into how the party was consolidating power in Germany. Here, and later in a security position at the Interior Ministry, he witnessed firsthand the infamous Night of the Long Knives in July 1934, when Hitler oversaw dozens of politically motivated murders. A couple of years later, Gisevius observed how the Nazis concocted scandals to drive two respected army officers, War Minister Werner von Blomberg and General Werner von Fritsch, from their posts.

The Nazis' disregard for the law, their efforts to destroy the careers and lives of respected officers, and the endless lies revolted Gisevius. Describing his work with the Gestapo during the early 1930s, he wrote, "We were living in a den of murderers in which we did not even dare step ten or twenty feet across the hall to wash our hands without telephoning a colleague beforehand and informing him of our intention to embark on so perilous an expedition."

Gisevius also had more than one personal ax to grind with the Gestapo and the National Socialists. Early in his work with the secret police, he angled for a promotion by spreading a rumor that the head of the organization, Rudolf Diels, was a Communist. The strategy seemed to work when Diels, under attack from numerous political enemies, was dismissed. But it backfired when Diels returned to the Gestapo and a warrant for the arrest of Gisevius was issued. Gisevius survived, thanks to the protection of a few powerful friends, but his upwardly mobile career had been permanently knocked off track.

Thus driven by moral revulsion and private ambitions, Gisevius soon fell in with those who shared his growing distaste for the Nazis. By the mid-1930s, he had struck up a friendship with Hans Oster, chief of staff to the head of the Abwehr, Wilhelm Canaris. They would sometimes meet in a rowboat in the middle of the Schlachtensee, a lake southwest of Berlin—one of the few places where they could avoid detection. Later, Gisevius formed what would be a lasting relationship with Hjalmar Schacht, who in the late 1930s served as the president of the Reichsbank and Germany's economics minister, and who abhorred the Nazis' treatment of Jews.

In 1938, Gisevius began working with a coalition of men and women with roots in the German army that was plotting to remove Hitler. The level of commitment of the members wasn't always obvious, but their primary objective was to organize a coup that would depose, but not necessarily kill, Hitler. With the Führer gone, they hoped to be able to quickly institute a democratic government and assume at least interim roles leading the nation.

Though the group was loosely organized, many of its members looked to Ludwig Beck, the former chief of the German general staff, for leadership. Hair thinning and still in fighting trim in his early sixties, Beck was a most unlikely rebel. A career officer, he devoted himself to the highest values of the army: loyalty, integrity, and love of country. Nor was he instinctively anti-Nazi. He had initially agreed with some of Hitler's more controversial beliefs. Something of an introvert, Beck was, in the words of one conspirator, a man "whose main characteristic was that he thoroughly studied any matter before attempting to pass judgment on it."

Beck broke with Hitler in 1938 when he learned of the Führer's plan to invade Czechoslovakia, a folly he was sure would mean war with Britain and France, which the German army was in no way prepared to win. So committed was Beck to his duty, and so convinced that Hitler was leading the country to ruin, that he opted for the only course his code of ethics would allow and resigned his commission. Within months he was plotting Hitler's downfall.

The key, Beck and others agreed, was to generate support for a coup among the officer corps of the German army. Respected by the general population, and holding ultimate power within the country, many army officers were dubious of the upstart Hitler and shared Beck's worries that Hitler was wholly unqualified to lead the troops.

Yet the plotters faced what seemed like an insurmountable problem in persuading army officers to rebel. Each had taken an oath of loyalty that, for many, constituted an unbreakable bond: "I swear by God this sacred oath that to the Leader of the German empire and people, Adolf Hitler, supreme commander of the armed forces, I shall render unconditional obedience and that as a brave soldier I shall at all times be prepared to give my life for this oath."

The words carried considerable weight, a solemn commitment that was a measure of an officer's manhood. "Though they themselves [German senior officers] were not active members of the Nazi Party, and were in fact either suspicious of or hostile toward the party, their very passivity supplied the Nazis with a tremendous momentum," Gisevius wrote.

Solid pockets of support for the Beck organization nevertheless remained scattered throughout the military. On the eastern front, where roving Einsatzgruppen razed villages and executed Jews and others en masse, a group of disgusted officers was open to joining a revolt. More surprising, a circle of Nazi opponents thrived within the military's intelligence service, the Abwehr, under the protection of its enigmatic chief, Wilhelm Canaris.

Short in stature and slight in build, Canaris had once supported the party and equally despised the peace terms that had ended World War I. Yet he was far from a prototypical Nazi. A renaissance man, Canaris was skilled in languages and held a deep appreciation of other cultures, especially those of southern Europe. Over time, as he saw the Nazis in action, his admiration turned to disgust. He found in the Abwehr an organization well suited to a secret campaign to bring down the regime. Under the cloak of its many clandestine activities, most any plot could be explained away.

Cautious by nature, Canaris was not the type to undertake subversive operations on his own. He had once installed Halina Szymańska, the widow of a Polish army officer, in Switzerland and helped her develop connections with the British intelligence service. And he encouraged Abwehr analysts to prepare battlefield assessments for senior generals in ways that made it look as though Germany would lose the war. But his real value to the resistance movement was to create a place where other men, such as Gisevius's friend Oster, could devise and execute their plots. By Dulles's reckoning, roughly 5 percent of the Abwehr's staff, many in key positions, were at any given time working against Hitler.

By the time Gisevius met Dulles in January 1943, Beck and his fellow conspirators had undertaken several attempts to remove Hitler from power, the most promising in 1938. As Beck had expected, Hitler advanced plans to invade Czechoslovakia that autumn on the pretext of protecting ethnic

Germans living in border areas known as the Sudetenland. The coming invasion, Beck believed, provided a unique opportunity to launch a coup back home. Such a naked display of aggression, he reasoned, would galvanize international opposition to the regime and, more important, incite the German public and officer corps.

Plans were drawn up with the precision one would expect of a Prussian general. Hitler was to be arrested at the chancellery—few could bring themselves to actually kill him. Key ministries, communications centers, and police and Gestapo installations were to be quickly occupied. Work had even begun on a new German constitution. Key army officers were enlisted to help, as was Wolf-Heinrich Graf von Helldorff, the Berlin police chief. Gisevius drove throughout Berlin posing as a sightseer, secretly studying police and military installations, estimating their strength, and mapping alternate routes to each through gardens and nearby buildings.

Thorough as the preparations were, they could not control the interference of an outlier, British prime minister Neville Chamberlain. Determined to prevent a war, Chamberlain made several trips to Germany in September 1938 hoping to negotiate a deal with Hitler.

Desperately, the conspirators passed word through trusted contacts to London urging Chamberlain to stand fast and describing their plans to take over the country. Yet Chamberlain, along with French prime minister Édouard Daladier and Italian dictator Benito Mussolini, met Hitler in Munich late in the month and agreed to the German leader's demands, including allowing Germany to occupy the Sudetenland. When the prime minister returned to London's Heston Aerodrome on September 30, 1938, he emerged from his airplane to an enthusiastic crowd and waved the document bearing the signatures that had averted the crisis.

For Beck and the others, Chamberlain's capitulation allowed Hitler to score a tremendous diplomatic triumph. A coup under such conditions was unthinkable. Several nights later, Gisevius, Schacht, and Oster gathered around a fireplace to burn their carefully constructed plans. "We spent the rest of the evening meditating not on Hitler's triumph, but on the calamity that had befallen Europe," Gisevius later wrote.

• • •

Throughout 1939, Beck and others in his group continued to nurture plans for ousting Hitler, and again hoped that a setback on the battlefield would generate wider support. Yet it was a lone individual, unknown to all of them, who came closest to achieving their goal, filling them with admiration and alarm.

Evenings in November 1939 found a Communist with dark, wavy hair and an inventive mind named Georg Elser hiding in Munich's Bürgerbräukeller. Here Hitler was to deliver a speech on November 8, and here Elser had placed a time bomb of his own design with which he hoped to kill him.

Elser planned every facet of the attack with meticulous precision. He took jobs in an armaments factory and a quarry to steal materials for making a bomb, which he tested several times. Then, over numerous nights, he hid in the beer hall after closing time, making use of his skills as a cabinetmaker to hollow out a portion of a pillar near where Hitler was expected to stand and which held up the restaurant's heavy roof. It was a painstaking job. To mask the sawing and hammering, he timed his work to coincide with noises outside the building. Before employees arrived each morning, he made sure to clean up any sawdust and carefully place a specially made cover over the hole he had carved out for his bomb.

The device went off as planned with spectacular precision and power, at exactly 9:20 p.m. Some eight people were killed and more than sixty wounded. Hitler, however, was not among them. He had changed his speaking schedule at the last minute when inclement weather grounded the plane that was to fly him back to Berlin. Instead, he took a train, a connection that forced him to leave the hall early. That evening Elser tried to cross the border into Switzerland. There he was found carrying technical drawings of shells, parts of a detonator, and a membership card of the "Red Front Fighters League."

When Gisevius and others heard of the attack, they quickly concluded that it must have been part of an unknown conspiracy, likely one including army officers. Only such men would have had the technical expertise and access to explosives to carry out the attack. But as the days passed, and no new arrests were made, the underground began to accept that Elser had indeed carried out the feat alone. His timing device, which could be set days ahead of time, was an amazing piece of engineering. "Self-taught in planting bombs, he could well boast of having achieved a masterpiece," Gisevius wrote.

Yet the attack unnerved many in the underground. They feared that another Nazi leader jockeying for power would simply replace Hitler if he were killed. "An assassination without a simultaneous *Putsch* would be senseless," Gisevius wrote. "Responsible political men could not go in for anything of the sort."

The next year went poorly for the resistance. Hitler seemed to be proving himself a military and diplomatic genius. In the spring of 1940, the German army stunned the Allies with an attack through the Ardennes forest in southeastern Belgium, a region that was supposed to be too rugged for German tanks to pass through. With German troops closing in on them, three hundred thousand British and other soldiers were evacuated from the French beaches of Dunkirk. Later in June, Paris fell. Delirious Germans celebrated the incredible sight of their troops goose-stepping down the Champs-Élysées. Attempting to topple Hitler at the height of his popularity and success, the members of the resistance had to admit to themselves, was almost pointless.

CHAPTER

4

"Roosevelt's Emissary"

Wearing a gray tweed jacket and puffing on his ever-present pipe, Dulles met Gerald Mayer, a prematurely balding officer of the Office of War Information, at the Hotel Bauer-au-Lac in Zurich one afternoon in December 1942. Set along a small park and overlooking shimmering Lake Zurich, the Bauer exuded wealth and style. The public rooms were particularly impressive—Tudor panels decorated with Gobelin tapestries hung from the walls, and massive fireplaces crackled with warmth.

A good-natured former NBC correspondent, Mayer had come to Switzerland to apply his peacetime skills in service of the war effort and had assumed the role of counselor and guide for Dulles. Agent 110 didn't need much help, though. He had hit the ground running.

In keeping with his diplomatic cover story, Dulles had initially taken an office near the American legation in Bern. But what he really needed was a place where potential sources could come and go without attracting attention. Within a few weeks, he found what would become his headquarters on a narrow cobblestoned street called the Herrengasse, or "Gentlemen's Lane."

Here, since the Middle Ages, the city's elite had built stately yet tightly packed homes laid out east to west, offering a maximum amount of sunlight and views of the blue-green Aare River, which flowed powerfully below. Perhaps none of these structures was finer than the villa that stood midway down its length, at number 23. Viewed from the front, where a small fountain split the street, a heavy wooden door suggested that those inside were citizens of importance. Three rows of arched windows, accented by planter boxes, gave way to a steeply tiled roof that hung slightly over the sidewalk. A vineyard blanketed the back property, while three distant yet glorious peaks of the Jungfrau range of the Bernese Alps—the Eiger, the Mönch, and the Jungfrau—lay beyond. Here Dulles rented a spacious apartment on the ground floor.

The location was perfect for his needs. A nearby shopping area with its steady stream of foot traffic allowed visitors to slip in unnoticed, while a little-used back door provided additional concealment. With help from the police and old friends in Swiss intelligence, he arranged to have the streetlights turned off to prevent nighttime callers from being easily identified. It didn't hurt that the villa, doubling as his living quarters, happened to be more than a little comfortable. Writing to his wife, Clover, Dulles described his new home as offering "the loveliest view over the river . . . and more space than I need."

Armed with a lengthy list of promising names from his days in law and diplomacy, as well as from the files of the OSS, Dulles quickly built up a network of contacts. Max Shoop, an old legal colleague who had moved from Paris to Geneva, stood ready to connect him with resistance groups in France and Italy. Royall Tyler, a friend who worked for the Bank for International Settlements in Basel, offered Dulles an entrée into the network of international financiers moving in and out of Switzerland. And an Austrian lawyer, Kurt Grimm, provided Dulles access to his network of legal professionals throughout occupied Europe.

One informant even helped him locate a tailor for a wardrobe makeover. Hanging up his Wall Street pinstripes, Dulles was soon seen around town in blazers, flannel slacks, and corduroy. In the fashion of the times, he tended to wear a fedora pushed jauntily down on his head.

Dulles's most important early contact was the man who would quickly become the number two in the Bern station, a German-American named Gero von Schulze-Gaevernitz. With the good looks of a ski racer—he also excelled in the sport—Schulze-Gaevernitz was the fortysomething son of an old Dulles friend who had once served as a cabinet minister during the Weimar Republic. Born to an American mother and a German father, he had grown up in Germany and built a successful career in finance. With the coming of war, the dashing and cultured businessman had taken American citizenship and moved to Switzerland to pursue his wide-ranging interests.

Schulze-Gaevernitz was universally described as calm, bright, and unfailingly loyal. Though an avid outdoorsman and sport lover, he nurtured intellectual passions that included the work of the Roman philosopher Lucius Annaeus Seneca. Even hardened American army officers walked away impressed. "He was a handsome, polished, well-mannered person . . . [who] . . . quickly attracted those around him," noted one American colonel.

Schulze-Gaevernitz was also a confirmed opponent of the Nazis and had once nearly pulled off a scheme to smuggle Schacht, the economics minister, to Washington, DC, for secret talks with Roosevelt. "Gaevernitz was deeply motivated by the conviction that Germany had never been so thoroughly permeated by Nazism as many were inclined to believe and that there were people in Germany, even in high positions in both the civilian and military administration, ready to support any workable undertaking that would get rid of Hitler and the Nazis and put an end to the war," Dulles wrote.

Most valuable for Dulles was that Schulze-Gaevernitz was immensely well connected. If Dulles wanted information on someone of importance, there was a good chance that Schulze-Gaevernitz either knew that person or knew someone who did. These contacts and others soon began offering a steady, though admittedly unspectacular, stream of information. Dulles collected details about German oil consumption, German weapons, and the mood of the German public.

Communicating this data back to the United States brought its own set of problems and pitfalls. One way to get documents and other information home was to ask diplomats from friendly, neutral countries to carry diplomatic pouches with secret correspondence when they traveled outside Switzerland. Leland Harrison had done that in the past, but such practices were unreliable, and the pouches occasionally went missing.

Another solution was a radiotelephone, and Dulles began to call Washington using a scrambling device loaned him by friends in the Swiss intelligence service. Scrambler or no, few doubted that the Swiss regularly listened in on his phone calls. Because some were suspected of regularly passing information to the Nazis, the radiotelephone could be used to communicate only the most mundane of reports.

That left the Swiss commercial telegraph system, clearly a case of being the best of the worst. Dulles's messages out of Bern were simply encrypted by changing the order of individual letters, and breaking the code was not especially difficult. Yet it was time-consuming, requiring members of his staff to labor for long hours over his messages. After casting about for better ways to code telegraph dispatches, Dulles landed on a solution. A number of American planes had crashed or been forced to land in Switzerland and, thanks to the country's neutrality laws, the crews were interned there. Turning to friends in the Swiss intelligence service, Dulles won permission to put a half dozen or so to work.

As Mayer and Dulles chatted over their meal at the Hotel Bauer-au-Lac, a woman in her late thirties strode across the restaurant, clearly expecting to turn the head of every male diner. Though her facial features were a touch too rounded for her to be considered a classic beauty, her short black hair, bright red lipstick, and skirt hemmed shorter than was the fashion were usually enough to ensure she was noticed. Her most distinguishing feature was how she carried herself—a confident person at home in her own skin.

Rising from his seat, Mayer introduced the woman, whose maiden name

Dulles may have recognized—Mary Bancroft. A daughter of Hugh Bancroft, the publisher of *The Wall Street Journal*, she was married to a Swiss businessman and worked as a freelance journalist.

The meeting was not a chance encounter. Seeking an outlet for her prodigious energies, Bancroft had volunteered to help Mayer with various writing projects in recent months. With the coming of war, she had written articles for Swiss and American newspapers that promoted the State Department's interests and had used her German skills to analyze speeches by Hitler and members of his inner circle, including the head of the German air force, Hermann Göring, and the minister of propaganda, Joseph Goebbels. "What I did not realize until many months later was that Gerry [Mayer] was scouting me among the several hundred Americans living permanently in Switzerland to see if any of them might be suitable to work for the Office of Strategic Services that was to be established in Bern."

Bancroft was not an obvious choice. She was notoriously unable to keep her mouth shut. She was also more than a little promiscuous, and around that time was carrying on an affair with a prominent Swiss professor. Neither quality was sought by the OSS in prospective employees. Yet Bancroft was insatiably curious, ran with an eclectic collection of friends, and was the sort who, in her own words, wanted to "go everywhere and see everything." She was also smart—she adored authors ranging from Thomas Mann to Thomas Wolfe—and was an unquestioned American patriot.

As they chatted, Mayer explained to Bancroft that Dulles was in Bern as an assistant to Harrison at the American mission. Bancroft appraised Dulles with a critical eye. "At that instant, I knew that if my friend thought of this man as his 'assistant,' he would shortly have a big surprise. Allen Dulles, with his piercing blue eyes and his deceptively open and cheery manner, didn't strike me as anybody's assistant, at least not for long," she wrote.

Bancroft recognized in Dulles a lifetime of privilege, ambition, and accomplishment.

The Dulles family had walked the corridors of power in American government since President Benjamin Harrison had appointed his grandfather

John W. Foster secretary of state. Though Dulles's father was a strict and fervent Presbyterian minister who would have liked to see his son follow in his footsteps, his grandfather exposed Allen and his ambitious brother John Foster to a wider world. In summers he spent time with the children at a family compound on Lake Ontario, in Henderson Harbor, New York, fishing and hunting and regaling them with stories and visitors from exotic lands. In winter, he invited the children to visit him in Washington, where they met more people of prominence and developed a taste for privilege and comfort. Allen's turn came when he was seven. Listening to grown-up conversation around the dinner table, he began to develop his own thoughts about the world and produced his first policy paper, a small book on the Boer War. Though the work was highly critical of the British fighting in South Africa, a view out of vogue among the American elite, his grandfather was so pleased by the effort that he had it published, spelling mistakes and grammatical errors included. Several newspapers, including the *Washington Post*, wrote brief, flattering reviews.

As Dulles grew into a young man, the connection between his family and American foreign policy became more tightly bound. After graduating from Princeton in 1914, where he spent almost as much time wooing coeds as cracking books, he made something of a self-guided global tour, finding teaching jobs in India along the way. Upon his return home, a career in the foreign service seemed the obvious course for a man of his interests and social skills, and he nurtured a dream of one day becoming secretary of state.

Life as a government employee imposed financial restrictions on Dulles and his growing family. After earning a law degree at George Washington University, he left the State Department in 1926 and joined his brother at the internationally famous law firm of Sullivan & Cromwell for paychecks that bolstered the family bank account.

His work with the firm first exposed Dulles to Nazi Germany. Desperate for money to pay the punishing obligations enforced by the victors of World War I, Germany was something of a paradise for American bankers hoping to arrange financing, and Dulles built up a lengthy list of business contacts.

In 1933 he even once met Adolf Hitler. At the time he had seen nothing more dangerous in the German leader than a love for his own voice.

During subsequent visits to Germany, however, Dulles's indifference turned to worry. By 1935, he was describing the "sinister impression" Hitler now made on him. Wooing clients on German golf courses, he learned of the devastating impact of Aryan laws on German Jews. By late in the decade, he developed a seething disgust for the Nazis, and he convinced partners at Sullivan & Cromwell to close the firm's office in Berlin. "I got the impression," Dulles told newspaper reporters after a trip to Germany in 1938, "that the intelligent Germans had allowed politics to slip out of their hands. As a result they lost their liberties."

Dulles remained drawn to diplomacy, traveling for months at a time as something of a freelance diplomat in the employ of the US government—for naval disarmament talks in Geneva and numerous conferences. And he became an active member of the Council on Foreign Relations, serving as a board member and writing several articles for the prestigious magazine *Foreign Affairs*.

Though a lifelong Republican, Dulles's views were not dictated by the party platform. In 1938, he ran for the House of Representatives and won the endorsement of the *New York Times*, which praised his fresh ideas and "liberal outlook." Unlike others in his party, Dulles refused to strongly condemn Roosevelt and the New Deal. He lost the campaign and returned to his work at the Council, promptly inviting Anthony Eden, former British foreign secretary, to speak about the risks of appeasing Hitler's aggression. With Princeton friend Hamilton Fish Armstrong, Dulles authored a book entitled *Can We Be Neutral?*. It argued that the United States, with its global interests, could not remain indifferent to world affairs.

After Mayer introduced Dulles to Bancroft, she returned home, pondering the implications of her assessment. If this confident and intelligent man wasn't working for Harrison, then just what was he doing in Switzerland? Before long, many were asking that same question.

Among reports of the war in the *Journal de Genève*, the nation's leading

French-language paper, was an article of considerable interest to Dulles. A reporter for the newspaper had learned that he was in the country and, in view of his past work in diplomacy, had considered the discovery a worthy news item.

Dulles quickly scanned the article, recognizing a fairly accurate account of his life so far. His eyes stopped when they came to one particular detail. Dulles, the newspaper reported, had been sent by President Roosevelt as his special emissary. It didn't mention his real position with the OSS, but it may as well have. Clearly the word was out that he was not in Switzerland simply to help Harrison. "Well I thought my career there was fixed; I thought I was 'blown'!" he wrote.

Once he calmed down, Dulles assessed the article with a different eye. He began to think he could actually benefit from the mischaracterization. The article enshrined him as a powerful figure who could speak and cut deals for the American government. It wasn't a perception he had planned or prepared for, yet he realized that the newspaper had given him a new cover story. "Despite my modest but truthful denials of the story, it was generally believed," Dulles later noted. "As a result, to my network flocked a host of informants, some cranks, it is true, but also some exceedingly valuable individuals."

CHAPTER

5

Unconditional Surrender

As Dulles settled into his Swiss post, Gisevius and the resistance group of military officers were progressing with a new and promising plot. Finally, they believed, Hitler was about to demonstrate to the German people that he was leading the country to ruin.

In the summer of 1942, the Führer ordered the German Sixth Army, under the command of General Friedrich Paulus, to take the southern Soviet city of Stalingrad, a key transport link strategically positioned on the Volga River and home to important factories. The battle initially went well for the Germans, but with supply lines stretched thousands of miles, the Nazi force was vulnerable to counterattack. By autumn, the Sixth Army was surrounded, and the coming of winter brought subzero temperatures, crippling frostbite, and deadly cases of typhus. Burrowed in basements, German troops stacked the frozen corpses of their dead comrades outside like wood. Those who could fight faced some of the fiercest combat anywhere in World

War II, creeping building by building through a city that was tenaciously defended. Frantic attempts to rescue the German forces and to resupply them with airdrops had failed.

From this catastrophe, the Beck group hoped to turn the generals against Hitler. Here, clearly, was proof positive of the Führer's incompetence and megalomania, they reasoned.

And this time, they hoped, there would be new allies. On the evening of January 8, 1943, Beck and others of his organization met with leaders of a second major underground movement in Germany.

Surrounded by rolling fields of potatoes, flax, and livestock about two hundred miles southeast of Berlin stood the country estate of the Moltke clan, one of Germany's most venerated military names. For decades, highly decorated family members had retreated to the estate and the mansion-like *Schloss*, or castle, at the center of the grounds to relax and entertain well-born guests.

Here in 1940, a member of the younger generation, Helmuth James Graf von Moltke, formed a branch of the German underground that would become known as the Kreisau Circle, named after a tiny village nearby. Standing six foot seven inches tall, reserved and opposed to violence, he traveled abroad frequently and had developed a decidedly anti-Nazi view. Like many who shared his beliefs, Moltke had in August 1939 secured a job in the Abwehr, which allowed him to safely nurture his fledgling group.

Compared with Beck's organization, the Kreisau Circle consisted of an eclectic collection of men and women—academics, theologians, diplomats, and labor leaders. Though the most important meetings were held at the Moltke estate, the majority of its work was carried out in apartments and homes around Germany. Small groups gathered to design the postwar reforms they wanted for the country, including the shape of government, the form of the economy, and the policies of agriculture and foreign relations.

Security required constant vigilance, as the circle was made up of civilians unaccustomed to military-like codes of secrecy. Only Moltke, who kept a poster in his Berlin apartment that read THE ENEMY IS LISTENING IN, and one other person knew of the group's entire body of work. Members were allowed to become acquainted with only two or three others, often not even learning their last names. All but their most important papers were burned at the conclusion of each meeting, and those documents deemed too important to destroy were hidden in what was considered an absolutely secure location—a beehive.

Moltke knew Beck and others in his organization, but until the Stalingrad disaster there had been little cooperation between the two major resistance groups. The time had come to work more closely.

Their meeting that night took place in a home in the Berlin suburb of Lichterfelde. Over yellow pea soup and slices of bread, the conversation began well. But around eleven o'clock, after "a few sallies," problematic differences began to emerge.

The disagreements seemed to stem from the generation gap between the two organizations. Members of the Beck group tended to be older and more conservative in their worldviews. Likely because of their military training, they were also more prone to taking action to depose Hitler. Members of the Kreisau Circle, on the other hand, were younger and more diverse, and often possessed left-leaning political views.

By the time the meeting broke up around midnight, members of both groups knew they would have a hard time coordinating their activities. For an hour afterward, Moltke and a handful of Kreisau members tried to come to terms with what had happened.

Nonetheless, plans for a coup moved forward. Beck and his group devised a strategy based on moral gymnastics that they hoped would ease the concerns of leading army officers. The moment the Stalingrad debacle was complete, the plan called for the field marshals Günther von Kluge and Erich von Manstein to decline to obey any more orders from Hitler. As Gisevius explained: "They would not renounce their oath to Hitler as head of the state or as their supreme commander, but simply refuse to obey him in his capacity of commander-in-chief in the East."

Once this occurred, a commander in the west, Erwin von Witzleben, would also break with Hitler. In the confusion that would follow, Beck and another officer, Friedrich Olbricht, chief of staff of what was known as the

Replacement Army—a force of mostly wounded soldiers, old men, and others not fit for the front—were to restore order by securing Berlin and arresting the Gestapo and party leaders.

As usual, Gisevius jumped at a chance to help. In the middle of January, not long after his first meeting with Dulles, he raced back to Berlin from Zurich. Working out of an office Olbricht had arranged for him, he attempted to map the location of SS bases. Though he was no stranger to clandestine operations, his project nearly gave the entire operation away when Olbricht accidentally broke off a key in the door where Gisevius was working, "thus making me the object of the curiosity of suspicious adjutants, stenographers, and so on."

All seemed ready when, on the morning of January 31, a sick and nearly incapacitated Field Marshall Paulus, who had set up his headquarters in the basement of a Stalingrad department store, declared the end was at hand. A radio message was made ready. "Russians at the entrance. We are preparing to surrender."

When news reached Germany on February 3, the country descended into a state of collective anger and depression. The magnitude of the defeat was staggering. Some troops had managed to slip through the Soviet net, but the Sixth Army and the Fourth Panzer Army were destroyed. Though estimates vary, Germany and her allies had lost at least half a million men. Soon newspapers around the world carried photos of the ninety-one thousand soldiers who had surrendered, trudging in an endless line through a snowy landscape to POW camps. In Nuremberg, weeping women ripped newspapers from the hands of kiosk owners. Men once afraid to whisper criticism of the regime openly questioned Hitler. Heinrich Himmler's security service reported that the entire nation was "deeply shaken." Graffiti appeared challenging Hitler as "the Stalingrad Murderer."

In Munich, an antifascist organization known as the White Rose, composed mostly of students at the University of Munich, undertook a bold attack that typified the country's anger. Not long after the surrender at Stalingrad, a pixie-haired biology student named Sophie Scholl brazenly dumped anti-Nazi leaflets from a staircase at the university. A janitor noticed and reported her. She and others were soon caught and guillotined.

Despite the energy unleashed at home, Field Marshals Manstein and Kluge balked. Kluge had hoped that Paulus, when captured, would make a proclamation to the German people that would help trigger the revolt. When he didn't, the two field marshals lost confidence in the ability of the coup to succeed. "The failure of the 'Stalingrad putsch,' as it was called, made clear that even in the face of military catastrophe the generals could not be counted upon," Dulles later wrote.

In early February, Gisevius, still stinging from disappointment over the failed putsch, arrived again at the Herrengasse with evidence of a security breach that could put him at serious risk. Sitting with Dulles, he reached into his pocket, withdrew a small black notebook, and began to read a short text aloud.

A coded American report transmitted to Washington from Switzerland, which nobody outside the OSS or the State Department should ever have set eyes on, had somehow fallen into the hands of the Abwehr. While Gisevius did not reveal all that the Germans had learned, he did say that Berlin had read, and acted on, one telegram out of Bern that focused on members of the resistance in Italy.

The message, Dulles later acknowledged, painted a "fairly accurate picture" of dissension in the Italian ranks. Several names were mentioned, among them the Italian foreign minister, Galeazzo Ciano, who was also Mussolini's brother-in-law. With the American message in hand, Hitler had sent a warning to Mussolini. Though it wasn't clear if there was a direct link with the American memo, Ciano was soon fired and posted to the Vatican, where he could be closely watched. Dulles himself had not sent the intercepted message, but he did sometimes use the same code.

The Americans soon took steps to tighten their security, and they used the knowledge that the Germans were reading their mail to feed them false information.

•   •   •

Why exactly Gisevius revealed Germany's ability to break an American code is open to conjecture. It might have been purely self-preservation, in case the inexperienced Americans began to discuss him over airwaves that the Gestapo were monitoring. He might also have shared the broken code in a display of goodwill to build up relations with Dulles. Either way, Gisevius and his friends in the underground still hoped to secure assistance from the Americans. Yet just a few weeks prior to the meeting, Churchill and Roosevelt had dealt a staggering blow to the ambitions of the resistance.

Meeting in Casablanca's Anfa Hotel in late January, the two leaders had originally set out to plan the next step in their military campaign, including identifying Sicily as the site of a major allied offensive that summer. At the conclusion of the meeting, on January 24, 1943, the pair sat down with reporters on the hotel grounds. Roosevelt, elegantly tailored in a light gray suit and gleaming black shoes, chatted amiably with his British counterpart, flipping through speaking notes and occasionally turning to exchange a brief remark with a phalanx of American and British military officers arrayed behind him. Their gold braid and decorations glistening in the North African sun, the military men shifted uneasily from foot to foot, looking decidedly uncomfortable in their role as background props.

As Churchill lit his cigar, Roosevelt began to read from a text that the two leaders had carefully prepared, each word vetted with their constituencies in mind. Calling the meeting "unprecedented in history," Roosevelt offered the appropriate level of specificity expected from a head of state on matters of military strategy. The talks, he said, had not been about just one arena, such as Europe or Asia, but "the whole global picture."

Toward the end of his statement, however, Roosevelt deviated from the script. Apparently speaking off-the-cuff, he said, "Some of you Britishers know the old story—we had a General called U.S. Grant. His name was Ulysses Simpson Grant, but in my, and the Prime Minister's, early days he was called 'Unconditional Surrender' Grant. The elimination of German, Japanese and Italian war power means the unconditional surrender by Germany, Italy and Japan."

Churchill tried to stifle his astonishment. He had indeed discussed the idea of unconditional surrender with Roosevelt, but he was still concerned about what exactly the term would mean in practice and had not expected it to be mentioned in public. Years later, striving to be as diplomatic as possible, Churchill wrote that it was "with some feeling of surprise" that he had heard Roosevelt's words.

The remark didn't bode well for the hopes of the resistance. Roosevelt's statement showed no flexibility, no willingness to consider anything other than defeating Germany on the battlefield. The Germans had seen harsh treatment by the Allies before.

Still fresh in their minds were the punishing terms of the Treaty of Versailles. Reparations payments that were part of the agreement had wrecked the deutsche mark, helping drive it to the outrageous exchange rate of 4.2 trillion marks to the dollar. Prices rose so fast in the early 1920s that diners could order a cup of coffee at one price, and when they finished drinking it, be presented with a bill that was significantly higher. Political and social instability, and later mass unemployment during the Great Depression of the 1930s, helped bring Hitler to power.

There was no point in unseating Hitler, some in the underground believed, if the country would be as badly off without him. One opponent of the Nazis, Ewald von Kleist-Schmenzin, said he would like to see both Roosevelt and Hitler roast in their own vat in hell. Albrecht von Kessel, a member of the German Foreign Ministry opposed to Hitler, worried that the president's remarks meant the German people could be "permanently enslaved."

Perhaps just as depressing for Gisevius was that Dulles, the man he hoped could convince Roosevelt to change his mind, fully backed the president's demand for unconditional surrender. In late January, using the code name "Burns," Agent 110 sent a long telegram through State Department channels to Donovan arguing that the Allies should use the unconditional surrender demand to demoralize the German public. It was important, he wrote, to make clear that innocent Germans would not be subject to humiliating treatment. But as an instrument of "psychological warfare," it was "absolutely sound," he wrote.

CHAPTER

6

"Because You're You"

Mary Bancroft walked through central Bern one evening not long after her first meeting with Dulles, passing through arcades, beneath the clock tower, and around the Kindlifresserbrunnen fountain, sculpted to depict an ogre who ate children. Reaching the Herrengasse, she turned and made her way partly down its length until she reached Dulles's villa.

Bancroft had heard stories about Dulles since Mayer had introduced them at the Bauer-au-Lac. That night, her husband told her that he was certain Dulles was a spy. Yet she struggled to reconcile the smiling man at the hotel with the archetype of a secret agent. In her reckoning, spies were "grim-faced, gimlet-eyed characters, wore gray felt hats with flipped-down brims and belted raincoats with turned-up collars." Dulles was a "cheery, extroverted man."

Dulles ushered Bancroft into the study, where a fire was roaring in the hearth. Sipping a martini, he explained that he had become an expert at fire building at Henderson and that he was also an excellent sailor. Bancroft said she preferred skiing. Taking in her surroundings, Bancroft noted a photo of an "attractive woman with wavy hair, high cheekbones, and a rather classic profile" on the mantel over the fireplace. "That's my wife," Dulles explained when he saw Bancroft studying it. "She's an angel."

Dulles met his wife, Clover Todd, in the spring of 1920 at a house party at the Thousand Islands, a resort near Watertown, New York. From the start, there seemed to be considerable chemistry between the two. Clover's blond hair, green eyes, and engaging smile had turned the heads of numerous young men. Her interests seemed to be a perfect match. She loved the outdoors, camping, riding, and canoeing.

Yet at a deeper, more troubling level, Clover and Dulles were ill suited. Where her husband was an extrovert, determined to get ahead in the world, Clover was inward looking and sensitive, with a highly developed sense of empathy for the downtrodden. Communication between the two was always strained. As Clover described it, "My husband doesn't converse with me, not that he doesn't talk to me about his *business*, but that he doesn't talk about *anything*. . . . It took me a long time to realize that when he talks it is only for the purpose of obtaining something. . . . He has either to be making someone admire him, or to be receiving some information worth his while; otherwise he gives one the impression that he doesn't talk because the person isn't worth talking to."

Over the years, their relationship had been punctuated with rumors of Dulles's infidelities and flirtations, often patched up with trips to Cartier, where a suitable piece of jewelry was purchased as an apology. "There were at least a hundred women in love with Allen at one time or another," his sister Eleanor once said, "and some of them didn't even get to close quarters with him."

As Bancroft and Dulles finished their drinks, dinner was announced, and they moved through a beautifully furnished salon to a large dining room on the other side of the apartment. Bancroft continued her private study of Dulles. "He struck me at first as a rather meat-and-potatoes type, quite uninterested in either food or his surroundings. Actually, as I was soon to discover, he was both a gourmet and a man who appreciated everything beautiful and elegant." The conversation skipped to their children, and eventually to each other. Bancroft began to get the feeling that Dulles had invited her with other intentions in mind, a situation that she well understood. By her own admission, she was "at the height of my sexual prowess and usually always on the prowl."

Yet, some ten years her senior, the man sitting across from her struck Bancroft as something of a dinosaur, a remnant of an Old World that was not her own. Men like Dulles, Bancroft noted, could remember another time when women were treated with deference, as rather fragile creatures that required protection. Men closer to her age were accustomed to "chaos, boom and bust, and the threat of dictators." They were not shocked by much, including the behavior of women.

During the evening, Bancroft had an opportunity to demonstrate the generation gap. As they chatted about work that she had done for Mayer, which Dulles said greatly impressed him, the conversation turned toward a section of German law that made homosexuality a criminal offense. "What do those people actually do?" Dulles asked rather abruptly.

Bancroft chose to enlighten Dulles with a story about an incident aboard a US Navy destroyer, and he flushed with embarrassment. "Where did you ever hear such a story?" Dulles asked, then briefly laughed. "Still, I'm glad to know." Bancroft later wrote, "Such innocence—and it was genuine—probably never would have been found in anyone of my generation."

The one thing that Bancroft really wanted to know was whether he might hire her to help with his mission. The prospect, though thrilling, seemed unlikely. "Nobody would ever think of somebody who talked all the time as a secret agent," she said of herself. Yet such work had long fascinated her. As a teenager, she had idolized the life of Mata Hari, the Dutch exotic dancer who captivated Paris and was shot in 1917 for allegedly spying for Germany.

By the time Dulles met her, Bancroft was a worldly and self-aware woman. Her first marriage, to Sherwin Badger, a US figure skating champion and Harvard man who competed in the 1928 Olympics in Saint Moritz, had ended in divorce over an affair. Not long thereafter she had met a Swiss businessman, Jean Rufenacht, aboard a ship to Europe. Pudgy and balding, Rufenacht was not really her type, but he had captivated her imagination with the lie that he was partly Turkish. "Believing as I did that Jean was a Turk, I fancied myself in some mysterious kind of danger. A delicious thought." Though she admitted to herself that she didn't love him, Bancroft accepted his proposal of marriage and made plans to move to Switzerland with her daughter, leaving her son with his father.

Not one for high tea and cucumber sandwiches with the expat wives in Zurich, Bancroft pursued interesting people in her new home with the tenacity of a big-game hunter. She became good friends with the wife of James Joyce, Nora. And she struck up an unlikely friendship with the famed psychologist Carl Gustav Jung, the pioneer of analytical psychology who had developed the idea of extroverted and introverted archetypes.

Bancroft first approached Jung about the sneezing attacks that had plagued her for years. He quickly discovered they were brought on by socially awkward situations, and their work together largely cured her.

Bancroft developed a small crush on Jung. Physically, she found the psychologist, who was then in his late sixties, "one hell of an attractive man." More impressive was Jung's "perfectly extraordinary wit," which she found "wicked, sometimes even quite cruel." Eager to learn more about his theories, and to spend time with him, Bancroft worked her way into a small circle of people who were devoted to the study of his research. Opinionated and outgoing compared with the prim-and-proper Swiss, she managed to create a few waves among the group, yet she also developed a close relationship with Jung.

As their first evening together concluded, Dulles told Bancroft she could be useful to his work. Possible informants visiting Switzerland might be able to meet at her apartment in Zurich without arousing much suspicion. She might also be able to meet others in public areas using her work as a journalist as cover.

Before she left, Dulles remarked that his home lacked enough household linen, a shortcoming difficult to rectify because wartime coupons were needed to exchange for such luxuries. Bancroft offered to share extras from a cabin that she and her husband had closed down for the war. Dulles made plans to personally pick them up.

At three o'clock one afternoon in December 1942, Dulles arrived at Bancroft's apartment in Zurich to collect the linens. Packing the sheets, pillowcases, and blankets into two large suitcases, he told Bancroft that he had a suite at the Bauer-au-Lac, the elegant hotel where they had first met, and suggested she come with him and wait until he was finished with some appointments. Saying that she had to wait for her daughter, Mary Jane, to return from school, Bancroft promised to meet him at the hotel later. At five o'clock that afternoon she entered the hotel lobby, tried to brush off the "insinuating look" of the concierge, and took the elevator to the second floor.

Bancroft found Dulles working in the large sitting room of his suite, his hard leather briefcase on the floor next to a table covered with papers. "What a nice room!" she remarked, gazing out the window at the canal outside. "Take a look at that sign over there by the window," said Dulles. "I've got to have some of those signs. Do you think you can get some for me?"

The placard carried a warning written in three languages. Two—in German and French—were letter perfect. The third, in English, read: THE SEAGULLS MAKING TOO MUCH NOICE, PLEASE DO NOT FEED THEM.

Though still early, the two left the hotel for a short walk to the iconic Veltlinerkeller. After a meal of Wiener schnitzel, they strolled along the tree-lined lakefront and finally stopped to sit on a park bench in the shadow of the massive clock tower of Saint Peter's church.

Removing his pipe from his pocket and carefully lighting it, Dulles told Bancroft that he thought they would work well together. Then, trying his best to strike a jocular tone, he added: "It *should* work out very well! We can let the work cover the romance—and the romance cover the work.

"Of course, I shall pay you a regular salary. Naturally, I have *millions* at my disposal. But because you're you, I am going to pay you only the minimum. You see, there may be a congressional investigation after the war. There usually is."

Feeling like a character in a play, she could only feebly reply, "Of course." She tried to organize her thoughts. What romance? What work? And what did he mean, "Because you're you"?

CHAPTER

7

"A Yankee Doodle-Dandy"

Dulles might have thought he knew a thing or two about espionage when he left the United States, but there was little in his background that could have prepared him for the complex world in which he had landed. New to Bern and eager to get his operation up and running as quickly as possible, he made a practice of meeting with any potential source, no matter the difficulties involved. He had developed this habit in his previous stint in Switzerland during World War I. Alone in the office one weekend, he received a message that a young Russian wanted to see him. Dulles had a tennis date that he was looking forward to and declined. The thwarted contact turned out to be Vladimir Lenin, the man who would soon play a leading role in the Russian Revolution. Dulles had long regretted that day and vowed never to make a similar mistake.

The result was a bewilderingly diverse stream of men and women who began arriving at the Herrengasse looking for number 23. Meeting there and at other locations were ex-politicians such as the leftist former German chancellor Joseph Wirth. Others were industrialists such as Walter Bovari, who soon delivered reports of experimental Nazi rockets. Diplomats stationed in Bern who wanted to maintain contact with the Allies, such as the Hungarian envoy Baron Bakach-Bessenyey, began to provide a steady stream of information about life behind Nazi lines. One trusted contact later wrote that Dulles's office "grew in time into a virtual center of the European Resistance. Not only Germans, but Austrians, Hungarians, Italians, Rumanians and Finns, not to mention citizens of occupied countries met there."

One especially promising contact named Eduard Schulte soon appeared. At age fifty-two, Schulte felt like a kindred spirit to Dulles. Both had been members of families that enjoyed the outdoors—Schulte's owned a private hunting preserve—and suffered physical handicaps. Dulles had struggled with a clubfoot as a child, and Schulte had lost his leg as a teenager in a railroad accident. Both spoke the language of international business, and at their first meeting the two even concluded they had met some fifteen years previous in an office of Sullivan & Cromwell's during negotiations on a business deal.

Most important, both men hated the Nazis. Schulte had met many of the party's leading lights, including the bombastic chief of the Luftwaffe, Hermann Göring, and recoiled at their thuggish behavior, their endless lies, and their violent ambitions.

Schulte, a confirmed individualist, didn't join conspiracy groups such as Beck's, but in 1942 he earned an iconic place in the underground. Working at one of his company's operations in Breslau, about two hundred miles southeast of Berlin, he learned that Himmler was visiting a little-known prison camp nearby. Auschwitz, an ancient trading center, had until recently housed little more than an old Austrian army barracks. But in recent months, the Germans had begun to expand the camp, erecting row after row of wooden huts and laying rail lines. German engineers had also constructed a number of concrete bunkers with narrow pipes running up through the ceiling.

Passed through friends in Switzerland, Schulte's report about the Nazi death camp eventually made its way to New York and Rabbi Stephen Wise, a passionate Zionist and the public face of the Jewish community in the United States.

Dulles never made the plight of the Jews a priority at his OSS station, but recognized the importance of such intelligence. He had been picking up his own reports about forced deportations since early 1943 and had reported to Washington on plans for mass killings, discovered by his contact Dutch theologian Willem Visser't Hooft.

Schulte clearly was a valuable resource, a proven anti-Nazi who was knowledgeable about Germany's rocket program, a subject of keen interest to Washington. This new source, Dulles concluded, was an ideal candidate for a list of Germans who might fill key roles in a new postwar government. Among the others were Gisevius; Otto Braun, a former social democratic leader in Prussia; and the economist Wilhelm Röpke, one of the fathers of the "social market economy." At one of their first meetings, Dulles decided to test Schulte's qualifications as a candidate for this illustrious group. He asked Schulte to prepare a position paper outlining his views, and the German eagerly jumped at the task.

Dulles extracted as much as he could from his informants by affecting a relaxed atmosphere, often inviting prospective contacts into his study, a homey and congenial room. Red drapes framed windows that overlooked the back garden with a pleasant view. A small table was stocked with "every imaginable alcoholic beverage." The centerpiece was a roaring fire in the hearth. "There is some subtle influence in a wood fire which makes people feel at ease and less inhibited in their conversation; and if you are asked a question which you are in no hurry to answer, you can stare at the fire and study patterns the flames make until you have shaped your answer," he later wrote.

Yet all too often the pressure of gathering information from such diverse sources, sorting it, and getting it to Washington led Agent 110 to take chances. From early on he was inclined toward reporting that Germany was on its last legs, before that was necessarily the case. He passed on absurd reports of threats to Britain, including one stating that German pilots were preparing kamikaze-style attacks on London. Later, just as the Germans were preparing a major offensive against the Soviets in the summer of 1943, Dulles informed Washington that Hitler would not attempt any more large-scale operations in the east.

Dulles also faced friction from an unexpected source. To the British, more experienced and more than a little disdainful of their transatlantic cousins, Dulles was an unwelcome partner. One British agent described him as "a Yankee doodle-dandy blow-in who has little to provide in real intelligence."

Part of the conflict was a difference in style. Well financed by Washington, Dulles had tried to jump-start his efforts to build an espionage ring by simply buying intelligence. The British didn't have the resources for such tactics and didn't believe they worked anyway; they were convinced that one couldn't rely on intelligence that had been purchased from strangers. A member of the British intelligence service operating out of Switzerland commented that Dulles "was like a man with a big bell who rang it to attract attention, saying, 'I've got plenty of money and I'm willing to buy information.' "

No Brit was more disgusted by what he saw in Bern than Claude Dansey, the deputy director of Britain's Secret Intelligence Service. Himself no sweetheart—even his own countrymen described him as rude, gruff, "an utter shit"—Dansey reserved special disdain for Dulles.

Before the war, the British spymaster had spent considerable energy building up a Swiss network, part of his so-called Z organization, and had stationed several of his best agents there. Over time, Dansey's interest in Switzerland had become a "fierce proprietary obsession," and Dulles's recklessness, Dansey feared, would ruin his carefully constructed work there. "He resented the installation of the OSS in Switzerland, and had lost no opportunity of belittling Dulles's work," one of Dansey's colleagues remarked.

The British might have been at least partially right about Dulles. It didn't take long for the Germans to learn he was in Bern. In January, German Foreign Ministry officials prepared a detailed analysis that was presented to Foreign Minister Joachim von Ribbentrop. The report chronicled Dulles's life from birth, each step of his career, and even his relationship with his brother John Foster, known as Foster. Dulles, it said, was "extremely intelligent, active and energetic."

Polling the opinions of German diplomats who had met Dulles before the war, the report cast him as not entirely unfriendly to Germany. He represented the "modern view" of Germany's political situation after World War I, the report stated, and as of 1925–1926, his personal views of Germany didn't necessarily reflect those of the State Department, though the author failed to spell out exactly what those views were. Dulles was attempting to establish contacts with emigrant groups, including some from Germany, the report went on.

The Germans were wrong about one thing. As had the Swiss newspaper, they incorrectly concluded that Dulles was serving a personal mission for Roosevelt. His job, the German report concluded, was to gain information about nothing more specific than conditions in Europe, focusing on the economy, and he was eager to return home.

Dulles's first few months seemed too scattershot, too uncoordinated, even too amateurish to be successful. Yet out of the chaos that appeared to prevail at the Herrengasse, one chilling theme began to preoccupy Dulles. It was reinforced when an old and most untrustworthy acquaintance unexpectedly materialized.

CHAPTER

8

"Utterly Without Scruples"

Dulles's car pulled onto the shoulder of a quiet road near Switzerland's eastern border in early January 1943. Prince Max Egon zu Hohenlohe-Langenburg slid into the seat next to him.

Prince Max, as Dulles called him, belonged to a world that few Americans knew. A Sudeten German with a family tree whose branches included generals and statesmen, Max carried a passport from the tiny principality of Liechtenstein. The neutral country provided the means for him to travel, necessary for an A-lister on the Riviera social circuit who owned homes around the world.

Able to move among the black uniforms of SS officers as effortlessly as among the tweeds of British aristocracy, Prince Max had pitched himself as a diplomat for hire before the war, though with disappointing results. Not many people trusted him. Carlton Hayes, the American ambassador to

Spain, described him as "utterly without scruples, lying to anyone without hesitation, including his German chiefs."

Prince Max initially proposed to Dulles a meeting on a remote ski run near the village of Les Diablerets in the western part of the country. Whether Dulles really was suffering from an attack of gout, which afflicted his left foot with painful regularity, or he simply hoped to avoid the embarrassment of admitting that he couldn't ski, Dulles had moved the rendezvous to their current location.

The prince wanted to discuss a delicate and serious matter, too complex to be resolved in a car. Further meetings were needed and security was paramount. They would need code names, and the pair soon agreed on "Mr. Bull" for Dulles and "Mr. Paul" for his informant. Another man was to join them, an SS officer named Reinhard Spitzy, who would take notes of their conversations.

Meeting Dulles in late March or early April, Prince Max began by taking pains to emphasize his disgust with the Nazis and their treatment of people in occupied territories. He hoped that Germany would one day serve as a bulwark against the expanding Soviet Union.

Then he got to the point: The Nazis had conquered vast swaths of Europe, yet with the Allies gaining strength, early 1943 was not a bad time to lock in as much territory as possible before the tide could turn. The Germans were willing, Prince Max explained, to consider some sort of peace deal.

What details had been provided to Prince Max are unknown, but as early as the middle of 1942, Reichsführer Heinrich Himmler, the head of the SS, had begun to consider peace overtures. Walter Schellenberg, head of the SS's foreign intelligence operation, later wrote in his autobiography that he had approached Himmler at his field headquarters in the Ukraine and outlined a stark scenario about where he believed the war was headed. With the United States mobilizing its massive economy for the production of aircraft, tanks, and ships, the outlook for Germany was not favorable, he told Himmler. At the same time, an opportunity to reach out to the Russians had presented itself. German intelligence had learned that Stalin was dissatisfied with his counterparts in London and Washington, and that Berlin might be able to play them off against each other. "It was important therefore to establish contact with Russia at the same time as we initiated our negotiations with the west," he wrote.

Himmler was intrigued enough to pull out a map of Europe. Using a green pencil, he and Schellenberg sketched out portions of the continent that Germany might be willing to cede to the Allies as part of negotiations, possibly including parts of France, the Low Countries, and territory to the east. Several countries, the two agreed, might be granted some autonomy but remain economically linked to the Reich. Hitler, Himmler hoped, could eventually be persuaded to go along with their plan. But keenly aware that, for the moment, the Führer might view discussion with the Allies as defeatism, Himmler warned Schellenberg to be careful, saying, "If you make a serious error in your preparations, I will drop you like a hot coal."

How much Prince Max knew of those conversations is unclear, but he presented to Dulles an insightful account of the situation in Berlin. He said that powerful figures in Germany were open to dealing with the West, but equally powerful others were prepared to "cast their lot with Russia." The logic behind an argument to tilt East was that Germany could eventually become a great power by aligning temporarily with Russia, whereas a Germany defeated and occupied by the Western powers would be reduced to a secondary position for generations to come.

In his official communiqués to Washington, Dulles dismissed Prince Max's warnings, writing that he was likely driven more than anything by some complex scheme to protect his vast property holdings.

CHAPTER

9

"Imposing Their Brand of Domination"

Prince Max was not taken seriously, and his motives, as Dulles pointed out, were likely self-serving. But their conversations did highlight a theme emerging from the strands of intelligence that Agent 110 was starting to collect. There were some within Germany who saw in the Soviets an attractive means to end the war.

The two nations shared considerable history. According to Marxist theory, Germany, highly industrialized with a large working class, was an opportune nexus for communism. As Lenin himself believed, "The revolution will not stop at Russia. The German proletariat is the most faithful and reliable ally of the Russian and worldwide proletarian revolution."

The kings of Prussia, as well as the Junker class of landowners, had long been "beguiled by the autocratic methods of the Czarist governments," Dulles noted. And though the Czar was long gone, Berlin and Moscow had found common cause in recent years. The Bolsheviks and the Germans both felt wronged by the Treaty of Versailles. In the 1922 Treaty of Rapollo, Russia and Germany reestablished relations and agreed to strengthen economic ties. In 1925 the Soviets provided facilities to train German pilots at a base 250 miles from Moscow. In an announcement that shocked the world, the two nations signed a nonaggression pact in 1939. The agreement lasted only until the summer of 1941, when Hitler without warning attacked his erstwhile ally, but the lesson was learned: wartime created unlikely bedfellows.

Moscow's rocky alliance with Washington and London likewise gave Stalin reason to consider dealing with Germany. The Soviet leader was frustrated that the United States and Britain seemed unwilling or unable to attack Germany on its western front, which would divert German soldiers and their weapons away from his forces to the east. The Western leaders had stiff-armed his hopes of controlling the countries of eastern Europe as a buffer against possible future invaders. Stalin also seemed to disagree with Roosevelt's stand on unconditional surrender. Almost a year before the Casablanca declaration, the Soviet leader had stated that his country's war was with the Nazis, not with the German people. "The experience of history shows that Hitlers come and go but the German nation, and the German state remain," he proclaimed in February 1942.

Even some senior Nazis had kind words for the Soviets. Heinrich Müller, the head of the Gestapo, spoke with admiration of the Communists, especially in comparison with what he referred to as the "spiritual anarchy of our Western culture." "The Communists' global aim of spiritual and material world revolution offers a sort of positive electoral charge to Western negativism," he told Schellenberg late one evening. Stalin, Müller said, was immeasurably superior to the leaders of the Western nations, and "if I had anything to say in the matter we'd reach an agreement with him as quickly as possible."

Dulles took the Soviet threat seriously. He belonged to a small cadre of Americans, along with the diplomat George Kennan and others from the State Department, who had observed the Soviet Union at close quarters and saw reasons to be suspicious.

In Bern during World War I, Dulles had witnessed the Soviet Union's hunger for expansion only a few months after the revolution that brought the Bolsheviks to power. Poles and Lithuanians came to the embassy pleading for American troops to help protect their countries. Later, in Paris as a young diplomat during the peace talks of 1919, he saw the Soviets angling to fill the political vacuum left by World War I. Then in Turkey, when eavesdropping on radio communications between Moscow and its agents abroad, he heard a Russian agent explain that economic hardships in South America—high unemployment and an influx of immigrants—made the area a ripe target for Soviet expansion, one that was "very favorable for us."

Sent to Berlin in 1920 to help reopen the dilapidated American embassy, Dulles watched as Russians swarmed in to solicit German sympathizers. They packed some three hundred employees into the Soviet embassy, transforming the diplomatic post into a central headquarters for exporting revolution. From Moscow, money and subversive literature arrived. Outside the embassy a large red banner was hung, emblazoned with the slogan "WORKERS OF ALL COUNTRIES, UNITE!" Radical leftists who called themselves Spartacists waged open gun battles around the capital with conservative militias known as the Freikorps. Bolshevik-inspired strikes—at which workers sang the Communist movement's anthem, "The Internationale"—shut down traffic and commerce.

One day in early March 1920, Dulles was caught up in such a street battle. Driving with a US Army colonel near Pariser Platz, he saw an armored car used by the Freikorps open fire on a car that had refused to stop, and "[clean] up the whole lot." Two days later, as he tried to evacuate Americans from Berlin, he learned of plans to establish a "Soviet government" in parts of the capital. Communist posters appeared around the city, and he was told that the Red Army was recruiting German men.

Dulles was not prone to the verbal pyrotechnics of his uncle, former secretary of state Robert Lansing, who once described the Bolsheviks as "the most hideous and monstrous thing that the human mind has ever conceived." Yet on his return to Switzerland, Dulles questioned the motives of the Soviet Union. On December 6, 1942, he wrote that antifascists in Europe were worried that Britain and the United States might fail to restrain the Soviets from exploiting social chaos at the end of the war and "imposing their brand of domination on Europe."

His suspicions grew as reports filtered back on the fate of the German soldiers captured at Stalingrad. Not all had been marched off across the tundra to POW camps. Some two thousand German officers had been plucked out and transported by train to comfortable quarters, where they enjoyed good food, soft beds, and well-stocked libraries and sports facilities. Why the Soviets were treating the men so well was a mystery. But Dulles felt he had a pretty good idea. On February 13, he reported to Washington that the Russians may have been preparing the German officers for "internal action" in Germany. Ten days later, citing reliable sources, he wrote, "It is considered possible in responsible German circles that the High German officers captured at Stalingrad may be in the mood to lead a German Revolutionary army against the present German regime in collaboration with the Russians."

Such reports were as yet mere snippets of the intelligence Agent 110 was gathering. But they would soon grow, and they would shape his view of the German underground and of America's wartime priorities.

10

Two Bottles of Cointreau

Around noon on March 13, 1943, Hitler's personal aircraft, a four-engine Focke-Wulf Fw 200 Condor, appeared over the thick forests near the Ukrainian city of Smolensk and landed on a grass strip. Waiting for him were officers of the Army Group Center, eager to deliver an update on the war on the eastern front and have lunch with the Nazi leader.

Also on the ground was a clutch of men who represented a new plot to depose Hitler, many of whom were known to Gisevius.

The leader of the operation was one of the more ambitious members of the resistance, Army general Henning von Tresckow. An athletic-looking officer with short-cropped hair, Tresckow had a familiar story. Once a supporter of Hitler and his campaign against the Treaty of Versailles, Tresckow had turned on the Führer after the Kristallnacht attacks on Jews in November 1938 and his learning of the brutal treatment of Russian prisoners of war. Quietly, he built a group of men who shared his growing commitment to overthrow Hitler; the group included his cousin by marriage, Fabian von Schlabrendorff. He had also begun working with Ludwig Beck, Hans Oster, and a civilian who was coming to play a larger role in the resistance, Carl Friedrich Goerdeler.

A pleasant-looking man in his late forties, with a genial personality, Goerdeler had spent a long career in politics. In 1937 he had resigned as mayor of Leipzig when the Nazis, against his express orders, tore down a statue of the Jewish composer Felix Mendelssohn. Since then, he had thrown himself into the cause of deposing Hitler, and had traveled widely, including to the United States, to sound the alarm about the Nazis. Naturally drawn to Beck and the others by their shared vision for Germany's future, Goerdeler brought a politician's sensibility to the resistance movement, and much-needed optimism, an outlook that many of those around him believed bordered on naïveté.

He and the other conspirators had realized early on that mounting an attack on the heavily guarded and wary Hitler in the German capital would be difficult, if not impossible. Their odds of success, they calculated, would increase dramatically if they could lure him out of Berlin, and by early 1943 they had persuaded Hitler's staff to do exactly that.

As in 1938, the planning was extensive. Assassination would not be enough. They would have to seize key government installations quickly, before senior Nazis took control.

The actual act of killing Hitler presented Tresckow with problems. Smuggling a bomb into a meeting would be easy, but it would kill many officers as well, including some who were needed to complete the coup. Shooting him would also have been possible, but the plotters feared that the German public would turn on a group that blatantly murdered their Führer. Instead, they devised a plan that they hoped would leave his death something of a mystery.

At the mess over lunch, Hitler tucked into his usual plate of vegetables, prepared as always by his personal chef and tasted first for poison by his physician. Watching Hitler at the table was, in the words of one, a "most revolting spectacle." He ate by bringing his mouth to the plate, rather than by lifting the food. Sitting nearby, Tresckow struck up a conversation with a member of Hitler's traveling entourage, Lieutenant Colonel Heinz Brandt. He had recently lost a bet with another officer at headquarters, Tresckow explained, and now owed that officer some bottles of Cointreau. Would Brandt take those on board the aircraft back to Hitler's headquarters near Rastenburg? When Brandt agreed, Tresckow said that Schlabrendorff would meet him at the airfield and hand over the prize.

The bottles of "Cointreau"—wrapped as a parcel—were bombs the coup leaders had acquired from the Abwehr equipped with a thirty-minute fuse. The choice of Cointreau was deliberate. It was the only brand that came in square bottles, similar in shape to their explosives. Of a British design, the bombs were ignited by a silent fuse and were extremely powerful; an explosive no bigger than a thick book was capable of destroying a fair-size room. Though the plane was specially fortified, Tresckow calculated that two bombs would be enough to blow Hitler and his aircraft out of the sky.

As planned, Schlabrendorff was able to arm the bombs and give them to Brandt shortly before Hitler's aircraft took off. In a matter of minutes, the Führer would be dead and the war soon over. Tresckow and Schlabrendorff rushed to a radio, where they expected to soon hear word of a tragedy in the air.

For two hours the pair waited with mounting anxiety, unable to comprehend why there were no reports of the explosion. Finally, a radio report broadcast that Hitler's plane had landed safely in Rastenburg. "We were in a state of indescribable agitation," Schlabrendorff later wrote. "The failure of our attempt was bad enough but the thought of what discovery of the bomb would mean to us and our fellow conspirators, friends, and families, was infinitely worse."

Tresckow quickly phoned Brandt. He could tell by his friendly voice that the device had not been discovered. He announced that he had given him the wrong package and asked him to hang on to it until Schlabrendorff could arrive and give him the real gift. The next day, Schlabrendorff flew to Brandt's office, his "blood running cold" as the officer casually juggled the package of disguised bombs back and forth in his hands before handing it over.

What prevented the explosion was never established, though it was concluded that most likely the heater in the plane's hold had malfunctioned—it sometimes did—and the cold of the altitude had affected the detonator.

With plans to take over the government still in effect, the resistance had to quickly shift to plan B, which centered on a suicide attack. Rudolf Christoph Freiherr von Gersdorff had volunteered to murder Hitler by blowing himself up during a tour Hitler was to take of enemy weapons in Berlin on March 21. As with the attempted attack on the plane, the scheme started well. Hitler arrived at the exhibit on schedule, and Gersdorff found an opportunity to ignite a new ten-minute fuse on a bomb that he hid in his clothing. He even managed to maneuver himself near the Nazi leader. Far off on the eastern front, Tresckow listened to a radio broadcast of the event, expecting at any moment to hear a report of a deadly explosion. As if he sensed danger, Hitler nervously sped through the show and exited the building after only two minutes. Gersdorff, still strapped to a ticking bomb, rushed to a men's room and pulled the fuses before they detonated.

Two opportunities to kill Hitler had come and gone in quick succession. Before the underground could regroup, the Nazis would strike back.

On April 5, 1943, Manfred Roeder, a Nazi attorney, and Franz Xaver Sonderegger, one of the Gestapo's best investigators, arrived in Berlin at the Abwehr headquarters, a gray five-story building on the Tirpitzufer overlooking the Landwehr Canal. Known as "Hitler's bloodhound," Roeder had developed a fearsome reputation for his aggressive and successful investigations, most spectacularly in 1942 when he broke up a ring known as the Red Orchestra that had been supplying information about Germany's military and economy to the Soviet Union and other countries.

Roeder had received a tip that an Abwehr agent, Hans von Dohnányi, was engaged in subversive activities, and Roeder planned to raid his office. There were any number of pursuits that Dohnányi could have been arrested for, but the one that Roeder had learned of was known as Operation Seven, a scheme to smuggle Jews and others out of Nazi Germany by passing them off as officers of the intelligence agency going abroad on missions. The investigator lacked many details of the operation, but he had been alerted to unusual money transfers made by the Abwehr.

Proceeding first to Wilhelm Canaris's wood-paneled office on the third floor, Roeder and Sonderegger presented papers authorizing them to arrest Dohnányi. Canaris was not surprised to see them. Though the raid was unannounced, Canaris had learned of it and had sent a warning to Dohnányi to make sure any incriminating materials were hidden. All seemed to be ready for the Abwehr men to survive the "surprise" raid.

With Canaris in tow, Roeder and his assistant walked to Oster's office, which adjoined Dohnányi's. At first, Oster refused to let them pass. If they wanted to arrest someone, Oster said, it should be him, as he took responsibility for the actions of his subordinates. The group pushed passed Oster and entered Dohnányi's room, catching him unawares.

Dohnányi either had never received Canaris's warning or had failed to take it seriously, and he could only watch as Roeder rifled through papers in his office, including those spread on his desk that described activities of the resistance. Dohnányi managed to catch the attention of Oster, and either with darting glances or by whispering "those papers, those papers" tried to alert him to the incriminating documents. Oster faced a terrible decision. As Gisevius later put it, "Should he ignore those pleas, or play the part of a correct superior and order his collaborators to be quiet? Or should he not try his best to take possession of the papers which lay on the desk?" Oster chose the latter course, sliding near the table where the documents rested and slipping them under his coat. The effort caught the eye of Sonderegger, who shouted, "Halt!"

Within hours, Dohnányi and two other Abwehr agents, Dietrich Bonhoeffer and Josef Müller, were arrested. Oster was soon suspended and later dismissed from his position at the Abwehr and placed under house arrest. Canaris was not directly implicated, but suspicions about his activities were raised that would not go away.

The arrests were a devastating blow to the conspirators within the

Abwehr. With Oster sidelined, Germany's resistance movement had, in the words of one member, "lost its managing director." Though Gisevius was prone to hyperbole, he probably had it right when he spoke of the "psychological shock" the arrests had caused and the "conspiratorial vacuum" the underground now faced.

CHAPTER

11

"Who, Me? Jealous?"

Bancroft spent part of the winter of 1942–43 at St. Moritz, the fabled resort where Europe's upper class had passed their winters for decades. Though she found the skiing there not as good as in other areas in Switzerland, St. Moritz held fond memories from 1928, when her first husband had competed there in the Winter Olympics.

Try as she might to enjoy the crisp air and stunning views, Dulles's park-bench proposal still rang in her ears. What did he mean by "because you're you"? she wondered. "Who did he think I was anyhow? Of course I was me!" Nor was she swooning over their encounters to date—a meeting with Mayer, the transfer of household linen, and a meal. "It certainly was not my idea of romance."

Yet the prospect of working for him—which seemed to go hand in hand with the romantic proposal—intrigued her. For the first time, she had found what she was seeking, "namely an opportunity to work with a man whose ability I admired, who saw situations exactly as I did and [who] had the authority to handle them as I thought they should be handled." St. Moritz, she realized, was not a bad place to try her hand at espionage. Whether the product of her imagination or observation, she concluded that a number of people around the village appeared to be of "rather unsavory reputations."

Returning to her room with her husband one day, she found a large bunch of yellow chrysanthemums, a gift from Dulles to thank her for giving him a copy of *De l'esprit de conquete et de l'usurpation* by Benjamin Constant, a Swiss-born French politician and writer. Bancroft asked Rufenacht if he was jealous. "Who, me? Jealous? Really! You Americans don't understand anything. You assume a husband is jealous when a man pays attention to his wife. It never occurs to you that he is even more annoyed when a man doesn't!"

If that's how Rufenacht really felt, he should have been delighted. Since their first meeting, Dulles had gently pursued his wife with not-so-innocent flirtations. On December 8, 1942, he wrote to thank her for the linens, including a payment of 250 francs for their use, but added: "Largely thanks to you I certainly enjoyed my first visit to Zurich and I hope to return again soon, or to see you here if you are in Bern. Meanwhile, I hold as hostage one large empty suitcase," the bag she loaned him to carry the white goods. A few days later, on December 15, he wrote asking when she was coming to Bern. And again on December 29, he wrote describing how he had braved snow flurries to get in a few rounds of golf.

Flattering though Dulles's attention may have been, Bancroft wanted to focus on her work. Viewing her wide circle of contacts no longer as just acquaintances and friends but as potential sources, she discovered that even seemingly unimportant snippets of information could hold rich meaning. She learned of an acute shortage of aluminum in Germany when her German maid Maria shared a letter from her brother-in-law Fritz, a soldier on the eastern front. He had lost his spoon in the snow and asked his wife to send an aluminum replacement. She couldn't help him, because there were no spoons available made of the metal, vital in aircraft production. Bancroft also gleaned important information from the Swiss husband of her American friend Mary Briner, whom she had gotten to know during ski holidays in Klosters. Briner's husband had just returned from a trip through Germany and Belgium, where he had learned that an RAF plane piloted by a Belgian had attacked the Gestapo headquarters in Brussels.

Gradually, Dulles gave Bancroft more challenging assignments. He asked her to poke around for information about Noel Field, a former State Department officer who lived in Geneva. Field had left the government when he found it impossible to square his work with his devotion to communism, and he had built up contacts with the French underground, many of whom were leftists. Bancroft, for reasons that are unclear, didn't much like Field, but Dulles was intrigued by his contacts. Bancroft, in fact, struggled with separating the likeability of possible informants from their real value, and cautioned herself that she would have to be on guard against letting her personal feelings cloud her judgment. She admitted, for instance, to having difficulty assessing the value of a deserter from the German army, a "nasty little man with shifty eyes and a sleazy manner" who claimed to have for sale the maps of a dozen German airfields, potentially of tremendous value to the Allies.

Bancroft's resourcefulness and her dedication—working for Dulles was "just about all" she did—quickly made her an important part of Agent 110's team. At 9:20 each morning, they would speak on the phone, Dulles giving instructions and requests for specific information, and trading news. Once a week she would take the train from Zurich to Bern, usually checking into the Hotel Schweizerhof on the Bahnhofplatz, and walk to the Herrengasse. There she would help Dulles prepare reports for transmission to Washington.

The two quickly built an easy rapport, able to confound any eavesdropping Germans or Swiss authorities who bugged the telephone lines. Bancroft "never ceased to be amazed" at Dulles's knack for catching the drift of what she was trying to convey with slang and inside jokes, and how astutely he could exercise judgment about the best way to handle even the most ticklish situation. "The speed with which he could think, the ingenuity with which he could find solutions to even the most complicated problems, were thrilling to me," she wrote. "I had never before found anyone who reacted as quickly to everything."

Almost inevitably, with the initial spark of attraction, the hours they spent together, and their open views of marriage, the relationship evolved into something else. Though Bancroft had initially feared the generation gap that seemed to separate them, she now found herself powerfully drawn to Dulles. His warm laugh was a quality she would remember for decades.

Most often their encounters took place during Bancroft's visits to the Herrengasse. They would prepare correspondence for Washington, usually have a meal, and then, as Bancroft called it, engage in "a bit of a dalliance." On one occasion, the couple was interrupted by the doorbell. Putting his hand over Bancroft's mouth, Dulles grabbed a notepad and scribbled, "DON'T MOVE, DON'T MAKE A SOUND." For ten minutes, the ringing and the knocking continued. When Bancroft lifted her eyebrows inquiringly, Dulles wrote a second note, "PERSISTENT BASTARD, ISN'T HE?"

After a few minutes of attempting to muffle their laughter, Dulles jumped from bed. "I guess he's gone," he said. Bancroft, aware of Dulles's eye for the ladies, replied: "How do you know it was a 'he'?"

Such playfulness attracted Bancroft. Her feelings for him grew into a love stronger than she had known for anyone. She believed that Dulles had fallen in love with her, too. Yet it would be wrong to conclude that there was anything particularly romantic about their budding relationship. There likely were no long walks holding hands and sweet whispers between the two.

Such an affair was not unusual for men of Dulles's generation, who considered such relationships an entitlement for the wealthy and powerful. But there were also unspoken rules. Divorce, for instance, was out of the question, a messy and unsightly prospect in the eyes of proper society. It was unchivalrous and shattered families. "I can't marry you," Dulles declared to Bancroft. "And I probably wouldn't even if I could. But I want you and need you now."

Bancroft saw their relationship differently. She was a rebel who enjoyed shocking people with tales of her sexual escapades. Even though Dulles had closed the door on any sort of formal relationship—something Bancroft accepted—she told her husband of the affair and asked to end their marriage. He replied with cold practicality. They should stay together, Rufenacht told her, but only for her own safety. Their marriage provided a certain level of protection from her work with Dulles. "I continued managing as best I could what were actually several very complicated situations," Bancroft concluded.

One evening toward the end of May 1943, as they prepared to get down to work on memos for Washington, Bancroft noticed that something was troubling Dulles. Without explaining why, he got up and closed the door. "Good God, what have I done," she thought. "Contrary to general opinion, I think you can keep your mouth shut," he said.

"I have been very satisfied with your work," Dulles went on. "But now you've really got to keep your mouth shut or five thousand people will be dead." Bancroft imagined five thousand people lying in their coffins, and blurted out "You are out of your cotton-picking mind. I can't. I have never been able to."

Dulles continued. "You've got to do this job for me. I've got no one else."

A member of the Abwehr had approached him, he said, with a fantastic story he was inclined to believe. Though he didn't explain why, Dulles refused to tell her that the man he wanted information on was Gisevius.

Agent 110 and the tall German spy had been spending so much time together that Dulles had given him a code name: "Tiny." Dulles had been impressed when, months before, Gisevius had shared with him that the Germans were able to read some coded transmissions out of Switzerland. "The incident of the broken code actually brought Gisevius and me closer together. For me, it was strong evidence of his sincerity." Dulles had also been pleased to learn that Gisevius shared his concerns about the Soviets, a view that was out of favor back home.

The specter of communism had haunted Americans during the Great Depression, and Washington didn't officially recognize the Soviet Union until 1933. Yet by the time Dulles was settling into his Swiss station, many Americans, especially in the White House, had warmed to the regime. The

Soviets, whose support was desperately needed in the fight against Hitler, were now seen as valued allies who deserved respect for their tremendous suffering. *Time* magazine reported that Stalin, once viewed as a "sort of unwashed Genghis Khan with blood dripping from his fingertips," had undergone a transformation in the eyes of Americans, and was now "increasingly benign," even a "nice old gentleman."

American newspapers extolled the heroic defense of Stalingrad and lionized brave Russian troops. The US Department of War produced posters of a beaming Soviet soldier, rifle slung over his shoulder, under the headline THIS MAN IS YOUR FRIEND. In late 1942, Americans cheered a female Soviet soldier, the "girl sniper" Lyudmila Pavlichenko, who was credited with killing more than three hundred Germans. Appearing in her Soviet army uniform on a goodwill tour, the woman with the big smile and the disarming personality received an invitation from Roosevelt to meet him at the White House. Ships flying the hammer-and-sickle flag, yet often crewed by Americans, regularly called at US ports, loading armaments and food for the USSR that Congress had financed with a $1 billion no-interest loan that was part of the American lend-lease program.

The Russians, Roosevelt now told an adviser, were actually misunderstood and had suffered after the revolution "at the hands of the west." Given time and a face-to-face meeting with Stalin, Roosevelt was convinced he could turn him into a solid ally.

Yet Dulles was still not sure about Gisevius's motives. That was where Bancroft fit in. "He has written a book about his experiences in the Third Reich," Dulles explained. "He wants this book translated so that it will be ready for publication the minute the war ends. I want you to translate it." Bancroft's mission was to establish a close relationship with the German. "With you working on his book, he may be off his guard and say things to you that contradict the story he is telling me." Dulles told her to expect a visit from "Dr. Bernhard."

The sky was threatening as Bancroft walked back to her hotel. Dulles's proposal weighed heavily on her mind. For all her brashness, Bancroft could exhibit a streak of self-doubt, and she wondered if she were up to the job of extracting and keeping secrets from an important German agent.

Passing under arches that extended over the sidewalks in the old part of Bern, she became aware of footsteps approaching her side. "You have such pretty legs," she heard a man say in French. "Are you not afraid to be out alone so late at night?"

"Young man," Bancroft snapped. "When a woman has reached my age, she is afraid of nothing!"

"Pardon," the man murmured and disappeared into the darkness, but the exchange, for the moment, bucked up her courage.

Back home, she felt the need to discuss her assignment with someone. At first she thought of taking it up with her husband, but she could not bear the inevitable mocking. "I could just hear Jean's snort of disgust, his comments about Americans and how little they knew about life." Instead, she turned to Jung, who, she had learned, had taken an interest in the phenomenon of the Nazis. In 1938, he had told an American journalist that the Führer reminded him of some of his patients who were so attuned to their own inner voices and visions that they wouldn't listen to anybody else.

Jung was more than willing to help Bancroft with her work. He had already been meeting with Dulles to pass on information obtained from his German contacts, details such as where Hitler spent his time and how he treated his senior officers. At Dulles's request, he had prepared a psychological analysis of Hitler that was used for profiles the OSS was preparing on senior Nazis. Among other things, Jung predicted that Hitler might commit suicide if his fortunes took a turn for the worse.

Bancroft was relieved to hear that Jung thought she was up to the challenge of keeping her project a secret, "[a]lthough probably only the prospect of five thousand corpses if you didn't would ever make you do it!" Even more of a relief was Jung's assessment of Agent 110. "Your friend Dulles is quite a tough nut, isn't he? I'm glad you've got his ear." He struck Jung as ambitious and used to power. Such types needed to hear the voice of a woman to moderate their views, so that they didn't go "off the deep end." From that moment on, Bancroft later wrote, she felt no hesitation about confronting Dulles when she felt he was "on the wrong track."

Not long thereafter, a man calling himself Dr. Bernhard phoned Bancroft to "pay his respects," and a meeting was arranged.

Greeting "Dr. Bernhard" at the front door of her Zurich apartment, Bancroft was at first taken aback by the stature of the man standing before her. Clad in a light gray suit, he was the "biggest man I'd ever seen." Yet his demeanor—his engaging manner and beguiling smile—put her at ease. Their conversation skipped through the usual array of first-meeting topics, such as tastes in literature, art, and music, and the beauty of Zurich. "There was scarcely a subject we didn't touch on, leaping from peak to peak like a couple of mountain goats, all the while eyeing each other appraisingly," Bancroft wrote. She evidently projected an air of honesty as well, for, after the initial awkwardness, Dr. Bernhard announced that he would go home and fetch his manuscript.

Bancroft's heart sank when she saw what he brought back—three parts of a four-volume book totaling 1,415 pages. "Of course, parts of the manuscript read like a detective story," he boasted. "But I assure you that the sensationalism is only incidental. It may help sell the book, but it interests me least of all." It was important, he said, to discuss his work with a woman, a viewpoint that he had sorely lacked over the last decade, as his relations with the opposite sex had been purely physical. Before leaving, he made Bancroft promise to read the whole thing from beginning to end (he would bring the final volume later) so she could best appreciate his accomplishment.

That night, Dulles called. "Did you see the doctor today?" he asked. "Yes . . . I saw him twice," she replied. "What's the prognosis?" Dulles wanted to know. "Good—but the treatment will take longer than we'd anticipated," she said.

The next night Bancroft and Dulles met for dinner. She needed help with all the work and wanted to enlist her friend Mary Briner. She reported the conversation she had with Dr. Bernhard. He had told her that everyone in Switzerland assumed he was Gestapo because he had begun his career in the Secret State Police in Prussia.

"That's what he claims when talking to me," Dulles said.

"Maybe it's true."

"Maybe," Dulles replied. "Let's see what you think after you've read his book."

Bancroft then described how her conversation with Dr. Bernhard had covered women and romantic relationships. Were he to marry, he told her, he believed it should be to a woman whom he loved but who wasn't actually in love with him. Only such a woman could manage him and keep him faithful.

"I have never heard such rot! What a man wants is a woman who thinks he's wonderful," Dulles said. "I guess there is more to you and Dr. Bernhard than meets the eye. I was afraid of that. He's a very attractive fellow. Are you sure you can handle that angle of it?"

Bancroft assured him she could.

"You haven't told me what you think of him. Do you trust him or not?" Dulles asked.

Bancroft wasn't sure.

"Well?" Dulles prodded.

"So far I'm sure of only one thing: He wouldn't do anything that you wouldn't do!"

"My God! I don't know if that's so good!"

CHAPTER
12

"There Is Just the Glimmer of a Chance
That This Man Is on the Square"

Gerald Mayer, the War Information officer who had introduced Dulles to
Bancroft, was studying official correspondence in his office in the American
legation's annex in Bern the morning of August 18, 1943, when a man calling
himself Dr. Brown arrived, requesting an urgent meeting.

Thinly built, with a long face, high forehead, and full head of cropped
hair, Dr. Brown introduced himself in accented English. He was, he said,
originally from Germany, but he had renounced his homeland and now
carried the passport of another nation. "For a long time I have been cau-
tiously seeking a reliable contact with the Allies. I have faith in their ultimate triumph and I should like to do what I can to hasten the victory."
Sounding like a businessman conniving for US government help, he annoyed the normally charming Mayer, who bluntly urged his guest to get
to the point.

The man reached into his jacket, withdrew an envelope, and extracted several typewritten sheets labeled "*Geheime Reichssache*," or "secret state document." Mayer accepted the pages with more than a small measure of irritation. But once he began skimming the contents, his mood rapidly brightened. The documents included copies of cables sent from Nazi ambassadors in Ankara, Paris, and Prague to Foreign Minister Joachim von Ribbentrop. Even a cursory glance suggested they offered a peek at Germany's military strategizing. Mayer asked where they came from.

Dr. Brown replied, "There is more from the same source. I am merely acting as an emissary for a friend who works in the Auswärtiges Amt [the German foreign ministry]. . . . He has much more information to give you."

Faced with the temptation to secure secrets and the more likely possibility that it was a trick, Mayer excused himself and rushed upstairs to where Dulles happened to be working that day. Dulles had been half expecting to hear something like this. The night before, he had bumped into the British military attaché, Colonel Henry Antrobus Cartwright. The British officer told Dulles that a man with a funny name, something with "-tal" in it, had paid them a visit. Cartwright had refused to talk with him and told Dulles that "he'll undoubtedly turn up at your shop in due course."

Dulles weighed three scenarios. One: It could be a ruse to break American codes. Two: The visitor was some sort of agent provocateur acting to get the Americans in trouble with Swiss authorities. Though Dulles enjoyed good relations with the Swiss, he knew they kept a close eye on foreigners and had deported some for spying, and that the Germans were scheming to get him in trouble. And three: "There is just the glimmer of a chance that this man is on the square."

Dulles instructed Mayer to return to his office and suggest that Dr. Brown and his mysterious friend meet him at his apartment that evening at midnight. Dulles would arrive shortly thereafter and introduce himself by the name of "Mr. Douglas." To ensure that the visitors wouldn't attract undue attention by asking for directions on the street, Mayer drew a detailed map showing his lodging in the Kirchenfeld district on the Aare River.

•   •   •

That evening Mayer returned to his apartment on the floor above the suite of the assistant US military attaché in time to mix himself a highball and relax with a magazine. He left the front door ajar so his visitors would not have to ring the bell.

At exactly midnight, the door was softly pushed open and in walked Dr. Brown and a gentleman wearing a leather jacket that was too warm for the evening, his shaven head glistening with perspiration. Standing about five seven, the second man possessed "Prussian-Slavic features," his blue-gray eyes set wide apart, his ears protruding from his round head.

There were no introductions, no shaking of hands. Then, to Mayer's horror, the second man abruptly reached into his jacket. Mayer quickly calculated ways to rouse the attaché downstairs if the man produced a gun.

Instead, he withdrew a large brown envelope with the stamp of a swastika embedded in dark red scaling wax. "Dr. Brown has told you that I had more material," he said. "You will find here, if I remember rightly, one hundred eighty-six separate items of information."

The man in the heavy coat was laying his papers on the coffee table when Dulles arrived. The tension in the room climbed a few more degrees, and Mayer, hoping to take the edge off, rose to mix more drinks while Dulles casually scanned the papers. The stranger, also sensing the need to earn their trust, revealed that he worked as an assistant to Dr. Karl Ritter of the German foreign office.

Dulles and Mayer exchanged glances. Ritter was well-known as a cold, ruthless diplomat. His current position, liaison officer between the Foreign Ministry and the German armed forces, was highly sensitive.

As the Americans examined the documents, their pulses quickened. Before them were verbatim copies of decoded telegrams to the German foreign office, a report on German troop morale at the Russian front, an inventory of damage inflicted by saboteurs in France, vital information about secret codes, and indications that the Germans had broken some American ones. Some of the papers were carbon copies of secret German communications; others were notes, scribbled in almost unintelligible handwriting. Most intriguing were sketches of Hitler's East Prussian headquarters. Producing a map and a pencil, the man provided the exact location of everything—Hitler's heavily fortified hideout, nearby railroad sidings where Himmler and Göring set up quarters, even the restaurant for diplomats located three hundred meters to the north. The materials, the man claimed, were copies he had made in his office working on Sundays when the Foreign Ministry was mostly empty. Volunteering to act as a ministry courier between Berlin and Bern, he had smuggled them across the border tied with a piece of string around his leg under his pants.

Seldom do sources carrying such damaging information simply walk in off the street, Dulles's instincts screamed. It was all just a little too good, and too fantastic, to be true. It normally required months and even years of careful cultivation to acquire a contact with such deep access. "We have no way of knowing," Dulles put in, "that you are not an agent provocateur."

The man in the leather coat agreed that suspicion was reasonable, but he countered that he would not have brought so many documents when one or two might have sufficed. The man calling himself Dr. Brown then leaned forward in his chair and cleared his throat. "If my friend will permit me, I should like to repeat a phrase he used when he came to my hotel yesterday. He said, 'It is not enough to clench one's fist and hide it in one's pocket. The fist must be used to strike.'" The comment broke some of the tension, and all lifted their glasses in a toast.

"What are the conditions?" Mayer asked.

"I hate the Nazis," the man from the Foreign Ministry said. "To me they are the enemy. I have a similar feeling about the Bolsheviks. They both menace the world. But we are in the middle of a war and this is no time to bargain. Try to believe that I am a patriotic German with a human conscience and that there are others. All we ask as payment for our services is help and encouragement and support after the war."

Dulles replied: "We can hardly divine now what will happen after the war. It must be won first." With that, he reached for the table and rapped it with his knuckles for luck.

Dulles and Mayer bore down on their questioning. What they heard and read was so highly detailed, so comprehensive, and so central to the German war effort that it was hard to imagine they had been invented—the locations of factories that would make good bombing targets, and information about German spies operating in London. Finally the Americans persuaded the courier to reveal his identity. His name was Fritz Kolbe. Neither Dulles nor Mayer had ever heard of him.

Born of humble roots in Berlin in 1900, his father a saddle maker, Kolbe had once belonged to a youth organization called the Wandervögel, which drilled into him a strong sense of idealism and stubborn tenacity to do what he thought right. After joining the Foreign Ministry in 1925, he served in several postings including Spain and South Africa, largely in support roles. Though he hadn't attained high rank within the ministry, his career was remarkable for one thing: he had refused to join the Nazi Party, firmly resisting considerable pressure. The man also revealed details of his personal life that would help them check his story. His first wife had died, and he had then married a Swiss woman. She was now in South Africa, and the two were attempting to divorce. His son, Peter, was still in Africa in the care of the family's former housekeeper.

As the hour ticked toward 3:00 a.m., the four men realized they should wind up their meeting. Many of the guests at Kolbe's hotel were German military and diplomatic officials. Eyebrows would be raised if he came back any later. They planned to reunite the next morning. If this man now calling himself Kolbe was on the level, Dulles was standing before one of the most important sources in the entire European theater.

The next morning, before catching a train back to Berlin, Kolbe briefly met with the Americans. If he was attempting to dupe Dulles, he had a flair for the dramatic. He had prepared his last will and testament before going to bed. Folded neatly in an envelope from the Hotel Jura, the paper included instructions on the care of his son. "Do not instill in him hatred of the enemy nor hatred of those who may assassinate me, but rather the unconditional will to fight and defend our ideals."

Kolbe also produced more nuggets. A couple of members of the German diplomatic mission in Switzerland, he said, might be convinced to work with the Americans. One was a bachelor with a taste for the ladies, which made him a blackmail target. Another had lived in the United States for ten years.

Dulles had something ready in return. Though still suspicious, he handed Kolbe a wad of money, 200 Swiss francs, to defray his expenses and to buy gifts for people in the Foreign Ministry who might aid his work. With time running out, he made arrangements for continuing their communications. In the future, Kolbe should introduce himself with the password "25900," a reference to his date of birth, September 25, 1900. Code names were discussed. One suggestion was that he go by the name of "George Summer," apparently for no reason more complex than because it was then summer.

The code name that would long be remembered in the United States, however, was the identification that Dulles soon began using in his messages to OSS headquarters. This informant would be known as "George Wood."

With Kolbe heading back to Berlin, Dulles returned to his office to begin preparing a report for Washington. Alarm bells thundered inside his head. This could easily be a classic game of deception: establish your credibility by supplying an enemy intelligence service with worthless bits known as "chicken feed." Mayer, too, was worried. Kolbe had seemed in a hurry; the information had "simply poured out of him." Why would a man take such grave risks and ask for nothing in return? "Did those selfless fighters against the Nazis really exist?"

With such nagging doubts, Dulles and Mayer began an exhaustive investigation. All their notes about his background, their opinions about his behavior and appearance, were fed to the OSS center of counterintelligence in London, down to the seemingly irrelevant prominence of his ears. Kolbe didn't seem especially intelligent or cunning, they reported, and he gave the impression of being "somewhat naïve and a romantic idealist."

On August 21, Dulles cabled Washington: "Every existing security safeguard must be observed and employed in spite of the fact that this may prevent desired action on certain revelations." Yet it was impossible to deny that the vast amounts of material Wood had delivered lent credibility to his story.

Two months would pass before Wood arrived in Bern again.

CHAPTER
13

"You Could Have Peace in Eight Days"

On the weekend of June 12–14, 1943, senior members of the Kreisau Circle descended on the Moltke family estate and settled into the book-filled Berghaus, perched atop a small hill. The unpretentious structure presented an ideal setting. A wide veranda offered pleasing views of the countryside, and in front the family had made a grassy terrace, rimmed by flowers.

Sunday was Pentecost, and the holiday weekend offered a natural cover. The security services would have little reason to question a gathering of men and women who outwardly wanted nothing more than some fresh air. Moltke and his wife, Freya, were well-known for their fine hospitality, and their guests could count on several days of delicious food.

On the work schedule for the weekend was the thorniest issue of the Kreisau's projects: foreign relations, a field that had largely been turned over to one of its senior members, Adam von Trott zu Solz. Tall and thin, a beanpole of a man, Trott had been born to an aristocratic family near Potsdam

and had made the most of the many advantages afforded him. A "bewilder-
ingly brilliant creature," he had attended Oxford, where he was a Rhodes
scholar in the 1930s, had lived for a brief time in the United States, and also
had traveled widely in Asia, where he studied the teachings of Confucius.
Talkative and outgoing, Trott was deeply religious and turned against the
Nazis early in the party's rise to power. In 1939, on a trip to the United
States, he had met with Assistant Secretary of State George Messersmith in
Washington, where he suggested a "durable peace settlement" that would
unite the Allies and strengthen the hand of anti-Nazi forces in Germany.
Not only did his suggestion fail to generate any interest, but he was secretly
followed throughout his trip by a pair of FBI agents, the bureau being con-
vinced he was a Nazi spy.

In 1941 and 1942, Trott began to travel more frequently to Switzerland.
There he struck up a working relationship with a promising British contact named Elizabeth Wiskemann. Wiskemann, who ostensibly worked in
Switzerland as a British journalist, gathered intelligence for her government
and was at first eager to meet Trott. His recklessness, however, soon caused
her "great anxiety." One day he called and in his near-perfect English announced, "It's Adam speaking." Wiskemann recoiled. Anyone eavesdropping
would know there were few people named Adam who spoke English so well.
Trained to identify people by their voices, she begged him to identity himself
as Tom, Dick, or Harry, but, as she lamented, he "could never bring himself
to take this simple precaution."

Like Gisevius, Trott learned of Agent 110 soon after he had arrived in
Bern, and through an intermediary—Dutch theologian Willem Visser't
Hooft—passed him a message.

In the note, Trott poured out his frustration with the Western powers.
London and Washington were taking a "high-handed" attitude toward the
underground movement in Germany. Many Germans, he warned, were
starting to wonder if their future lay with the Soviets.

Visser't Hooft, who had known Trott for years, was surprised at the
transformation in his young friend. "What worried me was not so much his
interest in the East, as his bitterness about the West," he later wrote. "And we

had received in those days other evidence of a growing anti-Western mood in the ranks of the German opposition."

Now, for the weekend meeting, Trott had prepared an extensive paper that laid out the key foreign policy questions the Kreisau Circle faced. How would the Allies respond to a new German government, and would the West be more willing to negotiate with it than would the Soviets? Several of the group argued that the Russians at least were "more reasonable" than Nazi propaganda was leading them to believe.

Trott had been privy to one of the most intriguing indications of Soviet willingness to negotiate with Germany. In late 1942, Peter Kleist, a senior member of Germany's Foreign Ministry with an honorary rank in the SS, traveled to Stockholm on a private mission to sound out Germany's enemies about a possible truce. Learning that the United States and Britain had no interest in talking to him, Kleist found his way to Edgar Clauss, a native of Riga, Latvia, who claimed to speak for the Soviets.

Clauss had no position in the Soviet government, yet he managed to impress the German with his knowledge of the inner workings of Soviet diplomacy and made a convincing case for himself as a go-between with the Soviet Foreign Ministry. To Kleist's astonishment, Clauss said the Soviets were eager to end the war as a draw. "I guarantee you," he said, "that if Germany withdraws to the 1939 borders, you could have peace in eight days." Kleist, who some historians believe was also in contact with Canaris, was unsure about how seriously to take the conversation and didn't pursue the matter any further.

Though some members of the Kreisau Circle expressed interest in dealing with the Soviets, Moltke and Trott concluded the holiday weekend ready to extend new peace feelers to the West.

Neutral Turkey was home to a large expatriate population that offered potential for go-betweens, many close to the Kreisau Circle. The British alone employed more than two thousand diplomats, military officers, and intelligence agents in the country. At least seventeen spy services were thought to operate out of Istanbul, and the Axis countries had some 1,500 operatives in

Turkey. Drifting among Istanbul's famous bazaars, mosques, and teahouses were White Russians, thousands of eastern European refugees, and countless professional informants.

Shortly after the weekend at Moltke's estate, Trott arranged a trip to Turkey as part of his work for the Foreign Ministry, ostensibly to gather information about Turkish attitudes toward Germany. Trott, who had never been to the country, looked forward to the exotic Bosporus, which offered "a touch of my old and best-loved Chinese homeland."

Trott met with sympathetic members of the German embassy, emigrants, and friends. Yet he apparently fell short of his ultimate objective of establishing contact with important representatives of Western governments. He returned to Germany with nothing of significance to report. Moltke decided to see if he could fare better.

With the help of friends in the Abwehr, Moltke devised a convincing cover story for his trip. He was to ascertain what had happened to ships that had gone missing on the Danube, and he would travel with another official. Once in Turkey, he would be free to establish contact with old friends, some of whom he believed could put him in touch with representatives of the OSS.

The American spy agency had been late to the game in Turkey, relying for a time on reports from American businessmen before sending an OSS agent in April 1943. Donovan had selected a savings-and-loan executive from Illinois named Lanning "Packy" McFarland, who seemed poorly cut out for the job. Accompanied by two deputies—a former journalist and an archaeologist who had visited Turkey a number of times for digs—Packy had no experience in espionage and took security lightly. He would famously enter Istanbul nightclubs waving his hands for the band to strike up the popular song "Boo, Boo, Baby, I'm a Spy."

Packy and his team, eager to get up and running, accepted hand-me-down informants from the British, one a Czech engineer who went by the code name Dogwood, who in turn ran his own informants. When Moltke landed in Turkey in July, he met two of Dogwood's men—Hans Wilbrandt, an economist, and Alexander Rüstow, a sociologist.

Moltke acknowledged to the pair that Germany would surely lose the war and unveiled a plan to help the Western Allies assume control. The scheme called for sending a German staff officer to England—faking an airplane crash as his means of entry—with papers and powers to strike an agreement. The western front, Moltke proposed, would be opened to an Anglo-American airborne invasion while the German army held off the Soviets in the east.

Nervous about dealing with Packy, whom he didn't know, Moltke asked if he could meet with Alexander Kirk, a polished and skilled American diplomat stationed in Cairo whom he had met before the war. A product of Yale and Harvard Law, with a finely cropped mustache and dark hair combed back, Kirk was an elegant man, every inch the diplomat.

He was also in no way a spy. Kirk didn't like the idea of throwing himself into the murky waters in which Moltke swam. Unconditional surrender was a well-known American policy, and Kirk was not about to meet with someone who wanted to explore ways around it.

For reasons that were not made clear to Moltke, Kirk refused to see him. They could possibly meet at a later date, he was told. Dejected, Moltke, like Trott, left Istanbul empty handed.

Moltke arrived back in Berlin in July, where friends were preparing a birthday party at an apartment. Hosted by Elisabeth von Thadden, a fifty-three-year-old former headmistress of a girls' boarding school with a severe expression and hair cut short above her ears, the gathering was a reminder of better times. There were luxuries seldom seen in Berlin in the summer of 1943. Laid out on a table decorated with flowers were cakes, and cream, and to everyone's surprise, filtered coffee, not the bitter grounds that were mixed with water and cooked in pots.

Circulating among groups of conversation were a number of people opposed to Hitler. Hannah Solf, the elegant widow of a distinguished Orientalist and the leader of a small, informal opposition group known as the Solf Circle, was there, as was Dr. Otto Kiep, a former consul general in New York. The conversation flowed easily among longtime friends and acquaintances.

There was one guest that evening nobody recognized. Dr. Paul Reckzeh, bearing a letter of introduction from a mutual friend, had met Thadden the previous day. After a brief chat, she extended an invitation.

Charming and poised, Dr. Reckzeh explained that he was a physician visiting from Switzerland to work at the Charité Hospital. Conversation inevitably drifted to the war. The Russian army had turned the tide in the east, and in July the Americans, the British, and the Canadians had successfully landed in Sicily. It now seemed that the war was lost, and Hitler, several guests argued, should be replaced with someone willing to negotiate a surrender with the Allies. Reckzeh expressed similar views, and before the evening was over had so enchanted the other guests that some gave him letters to deliver to Switzerland, as well as their names.

That evening, Reckzeh returned home knowing that his bosses would be pleased with his evening's work. He was a doctor, but he was also a Gestapo agent and had gone to Switzerland to pick up the trail of the resistance movement.

CHAPTER

14

"I Wouldn't Tell Dulles"

Divining the real identity of Dr. Bernhard became an obsession for Bancroft. How could a genuine agent of the Abwehr, she wondered, have as much free time as her charge seemed to enjoy? Clearly he was no ordinary German spy.

On a warm day about two months into their work together, she received her first clue. Chatting about his book, Dr. Bernhard removed his jacket to cool off. Bancroft noticed three small letters stitched into the fabric of his shirt: HBG. She immediately took note. The *H* might stand for Hans or Heinrich, she surmised, and the *B* for Bernhard. But the *G* could refer to almost anything.

Reaching about page 200 of the manuscript, a name materialized that matched the initials: "Gisevius."

She had heard of him already from her own sources. A couple of weeks earlier she had been told that the Nazis considered him "unreliable." If Hitler decided to invade Switzerland, she had heard, one plan called for German agents in the country to kill Gisevius and thereby justify an invasion on the grounds that the Swiss couldn't protect German citizens. Her imagination racing, she couldn't shake the fear that he might be hunted down and murdered right in her living room.

Bancroft was more right than she knew. Gisevius was deeply involved in the Operation Seven plot that had netted his friends at the Abwehr and aroused the suspicion of the Gestapo. "Tiny" kept a fund in Switzerland to help bankroll his activities with the resistance, and he triggered scrutiny when he withdrew a considerable sum to compensate Jewish refugees for assets they had been forced to leave behind in Germany, as well as to serve as a security deposit demanded by the Swiss for granting them entry visas.

Nazi attorney Roeder called Gisevius back to Germany in May to interrogate him about Operation Seven. Gisevius knew he faced a fearsome prosecutor, "pathologically ambitious, driven, ruthless with piercing eyes," yet to refuse the request seemed likely to incriminate his friends.

On May 12, Gisevius listened for a full day in the Berlin court with the self-described "spiteful smile of one who knew more than he cared to say" as Roeder barked questions and recriminations.

At first, Gisevius seemed to fool the prosecutor. Rather than appearing to hide anything, he conveyed the impression of being open and willing to answer questions and generally cooperate. On the second day of questioning, Gisevius stunned his interrogators by refusing to take an oath to tell the truth. He claimed that Field Marshal Wilhelm Keitel, the supreme chief of the Abwehr, had forbidden him to testify about classified Abwehr operations. Moreover, Gisevius told the court, Roeder should not have been interrogating him, or Dohnányi, or even Canaris. Rather, it was Keitel who should answer the prosecution.

The claim, Gisevius later admitted, was dubious, but it did allow the chief magistrate, the sympathetic Karl Sack, an opportunity to intervene. To Gisevius's relief, Sack ordered a postponement of the trial. Not waiting to see how things played out, Gisevius fled for Switzerland via an out-of-the-way border crossing. Any attempt to pursue him further faded when Keitel, who was also the titular head of the Reich military tribunal, transferred Roeder to another post. Months would pass before a new examining magistrate was appointed and the case restarted.

Still, as Bancroft had heard, Gisevius was not safe even in Switzerland. Soon after he arrived back in Zurich, Gisevius discovered evidence that suggested Abwehr agents had searched his apartment. He also received a number of "unofficial or friendly invitations" to return to Germany and one to visit France, all of which he had declined.

During the warm months of summer, when most Swiss families headed for the mountains and lakes for their holidays, Bancroft's work with Gisevius intensified. Nearly every day he arrived at her Zurich apartment on the Pestalozzi Strasse, where they labored for two and three hours at a time. To Bancroft's annoyance, the assignment was turning out to be onerous. Major parts of the book hadn't been written, or only crudely so. Gisevius wanted his book to be discussed, "and discussed from every possible angle."

But the larger struggle for Bancroft was her evolving education in espionage. For the first time in her short career, Bancroft was pulled into the duplicitous world of intelligence. She had to remind herself to be on guard, especially because Gisevius began pumping her for information about Dulles. Gisevius told her it must be "awful for a man of Allen's stature to be cooped up in Switzerland." He had seldom met anyone with "such inner restlessness," a quality he attributed to "great ambition."

Gisevius, as it turned out, was nearly as suspicious of Dulles as Agent 110 was of him. After preparing a memo summing up his political views, in which he had "torn the Russians limb from limb," he refused to give it to Dulles. If the Americans kept fighting Germany even after Hitler was killed, the Germans would have no choice but to make peace with the Soviets, he told Bancroft in the middle of August. If that were the case, he wouldn't want anything on record expressing his views about the Communists.

Gisevius also wanted to know her real motivation for dedicating so much time to his project, and during one of their work sessions he asked if she was being paid by the American government. "I'm working for you because I'm interested in your book," she replied.

In reality, Bancroft regularly fed Dulles versions of the book and phoned him constantly with updates about what she had learned. The two used the word "cub," their private code for Gisevius, so often she once quipped that she feared the Swiss police, presumably tapping their phone lines, would break into her apartment one day and demand that she hand over her pet lion.

Difficult as it was, Bancroft's work achieved her main objective of confirming that the German spy could be trusted. One summer afternoon she invited a friend, Elizabeth Scott-Montagu, whose cousin had been a British ambassador to Washington, to a work session with Gisevius. Together, the two tried to get him to open up about his current activities with the Abwehr.

"Of course, I get orders to send in reports [from his bosses in Berlin], but actually I haven't done a stroke of work for more than three years," Gisevius told them.

"You actually never send in a report?" Scott-Montagu asked.

"Maybe sometimes a fantasy . . ." Gisevius replied.

"Like what?"

"Oh, the kind of thing Hitler likes for bedtime reading. . . . How Dulles had been in trouble years ago for cutting up babies and putting them in ash cans . . . that kind of thing."

"Don't be silly!" Scott-Montagu said, laughing. "Do you really never send in a report?"

"Never. No sheet of paper exists in the Third Reich on which I have written anything that could possibly be construed as of the slightest use to the Nazis."

Yet he had not completely sold out, Gisevius clarified. He had no qualms about eliminating Hitler, but by his own code that didn't make him a traitor. "If I knew German troops were going over the Brenner Pass to Italy on a specific day, I wouldn't tell Dulles so he could order an Allied raid and get another feather in his cap."

The one thing Gisevius did want to talk about was the difficult work of the resistance. He complained to the point of tedium that, through naïveté and stupidity, the United States was driving Germany into the hands of those who favored an alliance with Moscow.

While the decision makers in the United States and England saw themselves as champions of justice and liberty and fair play, he argued, Germans of every class had begun to view the two nations as bloodthirsty oppressors bent on enforcing a "Carthaginian peace," a reference to the Roman army's victory in the Punic Wars, when most of the inhabitants of Carthage were killed or sold into slavery.

Roosevelt's demand for unconditional surrender seemed to prove this argument, Gisevius warned, and the Nazis had figured out how to use it to their advantage. On the evening of February 18, 1943, the Reichsminister of propaganda, Joseph Goebbels, appeared to have been enraged by Roosevelt's demand when he made the most compelling speech of his career. Many of the thousands of spectators had waited for hours to hear him speak at Berlin's Sportpalast, and the mood of the crowd bordered on delirium. Goebbels rose to the occasion. "The English [the United Kingdom and the United States] say that Germans want capitulation, not total war," he shouted. "Do you want total war?" he asked, shaking his fist. The crowd sprang to its feet cheering their commitment to fight, right arms stretched forward in the Nazi salute.

Reading the speech in German newspapers later, Dulles had to admire the German propaganda artist. The speech, he told one source, was a "masterpiece."

The Nazi-controlled *Völkischer Beobachter* made "unconditional surrender" a popular target. In one editorial, a columnist wrote: "The enemy at Casablanca proclaimed the Unconditional Surrender of the Axis and made it clear that their aim must be the total destruction of the German, Italian and Japanese peoples. It goes without saying that great people acknowledge only one unequivocal answer to such infamy: the total mobilization of all the vital forces they possess to achieve victory." The *Frankfurter Zeitung* added: "The unconditional surrender of the Axis Powers would leave entire nations in the same condition of devastation as were the southern states of America which had failed to recover after three generations and which the northern moneyed interests still exploit in many respects."

The Americans and British were backing up their hard-line attitude with actions. Led by British Lancasters by night and American Flying Fortresses and Liberators by day, Allied planes were now almost continually appearing over Germany, targeting not just military installations, but also German cities. In some of the most horrific bombing, a series of raids over Hamburg in late July and early August 1943, upwards of forty-four thousand civilians were killed in suffocating firestorms that produced hurricane-force winds, the heat so intense that it melted kitchen utensils. Bancroft's maid Maria expressed a widespread view when she explained to her boss how people had been cooked alive in their air-raid shelters. "God would surely punish those who were dropping phosphorous bombs on German civilians," she said.

Such treatment, Gisevius argued, made the Soviets look good by comparison and provoked Germans to look increasingly to the East for a way out of the war, exactly what Moscow seemed to be hoping for. Gisevius told Bancroft during one of their sessions that he was so upset, he wasn't able to sleep. Was Roosevelt really such a "fool," he asked her in early August 1943, that he thought that Stalin was fighting for "free peoples and humanity"?

The Russians, Gisevius warned, possessed a powerful trump card that might win over the support of the German army. They held hundreds of thousands of German soldiers as prisoners, giving them the power to return much of the German military intact. This might entice younger officers, whom he called "the captains," to favor cutting a deal. Though Gisevius didn't explain why, Dulles would later write that such younger officers were often predisposed toward a deal with the Soviets because they hoped the Communists, by keeping at least some of the German army together, would allow them to continue their military careers.

"What am I—and my friends—going to do after we've tried all these years to get rid of these Nazi gangsters and then just as we are about to accomplish our goal, the mask is torn off and we are confronted with this business of unconditional surrender?" Gisevius demanded. If the Western democracies weren't careful, the German people, disappointed with the West, could well "fling themselves in the arms of the Russians." The result would mean nothing less than "the end of Western Civilization."

Bancroft's phone echoed through her apartment. Picking up the receiver, she heard familiar warm tones on the other end. Dulles, as usual, had a request. Would it be all right with her if both he and Gisevius came over that evening? Her husband was away on business, and she readily agreed, offering to have a spread of cold cuts waiting at 8:30.

With the two making a simultaneous visit, Bancroft prepared her apartment and watched the clock slowly tick toward their arrival. First 8:45 passed, then 9:00, then 9:15. It wasn't like them to be so late. Had the Gestapo snatched the pair? Though such a move would have been highly unusual—the Germans were wary of provoking their Swiss hosts by attacking Americans—it could not be entirely ruled out. Bancroft went to the front door and peered into the quiet darkness of her street.

"My heart was going like a trip-hammer, my mouth felt dry, my hands icy," Bancroft wrote. Going back upstairs, she tried to read, but she couldn't concentrate on the words. Trying to pass the time, she paused for a moment to absently ponder the cold cuts and salad in the icebox. She then paced the floors of her apartment for another fifteen minutes.

As the wait wore on, the worry that she felt for Dulles and Gisevius transformed into a different emotion. "How dare they upset me like this? What right had they to disrupt my life? I wished I had never met either of them."

Angry at being stood up for so long, Bancroft had just about given up caring what had happened to either of them when Dulles arrived. "Sorry to be late," he said, charging into the hallway. "Where is he?"

"He hasn't come yet," Bancroft replied.

"He hasn't? Perhaps he's been killed!" Dulles said, roaring with laughter.

"Perhaps," Bancroft said.

"Good, then I can eat all the cold cuts. . . . I'm starved."

The doorbell rang again not long thereafter, and in stepped Gisevius. "Sorry, I was detained. . . . I—"

"Never mind. . . . It doesn't matter," Dulles interrupted, answering for Bancroft. "I just got here myself. . . . Get the food, Mary."

For two hours, Bancroft sat silently smoldering as the two men ate her food and discussed "absolutely nothing."

Though Bancroft remained loyal to Dulles, she often found his treatment annoying. One visit especially rankled. "Quick!" he said, as he pushed through the door to her apartment one day. "I've got a very tricky meeting coming up. I want to clear my head." Without making it to the bedroom, he guided her to the living room couch. "In scarcely more time than it takes to tell the story, he was gone again," offering his appreciation on the way out the door. "Thanks. That's just what I needed." Bancroft vowed to herself that the next time she saw Dulles she would tell him she was not going to cooperate again in "clearing his head."

Bancroft was also becoming aware that she was not the only woman to catch his eye.

Developing contacts with the Italian resistance, Dulles had met the vivacious countess Wally Toscanini Castelbarco. She had come to Switzerland to channel funds from her father, the eminent maestro Arturo Toscanini, then living in New York, to her friends and contacts in the Italian underground. Dulles, as with Bancroft, had seized the chance to advance both his professional and social ambitions. He happily passed coded messages between the woman and her father to help execute the money transfers.

Castelbarco added some spice to the routines of Herrengasse 23. Once, she noticed photographs in Dulles's office of Gisevius's book that Bancroft had supplied, and peppered him with questions. Dulles tried to deflect them, but in doing so mentioned Bancroft as "an American friend of mine," a remark that consumed the Italian with curiosity. Dulles's butler, Pierre, found her whirling energy too much and derisively referred to her as "La cirque"— "the circus" (Bancroft's use of the French gender). During Bancroft's weekly visits, she began to ask Pierre about the woman. If she hadn't been by, Pierre would announce that he had had a good week. If she had visited the villa, he would lower his voice, shrug and murmur, "La cirque was here!" When Bancroft finally asked Dulles about the countess, he laughed. "Am I supposed to have a romance with every beautiful woman I work with?" he asked. She replied, "No—just some of them!"

Even as Bancroft felt a twinge of jealousy about Dulles's female friends, her own work life was getting complicated. The woman who was "usually always on the prowl" was starting to pay more attention to her secret German agent.

It was Jung who noticed that she and Gisevius had much in common. Jung had heard quite a bit about him from Bancroft in recent months, and he concluded that Gisevius was "an honest and a decent man" but was "still drunk on revolution."

Jung's assessment of Gisevius came into clear focus when, in a meeting arranged by Bancroft, the two men got together at Jung's secluded home near Lake Zurich. The conversation was a difficult one for Gisevius. Jung spent part of their time together explaining his ideas on *Tier im Mensch* ("the animal in man"), which left the German feeling "kaputt."

After the meeting, Jung teased Bancroft. "Isn't he a nice boy," Jung said with a smile. "Isn't he!" He had intentionally taken a hard tack with Gisevius, he explained, to most quickly understand him. The best way to get the feel of somebody "is to punch 'em right through to the kidneys. . . . When I am doing that I can get my finger in." Bancroft, he warned, would have to be careful how she sought information. She should not attempt to extract facts from Gisevius bluntly; rather, she should let him engage in a "freewheeling, and associative way of communicating."

Jung's analysis also judged the compatibility of the two. He had concluded that they were "extroverted intuitives" and he thought their work together would be "an interesting experience." The two were exactly the same psychological type.

A product of the old school of European manners and courtship, Gisevius displayed a degree of tenderness that wasn't part of Dulles's makeup. He opened up to her in ways that Dulles never could. "Sometimes I think any personal unhappiness wouldn't matter if just once before I die I could create something that would make other people feel as alive as I so often feel," he wrote to her in October. "Here I am nearly forty. . . . And what have I got to show for it? Not even a chair I can call my own. . . . A library that your planes have destroyed [his apartment in Berlin had been hit in a recent bombing raid] and a thousand pages of my book. . . . But something inside me—my real life—just drives me on."

Gisevius also revealed his private ambitions. He was "basically a politician" who had been forced by circumstances into a strange life. Somewhat disingenuously—he had spent much of his life in security and espionage—he said he was fed up with "operating illegally." Once the war was over, he aimed for a job as an undersecretary in one of the government ministries, possibly in the foreign office, though he recognized that his police background left him better suited to a position in the Ministry of the Interior.

CHAPTER

15

The Committee for a Free Germany

Set in the heart of Bern's historic Old City, where it loomed over the river like an ancient castle, the Hotel Bellevue Palace had become a hub for spies. World famous for its exquisite service and magnificent view of the rugged Alps, the hotel had once been the preferred accommodation for visiting heads of state, movie stars, and anyone with the money for its luxurious suites.

When much of that business dried up during the war, Bern's expatriate community took over with a level of organization that would have pleased the hotel's methodical Swiss owners. According to unspoken rules, the hotel's La Terrasse restaurant was widely considered the domain of diplomats and agents of the Axis countries. Other parts of the hotel were the preserve of members of the Allied nations. At the bar, all sides mixed with Swiss politicians and journalists.

Here in the summer of 1943, among the clinking of fine china and the dignified staff, men and women traded information on secret talks in

Sweden to end the war. Word of a second meeting between the German Foreign Ministry official Peter Kleist and the apparent Soviet go-between, Edgar
Clauss, had found its way to Bern.

During the meeting at Stockholm's Strand Hotel, Clauss indicated that
the Soviets were still interested in negotiating and that he was ready to arrange a meeting with A. M. Alexandrov of the Soviet Foreign Ministry. Kleist
was skeptical. The tide of the war had now clearly shifted against the Germans. Why, Kleist wanted to know, would the Soviets be interested in cutting
a deal at this point?

Clauss explained that while Moscow was confident of an eventual victory, Stalin had grown weary of the constant stalling by London and Washington on launching a second front to take pressure off his forces. The Soviet
leader feared that continuing the fight against the Germans, which entailed
recapturing thousands of square miles of territory, would be a protracted
and costly exercise. They were interesting arguments, but Kleist didn't do
much more than listen, as he had at their first meeting in late 1942.

Apparently referring to the Kleist meeting, Dulles wrote Washington
on August 26 quoting several sources that German-Soviet peace feelers had
been exchanged, centering on the possibility that Germany would abandon
Bulgaria, Romania, and "Russian" territories.

At about the same time, one of Dulles's trusted sources helped solve the
mystery of what the Soviets were doing with their German prisoners of war.
Code-named "Kiss," probably for reasons of pronunciation as well as security, Gheorghi Kiosseivanov, the Bulgarian minister to Switzerland, delivered
word to Agent 110's doorstep that there was "a lot of talk" about an organization called the "Free Germany Committee."

Kiss was right. In July, the Soviet Union pulled leaders from the ranks
of POWs to form a "National Committee for a Free Germany." Outwardly,
the group was nothing more than an exercise to demoralize German troops.
Working with their Soviet captors, Free Germany Committee members and
a similarly created League of German Officers produced a manifesto that
stressed the "blackness" of Germany's aggressive attacks and urged German

troops, as well as members of the public, to overthrow the Nazi regime. Though some involved were exiled German Communists, the committee spoke of replacing the Nazis with a democratic government that would ensure personal liberties, property rights, and even a free press.

The Soviets were starting to drop behind enemy lines a newspaper prepared by the captured German officers. The *Freies Deutschland* featured articles urging German troops to surrender and testimonials promising humane treatment from the Soviets. In one early issue, a onetime Communist member of the Reichstag compared the German army's crumbling position to that of the army of 1918, but argued that Germany was now better off because the Free Germany Committee stood ready to lead them to peace. Some of these Germans were deemed so loyal to the Soviet Union that they were supplied with German uniforms and smuggled back behind German lines, along with paper and printing presses, to produce anti-Nazi propaganda.

Gisevius had warned that the Soviets would try to win the hearts and minds of German officers as a step toward an alliance. This looked like an attempt to curry favor with the German officers still in the field. And though the committee made all the right noises about a democratic future for Germany, few believed it was anything more than a sop to persuade more German POWs to join the organization. Some in Dulles's circle of informants began to fear a link between the Free Germany Committee and the Soviet Union's postwar ambitions.

Dulles's hardening suspicions of the Soviets soon became fairly common knowledge among his agents as well as the Germans spying on him. Inevitably, word reached the Soviets, too, and they planned a counterattack on the pesky American in Bern.

At his desk at MI6 headquarters in London, a dreary structure near Saint James's Park, an intelligence officer with impeccable credentials took special note of the transmissions that Dulles was sending to Washington about the Soviets.

Born in India and nicknamed "Kim" after the young boy in Rudyard Kipling's novel of the same name, H. A. R. Philby belonged to what would come to be known as the Cambridge Five, a ring of spies who had attended the University of Cambridge and who secretly worked for Moscow. By 1939 Philby had landed a position in MI6 and was working in counterespionage, a desk job that ensured he would see a steady stream of material of interest to his Russian handlers, and cables such as those Dulles was sending to Washington.

According to Gordon Thomas, an author and expert on intelligence services, it didn't take long for Philby to discern a hostile attitude toward Moscow from Agent 110. In addition to warning about the Free Germany Committee, Dulles frequently shared his suspicions about Soviet ambitions for central Europe. In one communiqué, Dulles wrote of Soviet designs in Yugoslavia and Bulgaria. Moscow likewise aimed to establish a socialist re- public in Poland, he warned. "It is calculated by Russia that when hostilities in Europe cease, England and the United States will still be at war with Japan, and Russia, as an attitude in the Orient, can be a bargaining point in accom- plishing objectives in Europe."

When Philby reported his findings to Moscow, the instructions back were clear: discredit Dulles.

In staff meetings at MI6 headquarters in the weeks that followed, Philby made a point of criticizing Dulles's work in Bern and challenging the cred- ibility of his sources. So convincing were Philby's assertions that the head of MI6, Stewart Menzies, took it upon himself to cable the British secret service's station chief in Washington, suggesting that he warn the US War Department about questionable reports from Switzerland.

Dulles began to pull together the threads of intelligence that he was hearing. Thanks to the stories from Gisevius and the reports from the informants who still trooped to the Herrengasse, he decided the German underground was more competent than he had first judged. At the same time, by refusing to cooperate with the resistance, the United States seemed to be handing the Soviet Union a golden opportunity to ingratiate itself with the conspirators and gain influence in postwar Germany.

On August 19, 1943, Agent 110 wrote his observation that "political warfare" was lagging behind "military warfare" in Germany. It was becoming clear, he continued, that the Casablanca declaration, especially as described by skilled German propagandists, was being used against the Allies.

Gingerly at first, Dulles suggested tweaking the course of US policy to offer a more optimistic vision of Germany's future. "Could not Allied leaders emphasize that while surrender is admissive of complete military defeat, it actually will inaugurate a new life for the oppressed in Axis and Axis-controlled countries; that it means the end of the war, the end of bombing raids, the end of the Gestapo."

It was a small step, but Dulles had crossed a threshold. His engagement with the resistance would steadily grow.

CHAPTER

16

"Twenty Percent for Liberation and Eighty Percent for Russia"

Italy had always been the weak link in the Axis alliance. As early as the spring of 1943, Italians began to complain about battlefield setbacks in ways that would have been unimaginable in Germany, holding strikes and demonstrations. In May, Dulles impertinently, and unsuccessfully, suggested that Stalin, Churchill, and Roosevelt offer a statement to Italian citizens making clear that the war was against their leaders, not the people. Dropping copies of this statement from planes and broadcasting it on radio, Dulles wrote, "might at least cause a sufficiently widespread disturbance to work as a continuing undermining factor for the Italian regime and the German forces of occupation."

As it would turn out, Mussolini was deposed in July even without Dulles's help. The Italian Grand Council of Fascism, nominally the main chamber of the Italian Fascist government, met on July 24, 1943, to debate the dismal state of the country's war effort. Hours of bitter argument ensued, culminating with a vote against Mussolini, one ballot opposing the dictator cast by his own son-in-law, Galeazzo Ciano. Later on the twenty-fifth, Il Duce was arrested and soon dispatched to a mountaintop hotel that was to serve as his prison. Italians celebrated, thinking that the war was over.

Yet Washington and London, Gisevius complained to Bancroft, had needlessly delayed a final surrender by failing to quickly sign an armistice with the new government under Pietro Badoglio. The aging former general was determined to rescue some shred of Italy's pride and hoped to flip sides to join the Allies. Not until September 8 was a peace deal announced, one that united the southern part of the country with the Allies.

Bancroft wrote that Gisevius was "berating me for the way the Allies had handled the situation in Italy, as if I were in some way responsible." The United States should not only have quickly agreed to a peace deal with Italy, but also followed it with offers to the Romanians, Bulgarians, and Hungarians, who were watching to see how the Americans handled the Italian surrender. Had the United States made such offers, Gisevius said, the countries would have fallen to the Allies like "ripe fruit." The real prize might have even been greater, he added. The psychological damage of losing so many countries would have devastated morale in Germany, and the country would have collapsed within seventy-two hours, he claimed.

There is no record that Dulles took Gisevius seriously. There was, however, one result of the Italian surrender that would consume Dulles to the final days of the war. As in Germany, he came to believe, the Soviets had designs on spreading communism.

Moscow's ambitions rested on the resistance movement that thrived in northern Italy. There, in the autumn of 1943, thousands of Italians—many ex-soldiers—began guerrilla campaigns against their German occupiers and a new German puppet state. Known as the Italian Social Republic, it was led by none other than Mussolini, rescued by German paratroopers in a daring raid in September.

Many of the partisans, Dulles was aware, were oriented toward Moscow.

By some estimates, up to half of the men and women fighting in the underground were members of Garibaldi Brigades, cells of Communist fighters named for the Italian hero Giuseppe Garibaldi. Helping lead the units were Communist Party cadres, some trained in the Soviet Union. It was made clear that anybody who wanted to advance up the chain of command must commit to communism.

Though driving the Germans from Italy was their primary focus, the brigades spent considerable energy on preparing to spread communism after the war. Italian Communists worked closely with the Communist Party in Yugoslavia, which supplied the Italians with arms and instructions and a communications link with the Soviet Union. OSS agents in Italy noted that sometimes the brigades took guns and ammunition parachuted to them by US aircraft and buried them to use after the war to secure political objectives, rather than use them to attack the Germans. As one OSS officer remarked, the Garibaldi leaders were "20 percent for liberation and 80 percent for Russia." Another OSS officer discovered that Communist partisans were plotting to have him murdered. Moscow had instructed Italian Communist resistance fighters to avoid helping American and British military efforts to advance up the peninsula.

Soviet influence on the Italian resistance was a subject of growing concern in Western capitals. Some feared a leftist government in northern Italy would take orders from Moscow. Others worried about Communist influence spreading throughout the entire country. The Italian population had grown disenchanted with what they had seen from the United States—its slow advance through the country and bombing campaigns that killed civilians.

For Dulles, this threat of a Communist-dominated northern Italy demanded action.

A steady rain beat against the windshield of Dulles's car as he drove into the hills above Lake Lugano, near the border between Italy and Switzerland. Next to him lay a memorial wreath, which Italian contacts had instructed him to take to the cemetery of a small village. He was to meet a member of the Italian resistance there.

Striding among the grave markers, Dulles was startled when an attractive woman in soaking-wet clothes stepped out from behind a mausoleum. "I am Countess de Grubelli," the woman announced. Dulles smoothly replied: "And I am very wet. Let's find an inn and get ourselves dry."

In the weeks that followed, punctuated by parties she threw for Dulles, the countess delivered a familiar refrain. Partisans in Italy were willing to fight the Germans, but they lacked weapons, food, and medicine. Engaged in a firefight with the Germans, a partisan had to think twice before every shot, knowing he had only a few rounds. Basic medical supplies were virtually nonexistent.

Allied planes did sometimes run supply missions, but they were too few and far between. When airdrops were arranged, the Germans might intercept the supplies or attack the planes as they flew low through the treacherous mountain valleys where the Italians hid.

Much of what Dulles heard was not news to him. Italian resistance leaders had been finding their way to Agent 110 in search of financial support. Among them was Ferruccio Parri, one of the most respected leaders of the underground group known as the Committee for the Liberation of Northern Italy. Dulles had done what he could to help Parri, but the result was paltry, especially compared to the support the Allies provided to resistance fighters in France or to Tito's partisans in Yugoslavia.

Dulles and the countess now developed a plan that seemed like a promising way to help.

Perched on a corner of Lake Lugano and surrounded by Switzerland—lake and land—the tiny Italian enclave of Campione had been a mecca for Europe's blue bloods before the war. At the lakefront casino, men in black ties crowded around clattering roulette wheels and took their chances at the craps tables. Restaurants echoed with the sound of popping champagne corks, and the waterfront buzzed with pleasure craft. All went quiet with the coming of war, and Campione had slumbered through the conflict in a state of tranquility, forgotten by the Allies, the Germans, and its own leaders in Rome.

In such a safe and cozy corner, reasoned Countess de Grubelli, the OSS could set up a training and communications center for the resistance. Supplies could be brought there and transported into the Italian backcountry. The OSS was working on some promising devices that the Italian underground was hungry to try out. One was a bomb detonator that could be triggered by radio or even by ground tremors during an air raid. The idea was for a partisan to plant explosives at a strategically important area and leave them to be detonated later during an air attack. When timed to go off during an Allied bombing, the Germans would not have reason to punish civilians or to hunt for the perpetrators.

Best of all, Campione looked like an easy conquest. Its six hundred or so citizens shared neutral Switzerland's disdain for fascism. The town was "defended" by six police officers who didn't feel the smallest measure of loyalty to Mussolini's puppet government. The countess and Dulles concluded that a small team of commandos, aided by partisans in the town, could "liberate" Campione in short order, probably without either side drawing a gun.

Dulles, who had never served in the military and was inexperienced in handling weapons, decided against leading the mission himself. He selected two OSS agents who were acquainted with the area and had worked with the Italians, one a former journalist named Donald Jones, whom Dulles referred to as "his man in Lugano." Jones had developed excellent relations with the Italian resistance as well as with the local Swiss police and intelligence services; both relationships would be invaluable for the scheme they were hatching.

Loading rifles for twenty men and a supply of hand grenades onto a small boat on a snowy January evening in 1944, the team slipped out of the yacht harbor at Lugano and made its way across the lake, peering toward the lights of their destination. As the group drew near, the silhouettes of partisans materialized in the darkness, a reassuring sign that all was unfolding according to plan. Reaching the shore, the men could see Campione's colorfully painted buildings peppering the steep hills, the narrow streets winding between them.

Stepping quietly from their boat, the small force met the local guides, who led them in search of the carabiniere. The surprised police, as expected, surrendered without a fight.

Word of the "invasion" quickly spread the following morning, to the delight of Campione's citizens. Without much prompting, many of the villagers gathered in the town square and jubilantly swore their allegiance to the new antifascist Italian government in Rome, which had allied itself with the United States and Britain.

There was one loose end that nobody—not the OSS men on the scene, or the countess, or least of all Dulles—had thought to consider. Now that Campione was freed by an American operation, the United States had to assume at least some responsibility for its welfare. And Campione was broke.

During the war years, Campione and its inhabitants had been living off their savings and small handouts from the Italian government. That nest egg had dried up by late 1943. Devoid of natural resources, unable to attract tourists during wartime, and lacking industry, Campione didn't have many options to fill its depleted coffers.

Yet Campione boasted an interesting history and an odd geographic position, a prized distinction for certain enterprises. Meeting with city leaders, Dulles agreed that the territory might be able to generate some income by printing a series of postage stamps celebrating its new freedom. Collectors around the world would pay handsomely to add Campione's offerings to their displays. The villagers heartily agreed.

Using OSS funds, a printer in Zurich was hired, and by May stamps began rolling off its presses, red, blue, green, and brown motifs depicting scenes of Campione and priced in Swiss francs. Campione's citizens busily wrote letters to stamp dealers around the world, and to the delight of all, checks began to arrive asking for the latest printings. "Enough were sold," Dulles later wrote with pride, "to carry more mail than Campione would send for generations and enough money was realized to meet the budget deficit."

CHAPTER

17

"A High-Tension Power Line"

The relationship between Bancroft and Gisevius was getting complicated. Bancroft felt as if they were linked by "a high-tension power line." They had grown so close that she believed she could summon Gisevius to phone her simply by thinking of him. More than once, Gisevius proposed the two get away and spend time together. Reaching for her hand, he would beg her to run off with him for a couple of weeks to "work on [his] book." Bancroft confessed she was sorely tempted to accept his offers, especially one day when he invited her to accompany him on a weekend away with a wonderful apartment at his disposal. He said he would be meeting the former chief of the Gestapo, Rudolf Diels. Diels was a famous ladies' man who had once had an affair with Martha Dodd, the daughter of the American ambassador to Germany in the 1930s, and he could have been a profitable source of intelligence. Gisevius joked that he was afraid to introduce the two because women found Diels so attractive.

There was no telling what she might discover in the company of two such men, she thought. The trip would offer the added benefit of being a private dig at Dulles. He had ridiculed her when she mentioned her telepathic ability to summon Gisevius. He snapped that he didn't want to end up being part of one of Jung's case studies. And it would have served him right, for all the demands he was placing on her, for her to run away with Gisevius, she later wrote.

Bancroft declined the offer, but she should have known better than to tell Dulles. He lashed out when she told him of the invitation. "Why the hell didn't you go? It might have been very interesting."

Dulles was growing ever hungrier for intelligence about the activities of the German underground. Though he now supported its work, he still had reason to doubt whether it could accomplish anything. Many of its members were running into trouble, the product of their own increasing desperation and the improved efforts of German authorities to discover them. One well-known resistance member, for instance, had recently risked a plan to overthrow Hitler that had gone terribly wrong.

Rather than purging Germany of leading Nazis, Carl Langbehn, a Berlin attorney, hoped to collaborate with one of the most prominent, none other than SS chief Himmler. Langbehn had known Himmler for years. Their daughters were school friends, and they lived not far apart in the affluent Berlin neighborhood of Dahlem. Meeting from time to time in relaxed social settings, the two enjoyed a relatively frank relationship. Langbehn, who opposed the Nazis, had once prevailed on Himmler to have an old professor, a non-Aryan, released from a concentration camp and sent to safety abroad.

Proposing to Himmler a plan to depose Hitler was a dangerous exercise. But Langbehn knew someone who he thought could help. Among his associates was the former Prussian minister of state finance Johannes Popitz. With a narrow face, large-rimmed glasses, and hair shorn to the skin on the sides of his head, Popitz knew Hans Oster from the Abwehr and was a fixture of the "Wednesday Club," a regular gathering of resistance leaders that included Beck. Yet his relationship with the leading lights of the group was tense. Popitz professed hard-chiseled views about what form of government and economy Germany should adopt after the war. Whereas men like Goerdeler favored a new Germany built on a representative government with a competitive market economy, Popitz believed the country would best be served by a regulated economy with a centralized state structure. Such differences or not, Langbehn reasoned, the man could help with his plan. Langbehn arranged a meeting between Popitz and Himmler at the Reichsführer's office at the Interior Ministry on August 26.

Sitting in an anteroom with a senior SS officer, the former public-relations executive General Karl Wolff, Langbehn eavesdropped as Popitz made his pitch. Gingerly, Popitz explained why he believed that Germany was headed for defeat, and his conviction that the United States and Britain feared Soviet intentions and would be willing to negotiate a peace deal with a German government led by someone other than Hitler. Though Langbehn knew Himmler, the conversation was fraught with danger. Few outside Hitler's inner circle understood the ever-swirling political currents there. And Popitz was in some respects ill-suited for the job. As one who knew Popitz described him, he was a man with "pure intentions but few sure political instincts." Wisely, Popitz stopped short of suggesting a plan to have Hitler assassinated.

Himmler apparently spoke little but at the end of the meeting authorized Langbehn to travel to Switzerland to see about striking up communication with the Western Allies. With considerable excitement, and deeply in over his head, the inexperienced Langbehn set off. Who exactly Langbehn met in Switzerland is unknown, but he returned to Germany hoping that his plan could move forward.

At some point during or shortly after his visit, the source he met with sent a message out of Switzerland describing the meeting and mentioning Langbehn. Unfortunately for him, German security services intercepted that transmission and were able to decode it. Soon the head of the Gestapo, Heinrich Müller, knew of Langbehn's traitorous overture.

A rival of Himmler's, Müller passed the message up the chain of command until it eventually reached Hitler. Such damning intelligence left Himmler no recourse but to sacrifice Langbehn. He denied any knowledge of what the lawyer had been up to, had him arrested, and then made sure that hearings into Langbehn's activities were kept out of public view.

Hitting even closer to home for Dulles, the German authorities had discovered his valuable contact Eduard Schulte, the industrialist who had exposed Auschwitz to the West.

At Dulles's request, Schulte had prepared a position paper on the economy and government of Germany after the war, a project he had undertaken in the Zurich office of a friend. Snooping through the waste bins where Schulte was working was a cleaning lady named Martha Rigling. A naturalized Swiss citizen, Rigling was originally from Germany and still felt loyal to her homeland. She was also the mistress of a member of the SS, a solid-looking man with dark hair named Johann Wüst.

Picking up in the Zurich office where Schulte had prepared his report, Rigling came across fifteen pages of carbon paper that had been part of his work and casually thrown away. She realized they might be of interest to Wüst.

Wüst immediately understood that he had some fascinating material—a report written by a leading German industrialist that not only assumed Germany would lose the war but also laid out a vision for postwar Germany that had nothing to do with the Nazis. Accounts of what happened next vary, but the pages that Rigling retrieved from the waste bin, and accompanying papers prepared by Wüst, found their way to Gisevius.

Gisevius devised a compelling plan to gum up the works of the Nazi bureaucracy. Allowed to see the Schulte papers by colleagues in German security services before they were sent to Berlin, he added his own assessment, intentionally writing it so poorly that intelligence analysts would have to ask time-consuming questions.

It was a stratagem sure to delay the investigation into Schulte. But he would not be able to employ such tactics forever, and Gisevius knew he needed to find a way to kill inquiries into Dulles's informant once and for all. The only way to do that, he reasoned, was to hazard a dangerous trip to Berlin, the city he had fled half a year before.

When Gisevius arrived at Abwehr headquarters in the early winter of 1943, he found that the proud institution bore little resemblance to what he had known before. Pessimism and gloom hung over the agency.

Sitting down with Canaris, Gisevius could see the strain of recent events etched on his face. Normally calm, Canaris appeared worn, the investigations of the spy agency taking their toll.

There was little he could do to extricate Schulte.

Another contact was only marginally more helpful. Colonel Egbert von Bentivengi, the head of the agency's counterespionage unit, met Gisevius but told him he had been removed from his job once before and believed himself to be under SS observation. The monocle-wearing colonel could not get involved in Schulte's case any more than Canaris could. But he did reveal some useful information. Schulte would probably soon be arrested. He added that Gisevius had to be careful if he aimed to warn him, as Schulte's phone was bugged.

The morning of December 2, 1943, Schulte was deep in a discussion with business partners on the company's coal operations. Normally extroverted, he had been in a glum mood all morning, reading about German military defeats. About an hour into the meeting, Schulte lifted his eyes as a secretary approached him. She whispered in his ear that he had an urgent phone call. Excusing himself, Schulte went to an adjacent room and picked up the receiver.

"This is Eduard," the stranger said. "Eduard who?" Schulte replied. "Surely you remember, we met a few months ago in Zurich when we had lunch." Schulte realized that the stranger was a friend of Gisevius's.

"I just had a call from our common friend. He thinks, and I agree with him, that your presence in Zurich is urgently needed. A critical situation has developed in the negotiations and your presence is required." Schulte offered to come the following week.

"Next week may be too late. You should come now, right away," the man said. Schulte hesitated for a second before he registered that this request would not be made unless he was in considerable personal danger. Schulte returned to the meeting and announced that he had to leave immediately. Without returning home for a suitcase, or even phoning his wife, he disappeared.

For the next several days, Schulte raced toward Switzerland with nothing more than the suit on his back, a frayed letter from his son to read and reread, a few magazines, and just enough cash to last him a week or two.

Reaching the border station at Basel, where the Rhine River separates Switzerland from Germany, Schulte made his way to customs control, a crossing he knew well. Though he tried to put on a confident face, the gravity of the moment was almost unbearable. Had the Gestapo issued a warrant for his arrest, and if they had, had it reached this point so far from Berlin? Handing his passport to the border guard, Schulte watched as the man flipped through the pages filled with stamps that showed he was a frequent traveler. Likely assuming that Schulte was again taking a routine business trip, the guard let him pass.

Not long after, Canaris traveled to Switzerland to see Gisevius. He knew *Der Lange* was increasingly in trouble, and he hoped his visit would bolster Gisevius in the eyes of other Abwehr agents in Switzerland. When Gisevius told him that an agent of the Abwehr's foreign counterintelligence service had searched his apartment, Canaris had the man transferred out of the country. Yet it was clear that Canaris could not protect Gisevius for long. It was time, the Abwehr boss counseled, for Gisevius to suspend work for the resistance, "to renounce all activity."

Gisevius knew that the odds of beating the Gestapo and the intelligence agents of the SS were growing longer every day. Yet professionally he had known little else than his work to unseat Hitler. There could be no giving up now. "My whole temperament and all my political views made it impossible for me to agree with the reasoning he outlined," he later wrote.

Though Gisevius didn't mention it, there was another reason to keep up his work. From the carnage of repeated arrests of his friends, a new figure was emerging. A decorated war hero with dashing good looks, yet full of controversial ideas about how to topple the Nazis, was about to inject a "new dynamism" into the entire German underground.

CHAPTER

18

"The Qualities of a Genius"

Claus von Stauffenberg exemplified the best the German army could produce. Born to one of southern Germany's aristocratic families, he excelled at whatever he put his mind to—school, work, horsemanship, and the pursuits of a Renaissance man. He spoke excellent English, and was an enthusiastic student of history. He enjoyed poetry.

Now in his midthirties, Stauffenberg was endowed with the dark hair and sharp features of a movie star. With a keen wit, an infectious laugh, and a well-developed sense of humor, and capable of shouldering tremendous amounts of work, he had been a darling of the German officer corps since the day he joined. In the words of one senior officer, he displayed "the qualities of a genius."

Stauffenberg was not impressed by his commander in chief. As with many senior officers of noble background, he found taking orders from someone he did not consider his equal to be an unsavory duty. Hitler was just such a man. The Führer's recent military blunders cast doubt on his leadership of the armed forces, to say nothing of the crimes that Hitler was ordering his troops to commit, orders that revolted the deeply religious Stauffenberg.

In the early years of Hitler's regime, Stauffenberg had been a figure of marginal importance in the resistance and had restricted his disagreements to small acts of protest. He kept an enormous portrait of Hitler in his office, not as a sign of respect but as the prop for a joke. Explaining the painting to friends, he would say, "I picked this one so that everyone who comes to my office gets some sense of lunacy and dizzying disproportion."

In April 1943, a chain of events began that would lead Stauffenberg to take a more active role. Early that month, as a lieutenant colonel in the Tenth Armored Division in Tunisia, Stauffenberg was conducting a reconnaissance mission when the pilot of an Allied fighter plane sighted the staff car in which he was riding. Swooping down in a strafing run, the plane riddled the car, hitting Stauffenberg several times. Evacuated to Munich, he underwent a series of painful operations and lost his right hand and two fingers on his left. He also lost his left eye, an injury that he covered with a black patch, and suffered damage to his left knee and ear. The man of accomplishment had to relearn simple tasks and teach himself new skills such as how to dress himself by using his teeth.

Reflecting in his hospital room and, later, in the serenity of his family garden in Lautlingen, Stauffenberg grappled with the inescapable conclusion that Germany would lose the war. It was only a matter of time, he believed, until the United States and Britain landed in France. There also seemed to be no answer to the Soviet advance in the east. The only question that remained was how much of Germany would be left when the end came. Eliminating Hitler, Stauffenberg concluded, was the only hope to preserve at least some of his beloved country.

There could be no half measures this time. Not only would Hitler have to be killed, but other senior Nazis would also have to die at the same time. The immediate hours after the attack would be crucial, as the conspirators would have to seize control of the German government before anybody else did.

•　　•　　•

From the start, Stauffenberg rubbed the leading lights of the resistance the wrong way, none more so than the ex-politician Goerdeler. The colonel found the aging former mayor too conservative for his views. According to Goerdeler's account, their first meeting was something of a disaster. He found Stauffenberg a "cranky, obstinate fellow who wanted to play politics." Goerdeler also concluded that Stauffenberg wanted to steer Germany on a "dubious political course with left-wing Socialists and Communists, and gave me a bad time with his overwhelming egotism."

Stauffenberg's real views are a matter of debate, but it was clear that under his leadership, the resistance was ready to act again.

CHAPTER
19

"Obviously a Plant"

The lights of a Triumph sports car blinked in the darkness as it approached the midspan of the Kirchenfeld Bridge, which arched over the Aare River. Gerald Mayer was right on time, eleven thirty p.m. on October 8. Waiting for a signal in the shadows at the southern end of the historic structure was Fritz Kolbe. "It's mighty good to see that you've made it again," Mayer said in a friendly voice as "Wood" climbed in.

Folding himself into the passenger seat, the German hoped to discuss the Triumph, a British make that one didn't often see on the streets of Berlin. But Mayer was focused on his driving, piloting the small car with the lights off down narrow cobblestone streets along the river and finally braking to a stop almost directly under the bridge where they had met a few moments earlier, its silhouette visible more than a hundred feet above them.

Mayer told Kolbe he was going to visit "Mr. Douglas" once again. He should climb through the back garden, up a steep path, and through dense shrubbery until he reached the back door of Herrengasse 23. "Go on alone," Mayer said. "I'll rejoin you up there in a little while. You're expected."

Kolbe carried with him some two hundred pages' worth of intelligence: a summary of the tense state of German-Italian relations, a list of French people whom the Nazis suspected of sympathizing with the Allies, a plan to smuggle tungsten disguised as oranges out of Spain, and U-boat movements in the Atlantic.

Equally important for Dulles was the fresh opportunity to try to trip Kolbe up. He subjected the German to a barrage of detailed questions about what he and Mayer had learned already, in hopes of discovering inconsistencies. At times, Kolbe's reaction seemed to support their suspicion. He had a difficult time talking about himself and frequently hesitated when describing his life, his youth, his friends, and his hatred of the Nazis.

Yet as he talked, his credentials continued to add up. He belonged to a small circle of men secretly opposed to Hitler, and two of his friends had died in concentration camps, he told the Americans. Many evenings, he met with a group of trusted friends in Der Schwabenwirt, a small but nice restaurant on Berlin's Motzstrasse. They had planned to blow up a train bridge near Werder, not far from the capital, but later thought better of the attack. His circle of friends included several doctors at the Charité Hospital, among them Ernst Ferdinand Sauerbruch, a famous surgeon and a pioneer in the development of prosthetic devices. Kolbe, awaiting his divorce, was engaged to Dr. Sauerbruch's secretary, Maria Fritsch.

Dulles had already made some inquiries into Kolbe. Since last seeing the German, he had sent a number of the Wood documents to Frederick Vanden Heuvel, a British agent in Geneva, and asked him to pass them to London.

Kolbe's papers were then delivered to the deputy MI6 director, Claude Dansey, who had resented Dulles from the start. Kolbe's story, he quickly concluded, was just too fantastic: a German informant with access to such sensitive information could not possibly make copies of top-secret documents, carry them on a public train across half the country, and walk across the border.

More to the point, Dansey could not bring himself to believe that the inexperienced Yank could have found something of value that his network had not. "The sight of the Berlin papers must have been a severe shock to [Dansey]," Kim Philby, the Soviet mole working inside MI6, later recounted. "It was clearly impossible that Dulles should have pulled off this spectacular scoop under his nose. Therefore, he had not." In Dansey's view, Kolbe's papers were "obviously a plant, and Dulles had fallen for it like a ton of bricks."

Washington, inclined to take its cue from MI6 on cases of such import, followed London's lead. The OSS treated everything sent by Dulles from this walk-in with considerable caution. But the OSS was intrigued enough to launch an investigation. Donovan formed something of a blue-ribbon panel to look into Kolbe's reports that included James Murphy, the head of counterintelligence, George Strong, the head of military intelligence, and Colonel Alfred McCormack, the head of special branch, the department responsible for deciphering enemy messages.

In the meantime, the OSS London station combed through Kolbe's documents paragraph by paragraph, word by word, before they were sent to Washington. Commentaries were attached detailing what could be confirmed and what couldn't. As Richard Helms, an up-and-coming OSS officer who evaluated the Kolbe files in Washington, later explained, "Kolbe was obviously an instrument of German intelligence, and his documents were probably the opening gambit in a deception scheme."

Kolbe made his third trip to Switzerland over the Christmas holiday in 1943, again carrying a trove of materials, some two hundred documents, including information about the construction sites of V-1 rockets in Belgium and France. The mountains of information he was delivering were almost overwhelming Dulles. It took days to code and send even portions of what Kolbe provided. There had to be a better way to get it all to Washington.

The method that Dulles devised was complex. Kolbe's papers began their journey in Geneva. There, the OSS had struck up a relationship with a locomotive engineer who frequently traveled between Switzerland and Lyon, and persuaded him to build a special compartment near the boiler of his train, just big enough to contain Kolbe's documents. The box provided not only a good hiding place but, thanks to another invention, also allowed the engineer to trip a special lever and dump its contents directly into the engine's boiler if he faced a nosy inspector. In Lyon, a member of the resistance met the engineer and transported the secret packet by bicycle to Marseilles, where a fishing boat took it to Corsica. From there, it was flown to Algiers, and on to London and Washington.

Gradually, the flood of material that made its way out of Switzerland began to win converts. Too much of it was supported by intelligence gathered from other sources. In late November, British counterintelligence concluded that there was no evidence that the material Kolbe provided was fake. "Wood," British analysts believed, should be encouraged but closely watched. At the same time, Norman Pearson, a counterintelligence expert with the OSS in London, wrote that if Kolbe were trying to fool Dulles, "it will have been far and away the most elaborate deception strategy so far known either to British or American intelligence services."

Dulles, too, was growing more confident. Schulze-Gaevernitz, his right-hand man who seemed to know everybody, had never heard of Kolbe. Yet he was able to learn much about Ernst Kocherthaler, the man who had first brought Kolbe to the Americans' attention.

Checking with sources that included the religious leader Visser't Hooft in Geneva, Schulze-Gaevernitz discovered details of Kocherthaler's life. Though born in Germany, Kocherthaler now carried a Spanish passport and had lived in Switzerland since 1936. He was well thought of in financial circles and had worked for a time at Warburg & Co. in Hamburg. He was either Jewish or partly Jewish, and had at one time tried to help establish a Christian university in Switzerland to educate German teachers after the war. He and his family lived in the small village of Adelboden, forty miles south of Bern.

Most compelling was the staggering amount of information that Kolbe was providing. Dulles could not escape the notion that if the Germans were attempting to dupe him, they would not provide so many details, because that made it easier to run cross-checks and discover if the information was outdated or fabricated.

On December 29, Dulles cabled Washington that he was now completely confident in Wood. He was providing so much accurate information that he had to be genuine. "I now firmly believe in the good faith of Woods, and I am ready to stake my reputation on the fact that these documents are genuine," he wrote.

Dulles was correct. The little man with protruding ears and the propensity to nervous perspiration was who he said he was: a German opposed to both the fascists and the Bolsheviks who wanted to help the Americans prevent either from taking over his nation.

Kolbe had been taking tremendous risks to help Dulles.

Once, on the way to Bern, Kolbe's train was attacked by a Mosquito, a light twin-engine British bomber. Clutching secret documents he had stolen for Dulles, Kolbe was forced to shelter in a ditch somewhere between Frankfurt and Karlsruhe for the better part of a night and a day.

On another occasion, Kolbe nearly started a fire in his office when he prepared a package for Switzerland. Afraid of strapping documents to his leg as he had on his first covert journey, Kolbe had devised a new means of smuggling materials by taking the official correspondence meant for the German legation and stuffing it into a larger package that included documents for Dulles. This he closed with red wax seals bearing the imprint of the Foreign Ministry. He had traded a box of chocolates for the stamping device. Once he cleared customs, he would go to a men's room and lock himself in a stall, open the outer envelope, remove the documents for Dulles, and place them in his coat. He would then burn the outer envelope and flush the ashes down the toilet.

Packing the materials, however, could be difficult. Afraid of working in the open, Kolbe once fumbled with his sealing device and a bit of flaming wax fell onto the papers in a desk drawer, igniting them. Barely managing to extinguish the flame before it spread, Kolbe rushed to the window and threw it open, waving the smoke out of the building before anybody was the wiser.

Kolbe was also proving to be a resourceful spy. In Bern, where German agents were likely to keep tabs on him, he accepted invitations for drinks or dinner from colleagues at the mission, visiting Dulles only late at night, and always varying his route. Hat pulled down nearly covering his eyes, he would pass through Bern's arcades, jumping on trams at the last second, slipping out the back doors of shops, and zigzagging across city streets.

He had developed a ruse to explain his meetings with Dulles that often went into the early hours of the morning. Kolbe made a point of bragging to colleagues about his sexual conquests. He spoke of "pretty Swiss women, who were not all that timid." And one evening, he spent a couple of hours in a local brothel, documenting the visit by making an appointment with a doctor who specialized in venereal diseases and making sure to save the bill.

This precaution likely saved his life. Returning from Bern after his August visit, Kolbe found an urgent message from a Foreign Ministry security officer. Surprised and nervous, he met with a pale-faced individual with deep-set eyes who displayed a telegram claiming that Kolbe had not been in his room the entire night of August 23–24.

"That is quite correct," Wood replied with a frozen smile. "One needs a little relaxation at times. You know how often one drifts around a strange city. A few drinks at a bar, a young woman . . ." He then extracted a doctor's certificate from his pocket stating that he had been given a prophylactic and a blood test on the morning of August 24. "Very well," the security officer conceded. "But take care how you waste your time in the future."

The risks were part of the attraction. A lifelong fitness enthusiast, Kolbe found his adventures intoxicating. They also suited the heroic ambitions he had set for himself. "He was an action guy, a physical guy. He would have loved to shoot somebody. He always dreamed of being the hero who would assassinate Hitler," Peter Sichel, an OSS officer, remembers.

Yet for all the background checks, for all the material that he brought to Bern, for all the sincerity with which he spoke, Kolbe was not yet able to satisfy one skeptic, the MI6 deputy director Claude Dansey.

CHAPTER

20

"Now All Is Lost"

In September, the Kreisau Circle's Moltke received disturbing news. The SS had requested a government official monitor the telephone of Elisabeth von Thadden, the woman who had hosted the birthday party attended by people privately opposed to the Nazi regime. The party-crashing Gestapo agent, Dr. Reckzeh, had made his report. Moltke, who learned of the phone tap from a friend, promptly informed Thadden and others whose phones were to be monitored.

A more skilled group of revolutionaries might have handled Moltke's warning by coolly watching what they said, but otherwise keeping up the appearance that everything was normal. Not Thadden and the others. Several abruptly refused to have any contact with Dr. Reckzeh, and most stopped using their phones. One guest concluded on his own that Dr. Reckzeh was suspicious and told him so to his face.

At first, their strategy of shutting down seemed to work. When September and October passed, and the Gestapo did nothing, some began to think they were in the clear. "We began to breathe more easily," one said.

Believing that a catastrophic security breach had been avoided, Moltke prepared to finally meet Alexander Kirk, the American diplomat in Cairo he knew from before the war, to discuss his peace plan. Arriving in Turkey in December, Moltke encountered the same OSS representatives he had met the first time, Wilbrandt and Rüstow.

Kirk still wasn't willing to meet him, the two told Moltke. Ever cautious, Kirk saw numerous security problems. Moltke, who stood more than six and a half feet tall, could be easily tailed by even the most inexperienced German agent. Air transport was likewise ruled out, as there was no commercial air service between Cairo and Istanbul, and arranging a military flight would have required informing the Turkish government, a step that opened up the possibility of a security leak.

The best the Americans could do was to arrange a meeting with the US military attaché, Brigadier General Richard G. Tindall, in Ankara. Disappointed, Moltke attended the meeting, but he found it a waste of time. Tindall didn't show much interest in the underground. Instead, he pumped Moltke for information about Germany's military, which he was in no mood to provide.

With that, Moltke left for what looked like an uncertain future at home. While he thought he had saved the birthday-party guests, he felt a deep sense of unease and didn't expect to avoid arrest for long. He explained to Wilbrandt and Rüstow that he wanted to spend Christmas with his family. "Now all is lost," he told them. He was more right than he knew.

Elisabeth von Thadden's party guests were wrong to think the Gestapo had lost interest in them. It was common practice for the secret police to wait as long as possible before arresting suspected traitors, observing them and hoping to learn as much as possible about their activities and membership. Yet there was no point in continuing surveillance if their subjects weren't yielding any information.

From January 10 to 12, 1944, Gestapo cars sped to the addresses of

Thadden and her friends, arresting dozens, including Hannah Solf and Otto Kiep, the former consul general in New York and a close contact of Moltke's.

The group was potentially a rich source of information about the resistance movement. Above all, the Gestapo wanted to know how they had been warned they were under surveillance. Dragged from their prison cells, members of the group, including a number of women, were brutally questioned and beaten. Most tried the best they could to keep their secrets. One, fearful he would break, strangled himself in his cell. Still, after a week the Gestapo learned about Moltke.

The evening of January 16, Moltke sat down with his diary. He had been to visit Johannes Popitz, the man who had worked with Carl Langbehn on the Himmler meeting. Despite the arrest of Langbehn, Moltke was impressed by Popitz. In his diary, he wrote, he was a "clever man" and a "brilliant talker." They were some of the last words the leader of the Kreisau Circle would confide to his diary as a free man. On January 19, 1944, agents of the SS appeared for him at his Abwehr office.

News of the arrests, especially that of the spiritual leader of the Kreisau Circle, sent shock waves through the German resistance. Somebody in the group of arrested partygoers was talking. Nobody was safe. Perhaps none was more nervous, and more inclined to panic, than a young Abwehr agent in Turkey.

Handsome, self-confident, and high-strung, Erich Vermehren had long opposed the Nazis. As a student, he had refused to join a Nazi youth group, even when doing so meant that he would not be allowed to accept a Rhodes scholarship to Oxford. His wife, the former countess Elizabeth Plettenberg, a devout Catholic thirteen years his senior, was even more ardent, already known to the Gestapo for distributing anti-Nazi literature.

A member of a well-to-do family of lawyers, and a friend to members of the Kreisau Circle, Vermehren had, after only a couple of weeks of training, been dispatched to the spy agency's station in Istanbul as a personal assistant to a friend of his father. There he quickly established contact with British intelligence and began slipping them copies of secret German documents.

News of the birthday-party arrests terrified the young German. He and his wife knew several of those taken into custody, and it was anybody's guess whether their names might be divulged under interrogation. When he received word that he was wanted back in Berlin, he and his wife assumed the worst.

On January 21, 1944, Vermehren sent a message to his office. He was sick and would not be in the following Monday. He also announced that he was moving and was changing his address. When Vermehren did not report for work the following week, German security agents discovered his apartment to be empty and the new address he had given to be fictitious.

With the help of the British agents, Vermehren and his wife had fled Turkey and were taken to London in what the British trumpeted as one of the great defections of the war. It wasn't every day that spies crossed over, and they carefully leaked word of the Vermehrens to the newspapers. The Associated Press reported that the couple had defected because they were disgusted by Nazi brutality.

In Germany, the news could not have been worse for Canaris, the head of the Abwehr. With alarming regularity, people who worked for him were being arrested. There had been Hans von Dohnányi in the spring. Moltke had been taken into custody after the birthday party. And now, an agent in Turkey, thought to have taken German codebooks with him, had fled to England. The diminutive head of German military intelligence was fully exposed and lacking anyone who could protect him.

Not long after returning from Switzerland, Canaris finally pushed the Führer too far. Asked to present a report on the situation on the eastern front, he offered a downbeat but accurate assessment. Hitler, who by 1944 believed his generals were overly pessimistic, erupted in anger, grabbing Canaris by the lapels and screaming at him. Shortly thereafter, Hitler ordered that most of the Abwehr's functions be merged into an umbrella organization—the Reich Main Security Office, led by Himmler's trusted lieutenant Walter Schellenberg. Canaris was dismissed and given the empty title of chief of the Office of Commercial and Economic Warfare.

•   •   •

One rainy night in late March 1944, Gisevius called on Dulles as he had so many times before, approaching Herrengasse 23 through the back vineyard. A maid greeted him at the rear door, an unusual occurrence, as Agent 110 was normally careful to keep his guests out of her view. On this night she had returned to work to retrieve a scarf left behind.

Ushering Gisevius into the house, she saw that his Tyrolean hunting cap was soaking wet and offered to take it into the kitchen and dry it. There she noticed three letters embroidered into the cap's lining: HBG. (Gisevius held a particularly risky fascination with monograms.) Intrigued, the woman pondered the significance of her discovery as Gisevius sat down with Dulles.

What the two discussed that evening is lost to history, but these were increasingly uncertain times for Gisevius. The ousting of Canaris was a painful blow. He had lost his most powerful protector. Gisevius was closer to other people in the underground, but none could shield him from the complex politics of Nazi security services as well as Canaris.

He would now be joined in Switzerland by another Abwehr man who, despite the downfall of Canaris, shared his views about the Nazis and was eager to strike up a relationship with Dulles.

Eduard von Waetjen would soon become a welcome visitor at the Herrengasse. Waetjen was a friend of Moltke's and traveled in circles familiar to Dulles—his father had been a successful German banker who worked for the Morgan Guaranty Trust in Germany. His sister was married to a Rockefeller. Waetjen also spoke English fluently, a welcome skill for the linguistically challenged Dulles. As Bancroft described him, Waetjen possessed a delightful sense of humor and a wide range of cultural interests, including translating the ancient Greek texts of Homer into German.

The meeting between Gisevius and Dulles that night concluded with no reason to think that anything out of the ordinary had happened, and Gisevius went home. A couple of days later, he arrived at the German legation in Bern, where he continued to work, despite growing suspicions about his loyalties. Before Gisevius had a chance to settle into his usual tasks, two men from the Foreign Ministry said they needed an urgent meeting. They had information that a "tall, heavy man" with the initials HBG had recently visited Allen Dulles, sneaking in by the back door. What, they demanded, was an Abwehr agent doing spending the evening with an American?

Gisevius, well acquainted with the powers of the German secret police, was ready for the interrogation.

The best reply was a mix of truth and lie. Gisevius acknowledged that he had dined with Dulles. But the American was the one supplying him with information, not the other way around. Dulles, he stated, was one of his best sources. If either of the two men now mentioned the maid's letter or anything to do with Dulles, Gisevius swore that he would see both drummed out of Germany's diplomatic corps.

Both agreed, and Gisevius considered the matter closed.

That evening Gisevius phoned Bancroft at her Zurich apartment at around ten o'clock and asked if he could come over to discuss the day's events. Ever the gentleman, he insisted that she first check with her husband.

Rufenacht and Gisevius, in fact, had struck up a friendship of their own. At their first meeting they had discovered they shared mutual friends and possessed the same sentimental feelings toward Germany. "Two more charming men you never saw, each saying exactly the right thing to make the best possible impression on the other," Bancroft noted. When the two waxed poetic about the beauties of Split and the Dalmatian coast, Bancroft remarked that she would rather go to Berlin. "Ach, Berlin!" they exclaimed in unison, their eyes misty with fondness for the German capital. Searching for common ground, they readily agreed that English was a beautiful language and that it would soon become a world language.

On this night, Rufenacht, already in bed with a book, readily gave his permission for Gisevius to visit.

Arriving less than half an hour later, Gisevius explained his close call to Bancroft and demanded that she take the earliest possible train to Bern and make sure the housekeeper was fired. Bancroft could not resist chiding Gisevius for the foolish mistake. He might hire her as an agent, she told Gisevius. But she certainly would not hire him!

Stepping out of Bancroft's apartment moments later, Gisevius slipped and dropped his briefcase, creating a racket that echoed down the empty street. Looking up from his French detective novel, Rufenacht commented drily: "I advise you to tell Gisevius to learn to walk downstairs quietly before he tries to kill Hitler."

CHAPTER

21

"I Trembled With Emotion"

Among the papers Kolbe delivered to Dulles over the Christmas holiday was a document containing a message from Franz von Papen, the German ambassador to Turkey, to Foreign Minister Ribbentrop, dated November 4, 1943. Papen wrote that he had been approached by a walk-in informant, a stranger who identified himself as "Pierre" but to whom the Germans quickly gave the code name "Cicero."

Cicero's real name was Elyesa Bazna. Short in stature with piercing dark eyes, Bazna had been born in the Balkans of humble roots, had performed a variety of odd jobs, and had once been sentenced to three years in a French penal labor camp for trying to steal weapons and cars. He also possessed considerable ambition and for a time saw a bright future for himself on the stage as a professional singer. He took lessons from a German music professor. Lacking either talent or luck, he never broke into the music business.

Instead, Bazna launched a successful career as a servant to members of the diplomatic corps in Ankara, working for a time as a driver for the American military attaché, among other dignitaries. Yet his ambition—or what others described as his arrogance—left him unfulfilled. In 1942, upon being employed by Albert Jenke, an aide to Papen, Bazna tried his hand at espionage. An amateur, he began by simply nosing through Jenke's papers and taking photographs of letters he found, using them to impress his wife and later a mistress.

Bazna's big break came when, without a thorough background check, he was hired by the British ambassador to Turkey, Sir Hugh Knatchbull-Hugessen. An old-fashioned diplomat who took a cavalier attitude toward security, Knatchbull-Hugessen occasionally left secret papers lying around his office. Bazna began taking photographs. Growing more bold and ambitious, he found the ambassador's key to the safe where the most-secret documents were stored, and he started photographing its contents as well.

With two rolls of film, Bazna decided to cash in on his work. In October 1943, he approached Ludwig Moyzisch, a member of the German intelligence service, with the seemingly outrageous claim that he had access to some of Britain's most closely held secrets and that he wanted the astounding sum of £20,000 for the rolls of film. More rolls, he promised, would soon be on offer for £15,000 each. The sums were fantastic, but his story was tantalizing enough that the Germans agreed, a decision no doubt made easier by their ability to print as many forged British notes as they wanted.

Among the documents that he now began delivering to the Germans, Kolbe's reports revealed, were conversations between British and Turkish leaders on whether Turkey would remain neutral or whether it would throw in its lot with the Allies. There were detailed reports of conferences in Cairo and Tehran, including indications that Churchill wanted to open a front in southern Europe. He also delivered information that painted a picture of the Allies' determination to totally destroy Germany. "I trembled with emotion before the spectacle of the vast historical prospects opened to me by those stolen documents," Moyzisch wrote later.

The most terrifying security break for the United States and Britain was
that Bazna had happened on the code word "Overlord"—the designation for
the planned invasion of France, the most closely guarded and important Allied military operation of the entire war.

The material was explosive, yet the Germans were unsure about whether
they could trust Cicero. Just as the Americans and the British had long
doubted Kolbe, the Germans suspected that Bazna was part of a British trick.
As Ribbentrop remarked to the German intelligence officer managing Cicero, it seemed "too good to be true."

Neither Kolbe, nor Dulles, nor anybody else in the Allied camp knew
that the Germans were ignoring the material, and all were deeply shaken
that such sensitive secrets were being passed to Berlin. When Donovan read
Dulles's report, he considered it important enough to pass on to Roosevelt,
who in turn forwarded it to Churchill.

The British were already starting to suspect that something was amiss in
Turkey. In early January, Knatchbull-Hugessen telegrammed London warning that his contacts suggested that Ambassador Papen knew more than he
should on a number of sensitive subjects, including talks on building radar
stations.

Prodded by Kolbe's memos, the British took action. Two investigators
were dispatched from London to Ankara to study the leak. It was a delicate
mission. Dulles worried that their arrival would arouse German suspicions
about where the Allies were getting their information. The British security
team also had to deal with a prickly and defensive Knatchbull-Hugessen,
who resented their questions and demands that he tighten his security.

In Ankara, the investigators studied the embassy's security procedures
and attempted to construct a trail of where the leak had originated. Their
queries found nothing. "Cicero," interrogated like many others in the embassy, was too smart. The valet handled their questions with skill and managed to avoid their traps, such as when they spoke to him in German, a
language he claimed not to understand. In the end, the investigators paid

him little attention, determining that he was too stupid to pull off such a scheme and didn't read English well enough to know what information to steal.

The British returned to London no wiser regarding the source of their leak, but confident that the embassy had at least tightened its security procedures. They were largely correct. Bazna must have realized that he was in over his head and not only stopped his photographic work, but also resigned his position.

Kolbe, even his critics now had to admit, was proving his sincerity beyond any doubt. The last lingering suspicions were dispelled by Philby, who saw in Kolbe's papers an opportunity to advance himself within MI6. The double agent went about conducting his own study into their authenticity. Using information Kolbe had obtained about conditions in Asia and comparing it against information the British had from other sources, he hoped to discover for himself whether Wood's documents were authentic. What he learned was remarkable.

Not only were Kolbe's reports accurate, they were of tremendous value to cryptographers, who could use the material to crack codes that had stumped them. Branches of the British military were similarly delighted by Kolbe's documents.

Philby arranged a meeting with Claude Dansey to discuss his findings. As Philby feared, Dansey was enraged. He bitterly complained that even if Kolbe's documents were authentic, the effect would be to encourage the OSS to "run riot all over Switzerland, fouling up the whole intelligence field. Heaven knew what damage they wouldn't do." After half an hour or so, Philby finally managed to calm Dansey down, in part by explaining that everyone who had seen the Kolbe papers thought that MI6 had obtained them, not the OSS.

On May 12, David Bruce, chief of the OSS London station, passed on congratulations from his hosts. "According to Broadway [MI6], the report [Wood on Japan] . . . is amazingly correct and there is small doubt as to its authenticity. They request that special congratulations be offered the source; these we hereby heartily send."

· · ·

For Agent 110, it was a moment of personal triumph. For the first time, in early 1944, Donovan began presenting to Roosevelt information Kolbe had gathered. Taking more credit than he probably deserved, Dulles would later boast, "Our rifling of the German Foreign Office safes in Berlin through an agent reporting to the Americans in Switzerland, put an end to the rifling of the British Ambassador's safe by a German agent in Turkey."

Yet the success Dulles scored with Kolbe was doing little to help him conquer his larger obstacles back home. Washington didn't take the German resistance movement seriously, and it would not accept that the Soviet Union was behaving rather suspiciously for an ally.

At one point, his communiqués about the Free Germany Committee had prompted the OSS and State Department to toy with the idea of forming an American version of the organization, tentatively dubbed the "Save Germany Group." Before the idea could gain any momentum, though, the Save Germany Group was quietly killed—its opponents arguing, among other things, that replicating the Soviets might appear as "a counter-move" to Moscow that violated the spirit of friendship sought by Roosevelt.

By December 1943, Dulles was having a hard time concealing his frustration. Early that month, he was shocked to read in a Swiss newspaper a report of a speech given by South African prime minister Jan Smuts that indicated how far the Western Allies would go to remain cozy with Moscow. Smuts was held in high regard by Churchill, and his words carried considerable weight. Europe, the South African said, would be turned on its head when World War II ended. Italy and France faced a long and hard road toward regaining the Great Power status they once had enjoyed. Germany would be "written off the slate for long, long years."

"We therefore are left with Britain and Russia. Russia is a new colossus that bestrides Europe," Smuts said. He described Russia as "mistress of the Continent" that would be in a "position no country ever occupied in the history of Europe."

Dulles was incredulous. How could an influential and respected member of the British war effort so blithely cede western Europe to the Soviets?

On December 6, he prepared a lengthy radiotelephone transmission to Washington describing the "real sensation" that Smuts had created. No speech given in the last year had caused so much excitement.

The remarks, Agent 110 reported, were accepted as an "authoritative statement of British policy" because they were given at almost the same time that Allied leaders were meeting in Tehran in November and December 1943. Many of Dulles's informants believed that the speech must have been approved by the US government and that Washington was now ready to deliver Europe to the Soviets. "It is possibly difficult for you in Washington to realize the extent of the real apprehension of Russia in this part of the world," Dulles complained.

A month later, with the Soviet military regaining vast swaths of its former territory, Dulles explained in a radiophone call to Washington that his contacts were now left with the impression that Moscow would become the "dominating force in determining the future of Europe."

CHAPTER

22

"I Do Not Understand What Our Policy Is"

Berlin's Tiergarten, once a private hunting ground for noblemen, had served for hundreds of years as a delightful wooded park in the heart of the German capital. Its winding paths, small ponds, stands of trees, and eponymous zoo were among the joys of living in the city, a place to take a walk on Sunday afternoons after visiting a local cake shop.

In the spring of 1944, under constant Allied bombing, the pastoral oasis resembled the no-man's-land between the German and British lines of World War I. Twisted and burned stumps were all that remained of its lush groves, the pathways were cratered, and most of the poor zoo creatures that had once entertained Berlin's children had been killed. Through this once magnificent park, a rare place where he could be sure no one would hear his conversations, Stauffenberg increasingly strolled.

The new leading man of the resistance had begun work on a clever plan to overthrow Hitler that had been approved by the Führer himself.

Code-named "Valkyrie," an appellation borrowed from Wagnerian opera, the strategy relied on the Replacement Army, the force that was established to protect against a domestic disturbance.

In his plan, Stauffenberg would assassinate Hitler and in the inevitable confusion persuade the commander in chief of the Replacement Army, General Friedrich Fromm, to issue the Valkyrie code, sending troops to seize control of government operations in Berlin and other major cities and to arrest leading Nazis. If everything worked, Stauffenberg expected officers in the regular army to side with him and complete the coup. It was a complex scheme of numerous moving parts, yet he had lined up an impressive array of supporters.

Aided by General Beck, Goerdeler, and other longtime members of the underground, Stauffenberg assembled numerous important officers. General Erich Fellgiebel, as the chief of signals at Hitler's military headquarters, the Wolf's Lair, was vital to control communications. Friedrich Olbricht, one of the original authors of the Valkyrie plan years before and now a senior officer in the Replacement Army, would run the early stages of the coup from Berlin. And recently joining the cadre, as Dulles reported, was the chief of the Berlin police, Wolf-Heinrich Graf von Helldorf.

Time was running short. The advancing Soviet armies in the east, and the expected Allied landings in France, signaled to all but the most self-deceiving that the war was entering its final stage. If the resistance wanted to save Germany from destruction and have anything left to negotiate with, they would have to move fast. Yet the question of the Allied response remained a bitter and unresolved problem.

In May, Gisevius and Waetjen met with Dulles to offer a bold gambit that Beck and Goerdeler hoped would be too tempting to refuse: a three-pronged Allied attack on their own country. Military commanders loyal to the resistance would help American airborne troops land in and around Berlin, support a seaborne invasion near Bremen and Hamburg along the north coast, and isolate Hitler and other high Nazi officials on the Obersalzberg, Hitler's mountain retreat.

Dulles knew that such an offer, well-intentioned though it may be, would never be accepted by Roosevelt. He told Gisevius that it would probably be seen in Washington as nothing more than a Nazi trick. Roosevelt, he knew, was determined not to upset the Soviets with anything that hinted of back-channel deals between the underground and the Western democracies. The United States, Dulles told his friend, "would abide by our agreements with Russia both literally and in the spirit."

Yet Dulles found it increasingly difficult to display such loyalty to American policy. In January 1944, he wrote Washington that the German group Gisevius represented, which he code-named the "Breakers," was "very eager to obtain political ammunition from our side," support that it so far had found "sadly wanting." The Breakers, he said, were strongly oriented toward the West, but they "[feared] their nation [was] being directed by events toward the influence of the East." No longer attempting to hide his anger, he added: "I do not understand what our policy is and what offers, if any, we could give to any resistance movement."

Not long afterward he fired off another missive. In a lengthy radio-telephone transmission on February 19, he wrote that with the German military collapsing on all fronts, "the only real question today is whether constructive regenerating forces will control and direct the fate of Europe, or whether forces of disintegration and anarchy will prevail." By making unconditional surrender the overriding goal of the war, the United States and Britain had lost sight of "social and spiritual factors," he argued. "As a result, it is Russia rather than the Western powers which is tending to dominate the scene."

Dulles was not alone in his frustration.

In Washington, Secretary of State Hull also believed the Casablanca demand would play into the hands of Propaganda Minister Goebbels and would only provoke the German people to fight on "long after calmer judgment had convinced them that their fight was hopeless." The Joint Chiefs of Staff were disgruntled and went so far as to establish a committee of intelligence officials charged with investigating the use of unconditional surrender as a tactic. Much like Dulles, the Joint Chiefs' committee called for the United States and Britain to stipulate that they did not seek to destroy the German state, and that the German people would not be subject to inhumane treatment. The ability to cooperate with ordinary Germans, the committee pointed out, was critical to establishing a lasting peace. Even Churchill was starting to wonder about the merits of Roosevelt's policy. In August 1943, the prime minister, noting how the war was going for Germany, had said there was no need "for us to discourage this progress by continually uttering the slogan 'Unconditional Surrender.'"

Though Roosevelt would never acknowledge it, there was precedent for allowing some nuance into his position. He claimed that Italy had surrendered unconditionally, yet the United States had negotiated with the new government for weeks on everything from jointly planning an invasion of Rome to Italy's status as a "cobelligerent" after the war. At Italy's request, the United States had agreed to remove the term "unconditionally" from the protocol peace document.

Dulles had watched the handling of the Italian surrender with a mixture of disgust and hope. "The Italian experience seems to indicate that unconditional surrender is a rather empty formula in practical application; a sort of pious preamble to the real business to follow," he wrote.

Yet Roosevelt would not be moved. He might be willing to publicly promise not to enslave German citizens, but nothing more. The president rejected the proposals of the Joint Chiefs' committee and, deflecting one protest from Hull, said there was to be no tampering with the underlying logic of the Casablanca statement. "Frankly I do not like the idea of conversation to define the idea of Unconditional Surrender." Reminding Hull of his reference to "'Unconditional Surrender' Grant" at Casablanca, Roosevelt said that any announcement modifying his stance would give the appearance of weakness or inconsistency.

Finally, in April, Donovan ordered Dulles to fall into line. "In attempting to drive a wedge between members of the Nazi Party, our only caution is to ensure that no encouragement is given to the idea that the military group or the party could expect anything short of an unconditional surrender."

Agent 110 nevertheless continued to probe for a hint that Washington, through a wink or a nod, might allow him to offer some solace to the Breakers. In a message dated July 13, among the longest of the steady stream that he fired off to Washington on a possible coup attempt, Dulles noted that offering "encouragement" could save thousands of Allied lives. The United States, he suggested, should publicly spur the German people to overthrow Hitler and assure them that innocent Germans had nothing to fear from the Western Allies. "I do not predict that this line will produce a revolution in Germany, but if there is any slight chance of it, and if we wish to help to bring it about, a statement of this nature would certainly be timely."

Whether Dulles took it upon himself to embolden the resistance is unclear. It would not have been hard, in his conversations with Gisevius or Waetjen, to speculate how American policy might change once Washington was presented with a new government. Meeting with a German informant, Dulles said he was convinced that Hitler's power was waning and that army generals would eventually lead the war without him. When that "psychologically important" moment arrived, Dulles said, options for negotiations would open.

Officially, Dulles insisted to a sometimes skeptical Washington that he abided by the strict spirit of his orders. The plotters would receive no support from the United States before, or after, they assassinated Hitler.

CHAPTER

23

"The Soviet Maintains a Steady Flow into the Reich of Constructive Ideas"

On April 10, 1944, Kolbe stepped off the train from Germany into the throngs in the Basel station. The Swiss passengers rushing to their seats were digesting horrible news: an American airborne raid had gotten lost attempting to bomb a German target and dropped its load on the city of Schaffhausen, a Swiss border town about one hundred miles northeast of Basel. Some one hundred or so people had been killed, outraging the Swiss and casting a shadow over American-Swiss relations.

Kolbe weaved his way through the travelers to the station's restaurant to meet with a member of the German Foreign Ministry. After a schnapps or two, Kolbe excused himself and went to a bathroom to separate the documents he had copied for Dulles from the official papers he was to hand over to his drinking partner.

Whether from the schnapps or the jitters—he could become nervous for a man who took so many risks—Kolbe fumbled with the key to his bag and watched in horror as it fell into the toilet. Only after offering a sizable tip to a bathroom matron to extract the key was he able to successfully secure the stolen secrets.

Kolbe had again brought with him a large collection of documents, which Dulles described as "valuable Easter eggs." On this trip, Kolbe had something more in mind than handing over German secrets. Since his last visit to Bern, he had begun to rub shoulders with the real leaders of the German resistance, such as Beck and figures like the economist Walter Bauer. Bauer worked for a major coal company in Prague and had recently made his office at Unter den Linden 28 a center for the underground to hold meetings.

Kolbe's surgeon friend Ernst Ferdinand Sauerbruch had also invited him to speak at the Wednesday Club, the regular gathering of members of the underground. Kolbe backed away from that opportunity, explaining that such an august gathering intimidated him. In reality, he felt the group was "too old" for him. Instead, he had crafted his own plans to overthrow Hitler. What was needed, he now excitedly told Dulles, was a *Volksmiliz*, or "people's militia," to help the United States and Britain mount an airborne invasion of Berlin, which he would lead. Composed of sportsmen and individuals who were Social Democrats and members of labor unions, his army could capture communication centers and other important points of infrastructure with lightning speed in the first wave of a major Allied airborne attack.

Each member would be issued an armband with the initials "VM," for *Volksmiliz*. His troops would get around on bicycles; the headquarters would be at Bauer's office; and he had devised a secret code, the password being "George 25900." The Americans, he hoped, would provide machine pistols, ammunition, food, signal flares, and helmets.

While the plan was driven in part by a desire to help, Kolbe had his postwar career in mind as well. The prospects for someone who had worked exclusively as a spy would likely not be bright, he figured. But as a member of the resistance, he would likely have "political status" in the new Germany.

Dulles listened impassively as Kolbe described his plan, puffing on his

pipe and looking as if he were not hearing a word. At one level, Agent
110 shared Kolbe's thinking. He was growing ever more uneasy about the
Soviets. Just days later he would communicate his latest fears about Moscow's intentions to Washington. Communist thought was finding fertile
ground in Germany, Dulles would write. People had lost all their material possessions, a fact that Moscow was exploiting. A central committee
of "the Communists" had been established within Germany to coordinate
activities. Millions of Soviet war prisoners in Germany and other occupied countries were being mobilized by a secret organization directed by
Moscow. "The Soviet [Union] maintains a steady flow into the Reich of
constructive ideas and schemes as a program to provide for the rehabilita-
tion of the Reich after the war. Such plans and ideas are being disseminated
widely among the masses of the German people through the whispering
campaign that the Communists have organized very well," Dulles would
write headquarters.

About the time of Kolbe's visit, the Soviets had also made an attempt to
gain influence in Italy. In mid-April 1944, "out of a clear sky," noted Secretary
of State Hull, the US State Department learned that the Soviet Union was exchanging diplomatic representatives with the fledgling Italian government.
Neither the United States nor Britain had yet taken this step, though both
had shouldered the fighting in Italy and occupied half the peninsula.

The Soviet move not only violated the spirit of cooperation the Allies
hoped to maintain, it was a direct breach of agreements they had made less
than six months earlier in Moscow, when it was decided that all matters concerning Italy were to be taken by the Allies as a group. "This unilateral action, taken without advance consultation with the British or ourselves, was
highly disconcerting," Hull would write.

Yet Dulles's concerns about the Soviets didn't mean the United States
needed Kolbe's militia. As Wood finished his proposal, he could discern no
hint of reaction in Dulles's face. For a long moment, the American stared
back at him. Then, taking one last draw on his pipe, Dulles spoke on an unrelated topic.

Kolbe steered Dulles back to his plan, and again waited. "We need you where you are," Dulles finally said. "Keep telling us what you find out at the Foreign Ministry; that is really where you are most useful for us."

For several hours the two went back and forth, Kolbe arguing he should give up his spy work, Dulles countering that the Allies were depending on him. There was also good reason to believe that Himmler had already penetrated the underground and that joining the group now would amount to a death sentence.

"Finally, he agreed to stay on the job, and I breathed a sigh of relief," Dulles wrote. Dejected, Kolbe returned to Berlin.

Smoldering after his visit with Dulles, Kolbe was coming to realize that it would be some time before he could make another trip to Bern. Foreign Ministry couriers crossing the Swiss border were now required to submit to body searches, or to have their briefcases examined. And the well-connected Sauerbruch had heard that the Foreign Ministry's chief of protocol, Alexander von Doernberg, had an eye on him.

Kolbe would have to communicate with Dulles indirectly. Employing his connections in the Foreign Ministry, Kolbe arranged for Willy Pohle, who often traveled to Switzerland on official business, to deliver private letters to a friend in Bern, Walter Schuepp, who could pass them on to Dulles. Dr. Sauerbruch likewise traveled to Zurich from time to time to attend medical conferences, and he agreed to carry private letters. Kolbe also invented his own code for messages to Dulles that didn't require tables or any sort of decoding device. Kolbe was so pleased with the system that he showed it to the coding department at the ministry and came away convinced that nobody could break it.

On another occasion, Kolbe suggested that messages to him be embedded in the personal columns of the London *Times*, to which he had regular access in his work at the Foreign Ministry. The BBC, he proposed, could convey messages during its evening broadcast at ten o'clock.

Dulles seemed happy to play along, knowing how much Kolbe enjoyed the cat-and-mouse games. To thank him for one letter, Agent 110 mailed a postcard with a mountain scene and a postmark from the ski resort of Parsenn. The card read that the writer had made "three ski jumps. As you know,

I am not a beginner. The weather is fine." The message, as understood by Kolbe, was that the Americans had received three letters from him, they had been able to decipher them, and the information was useful.

What Kolbe could not have known at the time he was pushing for a larger role was that the Allies had ambitious plans to topple Hitler—Operation Overlord, the invasion of the European continent.

For months, ships laden with supplies and equipment had arrived in English harbors from the United States. The joke went around that the weight of the American military, with its many soldiers, tanks, airplanes, and gallons of fuel, threatened to sink the island. For the American and English intelligence services, keeping secret the location of the coming attack on the French coast was the most important operation of the war.

To convince the Germans that the invasion would take place in the Pas-de-Calais, much closer to England than the actual landing beaches in Normandy were, the secret services rose to unprecedented levels of trickery and ingenuity. Artists, illustrators, magicians, radio experts—what later became known as the Ghost Army—were hired to perform the greatest sleight of hand ever attempted.

Inflatable tanks and fake airplanes were positioned in fields near logical embarkation points to fool German aerial reconnaissance and spies on the ground. The aircraft were so convincing that an American pilot once attempted to land near them, believing he had reached an operational runway. Recorded sounds of motoring tanks were broadcast from loudspeakers at night to give nosy spies the impression of ceaseless activity. General George Patton, the officer the Germans most feared, made a show of being driven to fake military installations far from the real ones.

Dulles's role was to help Allied soldiers once they reached French soil. From Bern, he worked with his contacts in the French resistance in the mountainous Haute-Savoie region that abuts Switzerland, supplying them with funds, organizing sabotage raids on German transport and communication installations, and uncovering highly valued order-of-battle intelligence. Sending almost daily reports in the weeks leading up to the invasion,

Dulles delivered data on German troop movements, the location of staff headquarters, communications networks, and even train traffic. In one telegram, he reported on May 13 that the Germans had concentrated roughly five hundred vehicles in the Paris Zoo.

When the invasion took place on June 6, D-Day, Dulles reported on how Germans were reacting. The public had learned of the attack only in the afternoon, and their attitude was one of grim apathy. The attack was seen throughout Germany as made "on orders from Moscow."

CHAPTER

24

"Aren't They Ready to Act Yet?"

By the summer of 1944, Gisevius was convinced that German agents were actively hunting for him. He spent most of his time moving from one new location to another. Work on his book with Bancroft had come to a stop.

Earlier in the spring, he had met her in St. Moritz, where he had been trying to lie low. Walking up the main street toward the chalet of a friend, Bancroft saw Gisevius coming toward her, "a frightful grey felt hat" pulled down over his eyes and a muffler wrapped around his neck and covering his mouth and nose. The two then darted around town together, weaving in and out of shops and alleyways, sometimes a yard apart, sometimes shoulder to shoulder. Gisevius chattered nervously. "Careful! Come this way! No, go that way, everyone can see us. Can everyone see us? When can we meet? Come down here. No, go down over there. Careful! Yes! Yes! No! No!"

Under the strain, whatever romance had sparked between them gave way to bickering and short tempers. Bancroft was increasingly annoyed with Gisevius's constant haranguing about unconditional surrender. She had long since decided against passing on very much from him on that topic to Dulles, fearing it would only rile him.

In recent weeks, the two had quarreled when Gisevius chided her on the simple subject of taking children out of school to go skiing.

"We here in Europe," Gisevius began.

Bancroft snapped "Oh, shut up! . . . I'm sick of 'we here in Europe.' If the kind of schooling that 'we here in Europe' have had can't get better results than the history of the last twenty-five years, I see no reason for anyone being subjected to that kind of schooling!"

A couple of months later, Gisevius was keeping a low profile in the mountain resort of Davos in eastern Switzerland when he received a phone call from an old friend in the Abwehr, Theodor Strünck. A lawyer and an insurance executive before the war, Strünck had long been one of the many members of the spy agency secretly fighting Hitler and had traveled to Switzerland to speak to Gisevius. There had been an "indiscretion," Strünck revealed, and Himmler now wanted Gisevius back in Germany by "hook or crook."

Though the Nazis trod carefully in Switzerland, there had been cases of their spiriting people out of neutral countries. Strünck suggested that Gisevius could buy some time by feigning illness. A physician had been arranged to certify that Gisevius was undergoing an appendicitis operation, or that he had broken his leg.

Gisevius was more interested in what Strünck might be able to tell him about the latest on a possible coup. "Aren't they ready to act yet?" he asked irritably.

"They claim the assassination will take place any day now," Strünck replied. "But you know how often we have been disappointed."

Not long after that phone call, Gisevius contacted Bancroft. He was going away for a few days, he said. "Homer," the code name the two had given Waetjen, would bring over a few pages of his book for her to work on that afternoon.

Later that day Waetjen arrived at Bancroft's apartment and laid Gisevius's manuscript on her table without any comment.

"Why didn't Gisevius bring that back himself?" Bancroft asked.

Waetjen replied, "I hoped you wouldn't ask. Actually, he's gone back to Germany . . ."

Bancroft understood what that meant. Gisevius had told her that he wouldn't make any more trips back to Berlin until the plot to kill Hitler was ready to go. Fearful that discussing it further would "put a jinx" on the operation, she changed the subject.

Gisevius's train came to a stop at the Potsdam station, on the outskirts of Berlin. Never mind that he was a wanted man eluding capture by the Gestapo; the journey from Switzerland to the German capital was a chilling reminder of what the war was doing to his homeland. It had been over a year since he was last in Germany, and as he looked out the window, the terrible effects of the bombing sank in. Rolling stock that had once been kept clean and in good working order was covered with dirt, windows blown out. Passing through Karlsruhe, he saw iron girders protruding from mounds of brick and concrete that had once been buildings and homes.

Nearing Berlin, Gisevius passed through his old neighborhood near Wannsee. Piles of rubble crowded sidewalks. He later learned that the approximate position of his home was a charred hole in the ground, a few family photos strewn among the smashed bricks and mortar. "The first impression was tremendously powerful," he wrote. "It was necessary to return to Germany from afar to see how inexorably the whole land was progressing toward utter annihilation."

Gisevius needn't have undertaken the risk. Though he was a core member of the group preparing to overthrow the government, his presence was not vital. He had felt compelled to return. "For years I had hoped for the great event—and now that the assassination was about to come off, was I to watch it from afar in Zurich? Every fiber of my being revolted against this paltry safety."

His ambition also factored into the decision. As a member of the resistance, Gisevius could count on a plum job in any post-Hitler government, and he no doubt wanted to make sure he was there to receive his reward when the time came. He had already been tapped to take a leading position in the police or security services of the new regime.

Gisevius met with Stauffenberg in the basement of Strünck's home late in the night on July 12, a location where they felt safe to speak openly. Gisevius had never met the colonel before but had heard a great deal about him.

The warrior-poet of high birth cut an unexpected impression in person.

Built like a man who had once been full of energy and strength, Stauffenberg initially reminded Gisevius of Otto von Bismarck, the "Iron Chancellor" who forged the German Empire from 1871. But as the evening progressed, he discovered a less flattering side to Stauffenberg. Gisevius noted how the coup leader, slumped in his wooden chair, limply dangling his arms and splaying his boots out in front, seemed frail.

Stauffenberg looked uncomfortable as he wiped perspiration from his brow. The wound to his eye still bothered him, and he occasionally lifted the patch that covered it and dabbed the area with cotton. Gisevius noted that Stauffenberg, far from his reputation as a cultured man, rudely demanded that Mrs. Strünck get him a coffee. "I would never have taken this young colonel for the model of the traditional officer, nor for the credible representative of that younger generation which had already been inwardly alienated from the Nazis," Gisevius wrote. "Undoubtedly this Stauffenberg was a swashbuckler who knew what he wanted; but he struck me as rather typical of the 'new' class of general staff officers: the kind of men best suited to Hitler's purposes—or to purposes of assassination."

Gisevius was disposed toward disliking the brash army officer. His friends had complained to him that Stauffenberg refused to share much of the assassination plan with them. Gisevius belonged to a cadre of men, one that had shrunk over the years, who had conspired against Hitler the entire war. Some Johnny-come-lately trying to call the shots rankled.

In Gisevius's telling of their conversation, Stauffenberg stared at the floor with "a meaningful smile on his face" as Gisevius explained his thinking about the policy of unconditional surrender. Reflecting Dulles's views,

Gisevius said there was no point discussing it any further; the Allies were sure to occupy Germany at the war's end.

"Isn't it altogether too late for the West?" Stauffenberg interrupted, and accused Gisevius of being a "hopeless 'Westerner.'"

Within a couple of weeks, Stauffenberg told him, the Soviets would be standing on the threshold of Berlin. The decision had been made for the resistance. All their political efforts would have to be focused toward the East. The more they talked, the more their conversation soured. Stauffenberg, Gisevius became convinced, was an army officer playing at politics, an occupation for which he was not qualified. He spoke "with an exaggerated sense of his mission, he thought he had to be everything at once: soldier, politician . . . savior of his fatherland."

As the night wore on, the list of grievances grew, at least in the eyes of Gisevius. Stauffenberg was likely to align a new German government with the Soviets. Stauffenberg was opposed to the idea of "purging" the new government of all its leadership, a step Gisevius thought vital to future relations with the West. Stauffenberg's plans lacked clarity. Even Gisevius's beloved book project was a bone of contention. Stauffenberg said it would have to be banned for how it portrayed certain generals. By the time the sun came up, Gisevius knew the two had to stop. "Perhaps our nerves were overstrained. At any rate, we quarreled almost at the last moment," he wrote.

That same evening, Dulles sent a sharp warning to Washington. "There is a possibility that a dramatic event may take place up north."

CHAPTER

25

The Wolf's Lair

On the morning of July 20, 1944, a Heinkel He III twin-engine aircraft droned over the heavily wooded, gently rolling landscape of East Prussia. Though the Heinkel's sleek silhouette was recognized by British civilians as the aircraft that dropped bombs on London during the Battle of Britain, this plane carried a human cargo of army officers: General Helmuth Stieff, Lieutenant Werner von Haeften, and Stauffenberg. Tucked inside two leather briefcases carried by the men was a pair of bombs.

Touching down just after ten o'clock on a secret airstrip not far from the city of Rastenburg, a small town noted for its fourteenth-century church and castle, Stauffenberg asked the pilot to wait for them. They would be back in a few hours and would need to return to Berlin as quickly as possible. The two climbed into a waiting open-top Mercedes for a brief ride through tall stands of pine, oak, and beech to one of the most secretive places in the entire Third Reich—the "Wolf's Lair," the heavily fortified command post from which Hitler directed the war.

Completed in 1941, the five-acre tract was, as one senior officer once described it, a cross between a monastery and a concentration camp. Cast in near-perpetual shadows by the canopy of tall trees, the area was protected by three security zones. The outer perimeter, sewn with land mines, was guarded by Waffen-SS troops. A second zone, where members of Hitler's staff and commanders were housed, included such comforts as movie theaters and a sauna. Surrounded by two rings of barbed wire, a minefield, electrified fences, and guard dogs was the third zone, reserved for Hitler and an assortment of personal staff and secretaries. Hitler inhabited an unadorned apartment in a one-story bunker, fortified with thick concrete. Nearby was an equally stout conference room where the Führer conducted military briefings.

Stauffenberg moved easily through the checkpoints at each perimeter. He was expected today to update Hitler and the senior staff on the Replacement Army. So easily did he penetrate the security cordon that he had time before the 1:00 p.m briefing with Hitler to eat a late breakfast. After months of careful planning, the lives of himself and dozens of accomplices, and the fate of his nation, would be forever altered by what was going to happen, one way or another, in the next few hours.

For all their planning, the putsch had some glaring shortcomings, starting with the role of Stauffenberg himself. As a result of his recent promotion to chief of staff of the Replacement Army, he had the best access to Hitler to carry out the attack. As the primary architect of the coup, he was also needed to organize the government takeover, a dual responsibility that was almost impossible to fulfill.

Moreover, relations with the Western Allies remained unsettled. Optimists such as Goerdeler believed that once Hitler had been eliminated, the United States and Britain would finally support his new government. Gisevius, who knew better, used his first few days back in Berlin to drum up support for a new idea to secure Allied support. Convinced that the Western democracies would never break ranks with the Soviets, Gisevius devised what he called the "Western solution." The scheme was simple enough. Rather than trying to force Roosevelt to change his mind, sympathetic German generals on the western front would approach the Allied commander in Europe, General Dwight D. Eisenhower, and surrender, or at least fall rapidly back toward Berlin.

Dulles had seemed open to the idea and had tried once more to persuade Washington to support the German resistance. Leaders of a possible coup, he reported, planned to organize an orderly retreat from the west and to dispatch their best forces to the east in an effort to prevent as much of Germany as possible from falling into Soviet hands. Dulles again pleaded for Roosevelt to offer his support to the German people, and in turn to the underground. "A presidential announcement to counter Goebbels' line about the Allies' plans for complete annihilation of the German people would encourage the anti-Nazi groups," he wrote.

The coup leaders rejected this idea. The "Western solution" failed to settle the issue of how Germany was to be treated after the war, and they believed it risked inflaming the "stab in the back" myth and could even lead to civil war.

A third area of uncertainty was the timing of the attack on Hitler. Stauffenberg had tried twice before, but he had called it off both times because all the details hadn't fallen into place. On July 11, he tracked Hitler to the Obersalzberg, but decided against carrying out the plan because other key Nazi targets were absent. Four days later, Stauffenberg flew to the Wolf's Lair and again found conditions not yet ripe.

Though Himmler wouldn't be at the Wolf's Lair on this day, Stauffenberg could not delay again. With so many people involved in the plot, the risk of detection grew each hour. At about the same time, Goerdeler had been forced to go into hiding when leaders of the coup received a tip that he would soon be arrested.

By the time Stauffenberg finished his breakfast, the temperature had begun to climb, leaving everyone hot and sticky. Ushered into Restricted Area 1,

Stauffenberg met Field Marshal Wilhelm Keitel, who informed him that the meeting with Hitler was now moved ahead to twelve thirty. Stauffenberg calmly asked whether, on account of the heat, there was a place where he could change his shirt and bring his aide Haeften to assist him. The two were shown to a lounge in Keitel's bunker. They closed the door behind them and proceeded to arm the bombs that Haeften had carried with him in his briefcase.

The devices were similar to those used in the attempt to blow up Hitler's plane more than a year earlier. Of British design, they were powerful and considered reliable, at least when not used at high altitudes. Best of all was the silent fuse. Rather than employing a mechanical timer, the bombs were armed by breaking a glass capsule filled with acid. The chemicals then slowly dissolved a wire that released the firing pin. For their purposes today, the men had selected the thinnest wire possible, one that set the bomb off after only ten minutes.

They had just completed this process on one of the bombs when there was a knock at the door. Major Ernst John von Freyend was growing impatient. "Stauffenberg, please come along," he barked.

Stauffenberg had time to stuff the one bomb into his brown leather briefcase. He didn't place the other unarmed bomb in with it, though the force of the first explosion would have set it off. Half-armed, Stauffenberg walked outside and past a high wire fence toward the meeting room.

One change to Hitler's schedule would have historic consequences. Rather than taking place in a heavily fortified bunker, the briefing with his generals was moved to a conference room with windows that could be thrown open to provide some relief from the oppressive heat.

Escorted by Major Freyend, who unknowingly carried the briefcase containing the bomb, Stauffenberg entered the new venue, a small space of roughly thirty feet by fifteen feet. All ten of the room's windows had been flung wide open to catch what wind there was to cool those inside. Hitler was seated with his back to the door at a massive oak table listening intently to General Adolf Heusinger provide an update on the eastern front. In one hand, the

Führer held a magnifying glass to read fine print on the maps spread out before him.

Not seeming to recognize Stauffenberg, whom he had met before only briefly, Hitler greeted him with a quick handshake and refocused his attention on Heusinger's briefing. Shown to a place near Hitler—Stauffenberg said he needed to be close on account of his bad hearing—he noticed that Major Freyend had placed his briefcase on the floor at his feet.

Hardly in the room for a minute, Stauffenberg muttered something about an important phone call that he had to make, a curious statement, as few things could have been more important than making a presentation to Hitler. With that, he slipped past a small table by the door on which other briefcases were laid and stepped out in the hallway, leaving his own briefcase behind.

Inside, the discussion on the eastern front continued. At one point, Hitler stood up to examine maps, causing a brief reshuffling of men around the table. In changing positions, Colonel Heinz Brandt, the officer who had unknowingly carried the bombs aboard Hitler's plane in March 1943, inadvertently knocked Stauffenberg's briefcase over with his foot. Bending over to set it up again, he repositioned the case next to one of the massive legs of the conference table.

Stauffenberg made his way to the communications center, where he briefly exchanged words with his fellow conspirator General Erich Fellgiebel, and then walked toward his staff car. As he reached the vehicle, where Haeften was already waiting for him, the tranquility of the forest setting was shattered by a tremendous explosion. Flames and smoke erupted from the conference room's windows, and splinters from the heavy oak table flew through the air like knives. In the distance, a man cried out, "Where's the Führer?"

To Stauffenberg, it was clear. The Führer was dead. Nobody could have survived the explosion. He ordered the driver to get them to the airstrip as quickly as possible, managing to pass through several security checkpoints.

Speeding down the dusty road, the pair jettisoned a small object from the car, the one bomb they had not carried into the conference room. At 1:15 p.m., the Heinkel took off for Berlin.

•   •   •

At almost the moment the bomb ripped through Hitler's meeting, Gisevius was standing at the window in the office of Police Chief Helldorff, gazing out over Alexanderplatz. Months of Allied bombing had laid waste to the area, once a center of Berlin's nightlife. Studying the "weary, gaunt people who moved slowly amid the ruins, I realized fully what perhaps was at stake now, perhaps this very second," Gisevius thought.

The tension was excruciating. According to the plan, another official participating in the conspiracy, Arthur Nebe, one of Gisevius's friends from his early days with the Gestapo in 1933, was to phone as soon as he had any news. That call was expected sometime after 1:00 p.m., the hour originally scheduled for Hitler's briefing.

Passing time with Count Gottfried von Bismarck, a grandson of Otto von Bismarck, Gisevius grew increasingly impatient and at 2:00 p.m. phoned Nebe. He said he was too busy to meet face-to-face, but offered cryptically that "something strange had happened in East Prussia."

Nebe and Gisevius, speaking in broad hints, tried to arrange a rendez-vous but failed to connect, the two waiting in different locations until 3:00 p.m. Returning to Helldorff's office, Gisevius resumed his vigil. Word on the assassination, he knew, would likely first come from the Bendlerstrasse, a complex of buildings just south of the Tiergarten that served as the head-quarters of the army, as well as the Replacement Army. The main group of conspirators had set up a base camp there under the leadership of General Olbricht.

Finally, at 4:00 p.m., Helldorff burst into the small room where Gisevius and Bismarck were waiting.

"It's starting!" he shouted. "Gentlemen, we're off." The three rushed to a waiting car to join the coup leaders. They arrived at the Bendlerstrasse headquarters with their hopes soaring. Hitler was now dead, and in a matter of hours Germany would be under their leadership and the war would soon come to an end. Instead, confusion reigned. General Fellgiebel was supposed to have phoned General Olbricht from his office at the Wolf's Lair after the attack and tell him to begin taking over the government. His call, however, was garbled. All that was clear in Berlin was that a bomb had gone off. Not until Stauffenberg landed back in the capital at 3:45 p.m. and phoned the Bendlerstrasse to announce Hitler was dead was the coup set in full motion.

Gisevius and his companions now learned there was doubt about whether Hitler had been killed. Stauffenberg, the only one present for the attack, was adamant. The force of the blast, he said, was as if a heavy shell had scored a direct hit to the building. Nobody could have survived.

General Fromm, however, refused to issue the order to call out the Replacement Army until he received confirmation. He reached Field Marshal Keitel at the Wolf's Lair. Hitler had not only survived the blast but was also not seriously hurt.

Gisevius exchanged looks of "utter consternation" with Helldorf and Bismarck as they were "confronted with the brutal reality of the *Putsch*."

Convinced that Hitler was alive, Fromm—who had walked a fine line between supporting the coup and remaining loyal to Hitler—now cast himself as a die-hard Nazi and bitterly demanded that Stauffenberg surrender himself. The conspirators then seized Fromm, the man they had counted on to help mobilize the Replacement Army, and confined him in a nearby office.

Other SS and police officers soon arrived at army headquarters, and they, too, were placed under detention. General Beck, the most respected member of the putsch, hit his forehead with the palm of his hand. "A number of things seem to be going wrong today," the old general dryly remarked to Gisevius.

Despite the turbulence, the coup leaders pressed on. Though lacking Fromm's signature, they transmitted the Valkyrie orders to military bases around Germany, Austria, and France; the orders were, in many cases, dutifully obeyed. In Paris, Carl-Heinrich von Stülpnagel ordered the arrest of 1,200 men, including leading members of the SS and German security services. Generals in Prague and Vienna likewise began to round up SS and Nazi Party leaders. Officers near Berlin complied and dispatched their forces to seize strategic points around the city.

Convinced that the outcome still hung in the balance, Gisevius urged bold action. It was vital to displace senior Nazis before they could regroup. He begged Stauffenberg to let him form an "officer's troop" that could drive from Bendlerstrasse to Gestapo headquarters on Prinz-Albrecht-Strasse to murder Heinrich Müller, the head of the Gestapo, and Propaganda Minister Goebbels. Stauffenberg refused, convinced that troops of the Replacement Army would soon arrest them.

Instead, General Beck had another job for Gisevius. The coup leaders needed to make a radio address to the German people, and he told Gisevius to get to a broadcast center to make an announcement. Typical of the growing confusion that surrounded the day, no one could find the text of the radio address that had been prepared in advance. While a search commenced, Gisevius was drawn into a new task. Helldorff, the head of the Berlin police, had returned to his office and phoned the Bendlerstrasse gathering, asking that Gisevius be sent over for an important meeting. Rounding up a car and driver, Gisevius set out for the short drive to Alexanderplatz.

Passing through the Brandenburg Gate, the massive neoclassical monument topped with a horse-drawn chariot, Gisevius observed a strange and disquieting scene. Heavily armed troops seemed to be emerging everywhere. "Down one street I saw several blocks of buildings surrounded. Every twenty yards I glimpsed one of those awe-inspiring warriors holding a submachine gun."

What the coup leaders did not yet realize was that key officers in the Replacement Army were learning the truth. A battalion of Grossdeutschland guards, who had been ordered to arrest Goebbels, had been convinced that Hitler was alive. Under the command of Major Otto Remer, twenty men burst into the propaganda minister's office with drawn pistols. Thinking quickly, Goebbels managed to call the Wolf's Lair and get Hitler himself on the line. Handing the receiver to an astonished Remer, Hitler asked if the officer recognized his office. Remer said he did.

Hitler assured the confused commander that he was in good health and ordered him to help put down the coup. Remer dispatched patrols to stop any other troops who might be headed toward the capital and personally set out to find the coup's ringleaders.

At about the same time, from the Wolf's Lair, Field Marshal Keitel sent by teleprinter a message to army commanders declaring that Himmler had been appointed chief of the Replacement Army and that only orders from the two of them were to be obeyed.

Finally tracking down Helldorff in an air-raid shelter, Gisevius pieced together what was happening. Where was he to go? The only idea that he could produce was to return to his comrades at army headquarters, knowing that doing so would probably spell his doom. Helldorff was dumbfounded. "Don't kid yourself, Gisevius. For years these generals have shit all over us. They promised us everything; they've kept not one of their promises. What happened today was right in line with the rest—more of their shit." Still, Gisevius wanted to be with General Beck and the others. He would not change his mind. Moments later, he ordered the chauffeur of a police car to drive him back to Bendlerstrasse.

Gisevius's car slowly made its way past wrecked buildings and damaged streets, its lone passenger "staring dully into space." Passing back through the Brandenburg Gate, his car was stopped by heavily armed soldiers. He would not be allowed to pass. The driver was to try a different route, past the Victory Column, a celebration of past German military glories. Gisevius lost himself in thought. "I am riding to suicide. I am riding to suicide . . ."

Gisevius imagined the look on Major Remer's face if he were to arrive at the Wehrmacht headquarters back at the Bendlerstrasse and demand that he be allowed to join the doomed men inside. About to veer left at the Victory Column, Gisevius was again stopped.

The way to Bendlerstrasse apparently blocked, Gisevius concluded there still might be a way to play a role in the putsch by making a radio address after all. The broadcast center, some distance away in Charlottenburg, became their destination.

His head swirled with questions. "What did I really have in common with these generals? Was I now to die for them?" He thought of other putsch attempts, such as the French coup of 1851, when Louis-Napoléon, nephew of Napoléon Bonaparte, reclaimed his uncle's throne as emperor of France. The radio station now came into view. There was no military guard, no police protecting the building. It might be possible to make the broadcast.

As he neared the transmitter, a new thought struck him. He was now close to the Reichskanzlerplatz, itself only a short walk from Theodor Strünck's cellar apartment and safety.

On the afternoon of July 20, Dulles was in Bern, talking with Elizabeth Wiskemann, the British journalist and intelligence officer whom Trott had met with from time to time. The phone rang and Dulles answered, listening to the brief message "as if accepting a piece of news he had rather expected."

Hanging up, he turned to his guest and announced, "There has been an attack on Hitler's life at his headquarters." Neither Dulles nor Wiskemann knew much more.

Bancroft, who was vacationing in a small cabin, was cracking some eggs to scramble for lunch the next day when her daughter tuned the radio to Beromünster, which was broadcast from a powerful transmitter and considered the "voice of Switzerland." Out of the speaker came a stunning announcement: An attempt had been made to kill Adolf Hitler. A number of officers had been arrested.

That evening, Bancroft and her daughter went to a nearby village and called Dulles from a public phone. "You've been listening to the radio?" he asked.

"Yes . . ."

"Well, I don't know anything more than you do. . . . You might drop in on our friend up on the hill [Eduard von Waetjen]. He'll be in touch. . . . How's the weather down there?" Dulles asked.

"Terrible."

"Well, cheer up. Things will work out somehow . . ."

In fact, Bancroft would soon learn, the coup had collapsed. Troops loyal to Hitler had surrounded the Bendlerstrasse army headquarters, and Fromm had escaped from his "imprisonment" to hunt down Stauffenberg, Beck,

Olbricht, and the others. After a brief shoot-out, they surrendered. But their fates were sealed.

Fromm moved quickly, likely to prevent the coup leaders from revealing that he, too, possessed at least tacit knowledge of the plot. Out of respect, the aging General Beck was given the honor of being allowed to shoot himself with his own pistol. After two failed attempts, the task was eventually finished by a sergeant.

Stauffenberg and three others were not long thereafter marched into the courtyard at the army headquarters. Forced to line up, their figures illuminated by the headlights of trucks, they watched as a hastily arranged firing squad was assembled. One by one, each was shot.

Yet there was no word on Gisevius.

CHAPTER

26

"Communism Is Not What Germany Needs"

One morning in September 1944, Kolbe sat down to breakfast in the mess hall at the Wolf's Lair in East Prussia. Arranged before him was an impressive offering of delicious food, including a plate of cold chicken. Tempting though the treat may have been, Kolbe made a display of refusing to eat. He wasn't feeling well, he explained.

Kolbe had been working at Hitler's headquarters since late August and hated the location, the scene of Stauffenberg's attack. He couldn't suppress memories of the failed July 20 assassination attempt. Several colleagues at the Foreign Ministry had been arrested and sentenced to death. His close friend Professor Sauerbruch had been questioned by the Gestapo on account of a conversation he had had with Stauffenberg. "Sauerbruch thinks that we are lost, he and I. He may be right," Kolbe had written Dulles.

Remarkably, Kolbe's clandestine work as Wood was not known to the Nazis. In early July, he had even been recommended for advancement. As part of the promotion process, the Foreign Ministry had written Nazi Party officials that Kolbe "worked tirelessly and well for the National Socialist State." Although Kolbe had never joined the party, his promotion was approved.

Kolbe was now employing a new technique to submit reports to his handler—photographing documents with a small camera that Dulles had provided him. The system was much safer than sneaking bulky papers across the border. Now photographs of up to sixty documents could be stored in small canisters, which could more easily be hidden. Yet the device presented new problems.

It was no easy matter to use the camera within the ministry. Photography was strictly forbidden, for obvious security reasons. And it was nearly impossible to do secretly, given the demands of lighting and framing his subjects. The only way he could conduct his work was to remove secret documents from the building, another violation of Foreign Ministry rules.

The Charité Hospital, where many of his friends worked, offered one possibility. Kolbe frequently visited Sauerbruch, and his secretary, Kolbe's fiancée, and had noticed numerous advantages for carrying out clandestine work there. The hospital often had electric power when other areas of Berlin didn't, and the lighting was good. It helped that his friends there were generally outside the radar of the Gestapo. One friend, Dr. Adolphe Jung, an Alsatian physician whom the Nazis had drafted to come to Berlin, was willing to let Kolbe, posing as a patient, use his office on the hospital's third floor. Carefully clipping documents to a cardboard background, Kolbe positioned them in order to catch outside light, or when working late at night, placed them under electric lamps. Often unable to complete his work in a single visit, Kolbe left the documents with Jung. "I was often very uneasy," Jung wrote. "In my room I had only an old desk that did not lock very securely. Usually I took the papers and put them in an envelope that I sealed. On it I wrote 'Manuscript pour le Journal de Médecine.'"

Such precautions helped, but removing documents from the Foreign Ministry remained a dangerous business. Working one day in March 1944, Kolbe told his colleagues that he wasn't feeling well and had to leave early.

What he really needed were a few hours to summarize documents about the anti-German activities of Hungarian prime minister Miklós Kállay for Dulles. He was just starting to lay out the documents and prepare them for copying when the phone rang. On the other end of the line was a panicked colleague from the ministry. "Where is the Miklós Kállay file? Ribbentrop is about to go to a meeting with Himmler. He needs the file right away."

Fighting back his sense of alarm, Kolbe replied that the files were in his personal safe and he alone had the key. Running back to the ministry, Kolbe bounded up the stairs to his office four at a time and, with his colleague standing feet away tapping his foot, managed to make it look as if he removed the file from his safe.

Walking the grounds of the Wolf's Lair, Kolbe saw something that restoked his worry about the Communists. Striding beneath the canopy of tall trees was a curious gentleman. Kolbe discreetly asked around and learned that his name was Peter Kleist, the man who had made contact with Soviet intermediaries in December 1942 and again in the summer of 1943. After a period of inactivity, Kleist was back in the peace-feeler business.

Though Wood didn't know the details, Kleist had visited Stockholm for five weeks in June and July and had again met Clauss, the Riga native working as a go-between. The Soviets seemingly had little to gain from the Germans at this point in the war, yet Clauss explained that Moscow was again worried that the Western democracies seemed poised to conquer Germany independent of the Soviet Union. With the failure of the July 20 plot, the Soviets felt they had lost many of their connections to the German resistance and were eager to explore alternatives.

The prospect of Soviet domination of his country was becoming more real for Kolbe as the end of the war approached. In a letter to Kocherthaler, his original intermediary with Agent 110, Kolbe warned of the threat of the advancing Russians. "Communism is not what Germany needs. . . . More and more people here are realizing that."

Desperate to get the news of his Kleist sighting to Dulles, Kolbe told his

boss, the Foreign Ministry's Karl Ritter, that he had developed a stomach ail-
ment as a complication from an appendicitis operation in 1940. The camp's
medical officer accepted the petition and approved Kolbe's leave. He hurried
back to Berlin and began working on a plan to meet Dulles.

On October 4, 1944, Kolbe prepared his package of documents and ob-
servations for Dulles. For this trip, he had hidden film with photos of about
thirty documents in the pocket of an overcoat. This he took with a parcel of
clothing to the Foreign Ministry mail room, where everything going abroad
was inspected and placed under a diplomatic seal.

Unfortunately, a zealous young staffer had replaced the regular clerk behind the counter. Striking up as friendly a tone as possible, Kolbe told him
the jacket belonged to someone in the ministry who needed it for the coming
winter. The mail room attendant nevertheless began what promised to be a
thorough inspection.

Kolbe watched with mounting panic, sweating profusely as the young
man went through the clothing item by item, shirts, trousers, even socks. Just
as he was about to unfold the coat containing the film, a colleague entered
the room. Kolbe jumped at the distraction and engaged the man in "an interesting conversation" that derailed the inspection. The clerk closed Kolbe's
bag, affixed the seals, and placed it in a large canvas pouch.

Kolbe returned to his office and poured himself a double cognac.

CHAPTER

27

"I Never Saw Them So Completely Downtrodden"

The evening of August 29, 1944, Dulles presented his passport to a Swiss guard at the small border crossing at Annemasse, two flimsy-looking wooden barriers all that separated him from France. For nearly two years, his crossing into the country might have resulted in imprisonment, possibly execution.

Not far down the road, the stern voices of one occupier had been replaced by those of another. The Americans had landed in the South of France and were pushing north. Crossing the barriers, Dulles was escorted to an OSS safe house in Lyon, about one hundred miles distant.

The botched events of July 20, and all they implied for his mission, weighed heavily. Wilhelm Hoegner, a German socialist exile in Bern and frequent Herrengasse contact, had seen Dulles and Schulze-Gaevernitz since the assassination attempt and had noticed a transformation. "I never saw them so completely downtrodden," he wrote. "They had always hoped that through the sudden downfall of Hitler, the war would be ended before the Soviet Russians entered Berlin. A quick peace agreement with a democratic German regime would have prevented that. But now all was lost. The continuation of the war would provide the Russians with a pathway to the Elbe River in the heart of Europe. American policy had suffered a terrible defeat."

With both the Kreisau Circle and the Breakers group shattered and thousands arrested, it was hard to envision anyone with the courage to stand up to Hitler. In one joke that circulated among members of the underground, it was asked, "Can Germany lose the war?" No, the reply went. "Now that we've got it, we'll never get rid of it."

Yet Dulles was wrong to assume that the failed coup meant all was lost. The closer the Soviets, Americans, and British drew to Berlin, the greater the urgency within Germany to end the war while there was still something left to save. Dulles and his OSS station in Switzerland would soon find themselves once again at the center of an ambitious new surrender plan, one that laid bare the deep divisions that existed between the Soviet Union and the United States and foreshadowed the Cold War.

CHAPTER

28

Reunion with Donovan

Situated on a hillside on the outskirts of Lyon, the OSS house was the first stop for Dulles on a quick trip back to the United States. Few American agents had spent so much time away from home, and analysts in Washington keenly awaited the backstory on the Breakers plot. A surprise awaited him.

OSS chief Donovan, who loathed sitting at his desk in Washington, had followed on the heels of American GIs when they invaded the South of France and made arrangements to see Agent 110. Dulles was at first delighted at the opportunity to catch up with his boss. As ambitious as ever, Dulles had heard that David Bruce would be leaving the London station soon and hoped his hard work would be rewarded with the job. Yet before boarding a DC-3 to London, Donovan pulled him aside. "I'm ordering David to stay on, just as I'm asking you to do the same," he said. "God knows what would happen if we had a change in Bern at this juncture. We just can't afford to lose you."

More bad news followed. Flying over the Loire valley, where Dulles worried that a German fighter plane would emerge from the sky, Donovan announced the OSS had some new ideas for the Swiss operation. He had brought with him on the flight William J. Casey, an OSS officer stationed in London, to explain plans to parachute agents "en masse" behind German lines. Such operations had worked well in France, and it seemed like they would in Germany as well. Listening as his colleagues shouted to be heard over the aircraft's noisy engines, Dulles learned that his Bern station was now to become "a salient" for launching such attacks into Germany and Austria.

Dulles recoiled as Casey explained the scheme. Speaking with "intensity and unshakable conviction," Dulles said such agents would never survive inside the Third Reich. The civilian population, as well as the German police and army, were on the lookout for spies. Any OSS agents would be quickly rounded up and executed. It would be much more effective, he argued, to establish a network of German informants as he had done. In fact, the outlook for such a program was as promising as ever.

Domestic opposition to Hitler, Dulles assured his boss, especially among army officers, was rapidly spreading. They were now required to offer one another the Nazi salute, which rankled. Wehrmacht officers now also had to give up their sidearms before seeing Hitler, a grave insult. Such men made inviting targets for the OSS.

Donovan's question about infiltrating the German lines was only a courtesy. Eisenhower's staff had already approved a scheme to parachute thirty additional agents into Germany to collect military and political intelligence. The operation represented for Donovan a "rebirth" for the OSS "in its truest sense," one that devised bold raids carried out by small groups of men on industrial installations and other targets.

The evening of September 8, Dulles and Bruce met for drinks at the American Bar at London's Savoy Hotel. It had been a momentous day in the British capital. Around dinnertime, the first of Hitler's advanced long-range V-2 ballistic missiles had hit London, killing three people in Chiswick.

• • •

OSS headquarters on Washington's Navy Hill would have been almost un-recognizable to Dulles. Small and tight-knit in 1942 when he had left for Switzerland, the agency now hummed with analysts, financial experts, and secretaries furiously transcribing secret correspondence from around the world. The OSS would at its peak in December 1944 employ thirteen thousand people, more than five thousand of them in Washington.

Those with the right clearances knew Dulles as something of a star. Their man in Bern was working about one hundred chief agents and had scored some impressive victories. His success with Kolbe was widely recognized. "Wood" had become arguably the OSS's most important intelligence asset. Dulles's work with the Breakers and the July 20 plot against Hitler were widely lauded, "sensational" in the words of Donovan. Some of his reports, Donovan told him, had been passed on to the president.

But there were also some who suspected that Agent 110 had overstepped his bounds by working so closely with the Breakers plotters. OSS headquarters had felt compelled to turn over all of Dulles's communications about the Breakers to the State Department and, oddly, to state that his work had been "merely the passive acceptance of intelligence" and that there had been "no bargaining of any kind." Dulles was instructed not to entertain any more members of the underground who wanted to organize a coup.

Shuttling between meetings in Washington, Dulles was giving more thought to the Soviets, and he began polling trusted advisers. His brother Foster was something of an expert on the subject, now serving as the principal foreign policy adviser to the Republican candidate for president in the upcoming election, Thomas Dewey. Foster approved of breaking Germany up as one means of preventing future aggression, but, he thought, the key to a peaceful world order, including relations between Germany and the Soviet Union, was a strong set of international organizations, none more important than what would become the United Nations.

Dulles met Emily Rado, an old friend, who had specific ideas about how to implement the inevitable occupation of Germany. One of the OSS's most gifted analysts, Rado had been educated in Switzerland, spoke numerous languages, and was widely admired as a "superior type person, one of the real unsung heroines [of the OSS]." The immediate days and weeks after the war ended would be vital, she said. The United States should turn to church leaders to help get the occupation off on the right foot.

The counsel that most coincided with his views, Dulles discovered, was that of his sister Eleanor. She had studied economics in Bonn in 1930 and now worked at the State Department as a member of the German Committee, a group that was considering alternatives for the country after the war. Some members, herself included, favored purging Germany of extremist ideas but wanted to restore its position in the world. They believed the punitive peace treaty that ended World War I was a mistake to be avoided.

Mulling over his experiences in Switzerland, the discussions he was now hearing in the United States, and the astonishing lack of preparation for the end of the war he observed in Washington, Dulles prepared a lengthy position paper for Donovan on October 7, 1944.

The end of the war, he wrote, presented the United States with two problems regarding Germany—how to punish the country and how to settle the peace. "These two must be kept distinct. There must be punishment, but if the settlement is itself a punishment, it will not be lasting."

The focus shouldn't be on preventing Germany from starting another war, he wrote, but preventing it from collapsing into social chaos. It would be a grave mistake, Dulles argued, to dismantle the German economy, as some, including US treasury secretary Henry Morgenthau Jr., were advising. Instead, he recommended that the United States help create jobs for German citizens to prevent social unrest. While firmly agreeing with the moral imperative to track down and punish leading Nazis, he also called for keeping the basic services of the economy functioning, especially the railroads, banking, and food distribution, even if some of the people with the right expertise had not necessarily defied the Nazi regime.

The role of the Soviets would be critical. Dulles expected Moscow to serve up a "ready-made" government in Germany based on the Free Germany Committee, and he counseled against accepting any such "made-in-Russia" solution.

Having dispatched his thoughts about Germany, and after writing another think piece on the position of Europe in general, Dulles prepared to return to Switzerland. His station, he knew, was in for radical changes.

CHAPTER
29

Light Had Gone Out

The unsupervised isolation Dulles had so enjoyed came to an abrupt end with the American invasion of the South of France in August 1944. He had never liked taking orders. In March 1944, for instance, he had refused to cooperate with the War Refugee Board and its plan to use Switzerland as a safe haven for Jews trapped in Germany. "Zealous individuals who are ignorant of conditions and do not have the necessary technical training can do the refugees the greatest amount of harm," he wrote. "There is a tremendous need for work now neglected, among refugees already here, especially Jews and Italians, without bringing in a new avalanche of refugees."

New logistical headaches emerged. The handful of staffers whom he managed mushroomed, and new duties were piled on. Suddenly he was tripping over code clerks, secretaries, and experts on various subjects. New posts were added in Geneva, Zurich, and Basel. There were even new cars to manage, a Packard and a front-wheel-drive Citroen.

Mundane chores now began to consume more of his time. The Sixth Army was hungry for information on changing levels of the Rhine River, which flowed into Germany, and an early reading could be obtained in Switzerland. To supply the information, an OSS representative was dispatched early in the morning to stroll across a bridge, note the water level, and phone in his report to the army.

To Clover, Dulles complained, "There is vastly more to do than when the frontiers were closed. . . . Meanwhile, they are flooding me with cables from all directions and asking generally that we do the impossible."

Those who knew Dulles best saw a sad transformation. Reminders of the July 20 debacle haunted him. In late January, he wrote Washington to say he had heard that Moltke, in prison for half a year, had been sentenced to death. Was there anything the OSS could do to delay his execution, such as finding a way to convince the Nazis that Moltke was more valuable to them alive than dead?

The plea came too late. Moltke was executed at Plötzensee Prison on January 23.

"Much of the sparkle and charm went out of Allen's personality," Bancroft observed. "It was rather like the way an exuberant young person behaves when his parents suddenly show up."

But Dulles had not been completely tamed. He was still running dozens of promising agents. Before Dulles left for Washington, for instance, Schulze-Gaevernitz had brought in a young former German soldier with impeccable credentials. A member of anti-Nazi groups in Vienna before the war, Fritz Molden had served in a punishment unit on the eastern front before somehow managing a transfer to Italy. There he had promptly gone AWOL and fought for a time with the Italian resistance. Finally, in 1944, he had sneaked across the border into Switzerland, where, with the help of Swiss intelligence, he sought out representatives of the Allies. Arriving at the Herrengasse late one evening, Molden entranced Dulles for three hours with his personal story and promises of how the Austrian resistance could help the Allies. "Dulles was most affable and, on saying good-bye late that night, he told me that he would do his utmost to help us, but first we must show that we could produce results," Molden later wrote.

Trying to prove his worth, Molden traveled to Austria under the guise of a German sergeant. The rank, he reasoned, would allow him a measure of anonymity that an officer's uniform could not provide. Most patrols were led by sergeants, who tended to treat others of their rank with cordiality and usually asked few questions. He also spent considerable time memorizing a personal history of the identity he had assumed, asking friends to abruptly wake him from a sound sleep to see if he could present details of his CV accurately and without hesitation. Spending several days in Vienna, Molden met with members of the resistance to discuss ways to unify their work, and he memorized a lengthy report that he could later present to the Americans.

Now, in October, he came again to the Herrengasse, Agent 110 suffering from gout that kept him in his chair during their visit. Over the next two days, Molden impressed the American enough to win promises of further help.

Dulles, with Schulze-Gaevernitz, was also working on a plan to persuade German commanders to give up their troops in small-scale surrenders. Some of the many high-ranking German officers the Allies had captured on the western front, Dulles and Schulze-Gaevernitz knew, were known critics of the Nazis. Such men could probably be persuaded to tell the OSS which German generals still fighting shared their views. Visiting POW camps in Belgium and England, Schulze-Gaevernitz and an army intelligence officer found several senior officers whom they hoped could form the basis of an advisory group on how to carry out their plan. The major obstacle, they learned, was making contact with potential German turncoats. Radio communication was impossible. Equally out of the question was sneaking such men through German lines. More-junior officers, they reasoned, might be able to slip into German territory claiming they had escaped from POW camps and, once close to the German generals, present the details of how to surrender.

Everything about the plan seemed to make sense, and Schulze-Gaevernitz presented it to General Eisenhower in December 1944. Schulze-Gaevernitz might have received authorization had it not been for a stunning German attack on American forces in the densely wooded forests of the Ardennes in the middle of the month. The ensuing battle, later known as the Battle of the Bulge because of how the attack appeared on the maps of commanders, was the bloodiest of the war for the Americans and left Allied generals convinced there was no dealing with the Nazis. "Washington was now pretty well convinced that the Germans would fight to the bitter end and that voluntary surrenders were most unlikely," Dulles later wrote.

All the while Dulles was tackling these projects, the fate of Gisevius was never far from his mind. Meeting one cool evening shortly after he returned to Switzerland, Dulles and Bancroft discussed whether they would ever see their old friend again. Bancroft explained that she was working on an introduction to Gisevius's book, which she believed was his obituary.

Yet the simple fact that there had been no report of his capture—Nazi newspapers never missed an opportunity to tout a new arrest—seemed to indicate that not all hope was lost.

CHAPTER

30

"I Felt That the Walls of the Cellar Were About to Collapse Around Me"

Late in the evening on July 20, the coup crumbling, Gisevius alighted from his car and set off on foot to a radio transmitter to broadcast a call for public support. Passing a tall picket fence, his mind raced. Increasingly, the course in front of him looked like a futile suicide mission. Examining a pass given to coup members, Gisevius achieved a moment of clarity. He destroyed the ticket, threw the shreds over the fence, and set off for the temporary safety of the nearby apartment of his friend Theodor Strünck.

The two spent that night huddling close to the radio. Repeatedly they heard announcements that Hitler himself would make a brief statement, but delays in the broadcast raised their hopes that it was a hoax. Finally, around midnight, Hitler's unmistakable voice crackled. "A very small clique of ambitious, dishonorable and at the same time criminally stupid officers have conspired to remove me and at the same time to overturn the staff leadership of the German armed forces. A bomb that was planted by Colonel Graf von Stauffenberg exploded two meters from my right side. It very seriously wounded a number of my faithful staff members. One of them has died. I myself am absolutely unhurt, except for very light scratches, bruises and burns. I interpret this as a confirmation of the order of Providence that I continue to pursue the goal of my life, as I have done up to now."

Hitler signed off and marching music was played.

Gisevius went to bed that night plagued by the horror of opportunity missed and the revenge that would follow. "I felt that the walls of the cellar were about to collapse around me, so oppressed was I by the memory of all the hopes, fears, and disappointments that had engrossed us in our talks within these four walls during the past few days and hours."

Gisevius spent the next several days consumed by terror. Desperate for information and a place to hide, he moved as inconspicuously as possible around Berlin from one friend's house to another, expecting at any moment a tap on the shoulder and the face of a Gestapo agent. Old friends and coconspirators greeted him in their doorways with nervous smiles and warnings to keep moving. There had not been many arrests *yet*, but all involved in the plot feared a brutal and horrific bloodletting.

Gisevius concluded that to remain in Berlin would be foolhardy. He was too well-known among those in the security services who, even if they weren't looking for him, might well notice him simply by accident. It would be dangerous, but Gisevius, Strünck, his wife, and a coconspirator, Arthur Nebe, who had a car, decided to flee to the countryside near Potsdam.

Traveling during a night made even darker by a blackout, they repeatedly got lost. More than once, they had to stop and get out of the car to consult road signs. Quietly discussing their route, the four could hear the drone of Allied bombers high overhead. Adding to the tension were the dozens of checkpoints, each of which required them to offer up carefully constructed lies.

Their plan was to seek shelter with religious leaders who were thought to be sympathetic to the resistance. Yet knocking on church doors, the four discovered that pastors considered it too dangerous to take in anybody sought by the Gestapo. One churchman explained that townspeople were required by law to report any new faces they saw. "I implore you for the sake of my wife and children not to come here again," one called out as they left his home.

Rebuffed at every turn and low on gasoline, the four decided to give up their hunt. The only thing left to do was to abandon the car, hiding it in thick underbrush, and take a train back to Berlin, though the thought of traveling in public filled them with "sheer torment." They would have to change trains no fewer than five times, providing ample opportunities for police officers monitoring passengers to spot them. Traveling as a group, they realized, made them more conspicuous. They said quiet good-byes and split up. They would not see each other again.

In Berlin, Gisevius made his way to a home belonging to a lady friend. It was risky; the house was located close to Gestapo headquarters, where many would be likely to recognize him. But he lacked alternatives, and there was no reason that anybody would think to look for him there.

For the next few days it appeared that Hitler, in an effort to play down the coup, would not aggressively hunt down the plotters. On July 24, Ulrich von Hassell, a German diplomat who had joined the conspiracy, met with Gisevius and said he wasn't even trying to hide. It was impossible for him and his family to escape, he reasoned. Apparently still stewing about Stauffenberg, Gisevius complained that he and his close friends had been excluded from the final phase of planning for the attack. Hassell left the meeting feeling depressed, too, not only by the missed opportunity but also by Gisevius's bitter attitude.

Days later, the manhunt began. All over Germany and beyond, thousands were arrested. Yet the Gestapo seemed unable to find Gisevius.

From his Berlin hideout, he was not entirely cut off from the outside world, or without help. Members of the resistance had set about devising plans to get him back to Switzerland. Some began raising money, and one early scheme called for him to leave Germany in the company of a member of the underground disguised as a Red Cross worker.

At first, Gisevius had reason to think that his rescue might not take long. In the middle of October, a member of the underground got word to him that he would soon receive "a book" that would indicate he could trust whoever brought it. Another month passed before a woman turned up at the house and gave Gisevius the book, yet she offered no explanation or information on what was being done for him. There was only a terse note that a further message would arrive "shortly." Gisevius read each page over and over, looking for some hidden message, and when he couldn't find anything, he tore open the binding.

The wait for more information was filled with torment. Bombing raids had blown out the windows of the house where he was hiding, and temperatures, especially at night, dropped sharply as autumn progressed. Hours turned to days and days into weeks.

There were occasional visitors—old friends from the resistance—but he otherwise had little to keep himself occupied. Possibly tuning in to foreign radio broadcasts to kill time, Gisevius might have been startled to hear the measured tones of his old friend Beck exhorting Germans to keep up the fight against Hitler. It was perplexing. The Nazis had told the German people that Beck was dead, yet the voice sounded authentic. The broadcast was actually part of an OSS operation designed to discredit Hitler's regime, the voice that of a German POW in England.

The one project that he tackled, his book, left him feeling ill. Many of the people he wrote about, friends and conspirators, had been rounded up and were being tortured and executed. On the eastern front, Tresckow, who had tried to blow up Hitler's plane in the spring of 1943, killed himself with a hand grenade. Hassell was picked up on July 29. Shortly thereafter, Strünck was taken into custody. Goerdeler was arrested on August 12 after an innkeeper notified authorities that she had seen him in the area visiting the graves of his parents. Trott, of the Kreisau Circle, who had helped with the planning for the coup, was arrested and hanged in August. Oster and Canaris were arrested days after the attack and sent to prison, where they would eventually be executed.

The Gestapo liked to target the family members of the underground.

Gisevius had succeeded in getting his mother safely to Switzerland. But from a friend he learned that the authorities had taken his sister into custody in mid-August, and nobody knew what they had done with her. They had also sent a plane to apprehend his cousin, then fighting with German forces on the Baltic front. The so-called arrest of kin was, Gisevius had to acknowledge, an effective tool to combat the resistance. "Everyone has the moral right to risk his own life, but can he justify himself before God and man if he also hazards the lives of his wife and children?"

With too much time on his hands, Gisevius concocted one explanation after another for why his rescue was taking so long. Perhaps Dulles and his friends were waiting to sneak him out of Germany during the dark of the moon. Yet when the period passed and the moon became full, he wondered if part of his rescue plan depended on good moonlight, so as to escape through the underbrush and swamps along the Swiss-German border. More weeks passed and Christmas approached with no further word. Surely they had planned for his escape on Christmas Eve, when Gestapo patrols would be reduced. By the middle of January, he was giving up hope.

Spiriting Gisevius out of Germany was proving to be harder than expected. His name and description had been widely disseminated to police and border guards within weeks of July 20. At six feet four, and needing his thick glasses to see, Gisevius would be hard to miss.

The Germans were also becoming more aware of the connection between Dulles and the July 20 plotters. In November, the chief of the Berlin security police wrote a report to Martin Bormann, one of Hitler's most trusted aides, which aimed to shed light on the ties between the conspirators and foreign countries. Gisevius, the report said, was closely linked to the now-disgraced former Abwehr chief Canaris as well as to members of the resistance, including General Beck. The report also identified Eduard von Waetjen, Bancroft's "Homer," as a confidant of Gisevius's and someone who worked with opposition groups "in the same dubious way."

Gisevius and Goerdeler were both on good terms with Dulles, the Nazi report went on, and had worked closely with him shortly before the July 20 attack on Hitler. "It was obvious that conspiracy circles hoped to profit considerably from the connection with Dulles," the security police chief wrote.

While the Nazis ramped up their investigation into the attack, news of what had happened began to find its way into briefing papers in Washington, and eventually into American headlines. Remarkably, the plotters received little more sympathy than they did in Germany. The *New York Herald Tribune* opined that Hitler would now help the Allies by hunting down and executing German militants, a job American troops would otherwise have had to perform. Another newspaper wrote that details of the plot "suggest more the atmosphere of a gangster's lurid underworld than the normal atmosphere [of] an officers' corps and *a civilized government.*" There were even suggestions from the OSS that its officers provide the SS with names of men and women known to have taken part in the attack on Hitler so as to sow discord. By contrast, in the Soviet Union the putsch leaders were shown respect, Radio Moscow sensing a propoganda opportunity by hailing the "courageous men" who rose up against Hitler and calling on others to continue their work.

That the Bern station chief did not share the sentiments of his countrymen would not have surprised his superiors, and Dulles pressed ahead with plans to sneak Gisevius out of Germany. The best bet, he decided, was a technique the Allies had used in similar circumstances. Posing as a Gestapo agent, a quick-witted member of the resistance could bluff his way out of most tight situations.

Agent 110 tapped trusted colleagues to begin making arrangements.

Employing contacts in the German embassy in Bern, Schulze-Gaevernitz obtained examples of the identification cards and travel documents that Gisevius could use to pass himself off as a member of the Gestapo. These could easily be copied by MI6 forgers in London. More difficult was the identity badge carried by each officer of the secret police. Oval shaped, about the size of a belt buckle, the disk was made of an unknown silver alloy that was difficult to copy. Further complicating things, an official number, which could be checked at any Gestapo office, was engraved into the reverse side. The British forgers would have to pick some number at random and hope for the best.

A further delay came when the travel documents arrived in Switzerland. It was discovered that they lacked a special travel stamp that could be prepared only in London. Carrying the documents back to the English capital, a courier incredibly presented the faked Gestapo papers to an Allied military policeman in Paris and was promptly arrested. More time was lost while the OSS smoothed things over.

Finally, around the turn of the year, the completed travel documents arrived back in Switzerland, and Dulles made plans to send them to Berlin. Unable to use the normal postal service, he employed a secret courier service developed by friends in Swiss intelligence, code-named Viking.

On the evening of January 20, 1945, the doorbell rang at Gisevius's hideout. At the door stood the same woman who had delivered the book months before, breathlessly asking if everything was all right. When he replied that all was well, she ran into the darkness.

A few moments later, the bell rang again. Gisevius rushed to the door in time to see a car, its headlights turned off, speeding away. A fat envelope stuck out of the mailbox. Quickly grabbing the package and returning inside, he opened the flap and emptied the contents. Gisevius retrieved a passport with a picture of himself on it under the name of Hoffmann. There were also a special pass and a letter from Gestapo headquarters instructing all officials of the government to assist him on a secret mission to Switzerland. It appeared that the OSS had thought of everything. He would leave right away.

Walking into a bustling train station at about 5:00 p.m. the next day, Gisevius saw how difficult the journey would be. Across the platform from his train was another, bound for Vienna, with a number of SS officers waiting for it. He hoped that none would recognize him. What's more, his train was already overflowing with passengers. At first, Gisevius considered bribing the conductor to find a seat for him. Before he could decide, loud shouting and arguing broke his concentration. The baggage car on his train had just been opened to allow arriving passengers to retrieve their suitcases. Many more people, though, were attempting to use the open car as a means to board the train.

Seizing the advantage of the confusion, Gisevius made his way to the commotion, withdrew his fake badge and displayed it for all to see. Shouting "Gestapo," he elbowed his way through the crowd and momentarily cleared the car out. Having boarded the train, Gisevius made his way into a passenger compartment, scarcely looking over his shoulder as the crowd again surged toward the luggage car. With the seats all long since taken, Gisevius noticed two small children and moved toward them. Lifting each up, he took their place and perched the youngsters on both of his knees, hiding his face behind them.

At 6:00 a.m. the morning of January 23, 1945, a bedraggled Gisevius stepped into the small waiting room at the Swiss-German border crossing near Lake Constance. Two officials, one a Gestapo man, peered up at him. It was odd to have anybody cross the border this time of the morning, let alone one claiming to be a high-ranking Gestapo agent. The suit that now hung from his large frame was the same one that he had worn on July 20, and in fact had worn almost every day since. His coat was dirty, and he wore a hat stolen on his rail journey that was several sizes too small. His thick, dark hair, which he cut himself with a pair of nail scissors, was rough and uneven. He wore a pair of fur-lined boots.

He hoped such a shabby image might lend credibility to his story. Nobody but a Gestapo agent on a secret mission would dare attempt a border crossing. "I raised my arm limply in response to their greeting, for the two of them stood stiffly to see me out of the Gestapo's Germany. And I was free!"

A few nights later, Gisevius walked as he had so many times before toward the Herrengasse villa. The months of tension and hiding had taken a toll. He was much thinner, and his hair had grayed considerably. Ushered inside, he sank into one of the two leather chairs by the fireplace. Dulles quickly came in, extending both hands in warm welcome. "I felt as if my pilgrimage through the Nazi millennium was over at last. I was deeply moved, profoundly grateful. I thought of my friends, of the dead, of the living."

One morning a day or two later Gisevius showed up at the door of Bancroft's Zurich apartment. "Well, here I am!"

"Yes," Bancroft replied. "And it's high time you came back too!"

CHAPTER

31

"An Implacable Enemy of Bolshevism"

The peace feelers Kolbe discovered at the Wolf's Lair during the late summer of 1944 were examples of a growing torrent of attempts by leading Nazis to surrender themselves, their armies, and their country. Some, as Gisevius had been warning, were looking to the East. Foreign Minister Ribbentrop, who had arranged the nonaggression pact with the Soviets in 1939, favored a deal whereby the two countries would share domination of Europe. Propaganda Minister Goebbels suggested that if Germany had to choose between East and West, the answer should be East. The Soviets were an increasingly attractive partner. With their armies closing in, the conventional wisdom among many close to Hitler was that the Russians would display an accommodating attitude toward the horrors they would uncover when they arrived at the concentration camps.

The West, though, still exerted the strongest pull for the majority of senior German officers. A number reached out to American and British contacts through neutral intermediaries in Stockholm, the Vatican, and, of course, Switzerland.

Bizarrely, none was more aggressive than Himmler. Demonstrating a spectacular lack of awareness of how his crimes were regarded in the West, the Reichsführer surrounded himself with a cottage industry of men who established contacts with Washington and London.

Himmler's strategy began with attempts to whitewash his image by showing a humane side that he had given no evidence of possessing. Between the summer of 1944 and early 1945, he agreed to transfer nearly 2,700 Jews to Switzerland (albeit for a hefty price) and issued strict orders to concentration camp commanders to improve conditions and prevent the outbreak of disease. Early in 1945, with the help of his physical therapist, Felix Kersten, he struck up a relationship with the vice president of the Swedish Red Cross, Count Folke Bernadotte, and reached an agreement that led to the rescue of Norwegian and Danish prisoners held by the Nazis.

In February, Ernst Kaltenbrunner, the head of the Reich Main Security Office and another member of Himmler's outreach team, dispatched an SS intelligence officer in his twenties to meet Dulles. Wilhelm Höttl, accompanied by an Austrian industrialist, Fritz Weston, met Agent 110 with the goal of painting Martin Bormann, another Nazi Party leader, as the one to worry about, and Himmler as the man who wanted peace with the West. Playing to Dulles's well-known antipathy toward the Soviets, Höttl reminded him of the threat from the East and promised that Field Marshal Albert Kesselring, the commander in chief of Army Group South, and Field Marshal Gerd von Rundstedt on the western front supported the idea of negotiating with the West.

Höttl found that Dulles "showed himself to be not only a man of high intelligence, but also an implacable enemy of Bolshevism, whose opposition was based on knowledge, reasoned argument and clear-sighted vision." Such attitudes toward the Soviets established a common ground that marked Dulles as somebody Himmler's team could work with.

A month later, Höttl returned to Switzerland with a variation of the theme he had floated in February. Under the impression that the United

States planned to set up its own occupation government in Austria, he put forward Kaltenbrunner as a candidate to work with the Americans. Höttl seemed to think the conversation had gone well and urged Kaltenbrunner to arrange a meeting with Dulles. There the effort fizzled, Kaltenbrunner apparently distracted by other things.

In April, Dulles received another peace overture, this time from Walter Schellenberg, through one of his contacts in the Swiss security services, General Roger Masson. Again hoping to tap Dulles's concern about the Soviets, Schellenberg suggested that the German army could open the western front to the Americans as long as they could continue the fight in the east.

Dulles treated these maneuvers with skepticism. Himmler was a war criminal whose days were numbered. In reporting the Schellenberg overture, he wrote Washington that it was obvious the SS officer was trying to buy immunity from his crimes. Nor did the Germans have much to trade at this point. "I told Masson [the] west[ern] front was already opened up without Schellenberg['s] help."

CHAPTER

32

"A Common Desire to Know What the Germans Were Planning"

February 25, 1945, dawned cold and gray. It had been a difficult winter for Dulles. In December, he had complained that it seemed to have been raining for weeks without letup. And he had been stricken with painful gout, which made it hard to move around and left him in a surly mood.

The job he faced that day gave him no reason to feel any brighter. He and Schulze-Gaevernitz were to drive to Hegenheim, an Alsatian village in France near the intersection of Switzerland and Germany, to meet with General Gene Harrison, chief of intelligence for the US Sixth Army. The army had lost a truck near Colmar, a few miles away, that contained a safe filled with important military papers, and Harrison needed help finding it. It was not the sort of assignment that Dulles relished, drudge work by the standards he set for himself.

As Dulles discussed the problem at General Harrison's office, an urgent message reached him from his team in Bern. Major Max Waibel of the Swiss military needed to see both him and Schulze-Gaevernitz on an urgent matter.

No doubt happily leaving General Harrison and France behind, Dulles and Schulze-Gaevernitz drove halfway across Switzerland to see Waibel. (The missing truck was later found half-sunken in a stream, its contents intact.) Dulles felt "a strong bond both of friendship and professional trust and understanding" with Waibel, and the two "shared a common desire to know what the Germans were planning." With the Wehrmacht in retreat in Italy, Waibel and many others in Switzerland were growing nervous about the prospect of thousands of Nazi soldiers showing up on their borders seeking asylum or safe passage through to Germany. The Bern government was keen to make sure that the economy of northern Italy survived the war, especially the port of Genoa, through which food and supplies passed to Switzerland.

Waibel, who wore his hair short and framed his eyes with a pair of wire-rimmed glasses, greeted the pair at a quiet restaurant near Lake Lucerne that served excellent trout. He explained that two civilians had recently contacted him with a peace offer from senior German officers based in Italy. One was Baron Luigi Parilli, an Italian businessman considered a "cheerful but cunning gentleman," and the other, Professor Max Hausmann, was head of a fashionable Swiss boys' school.

The connection to Italy intrigued Dulles, a country he felt required "careful handling." Though the "great majority" of Italians favored building their future around the West, the Communist movement there remained strong, especially in the underground. Dulles believed it was important that the north of Italy be freed by American and British forces rather than by Russian troops advancing through Yugoslavia. If the Western Allies failed, the tendency of "north Italy to go communist would be very strong."

Yet the more Waibel explained, the more Dulles regretted driving so far. The story he now heard sounded like the pipe dream of an Italian industrialist with no real pull with the Germans. Dulles had seen it before, excited men so desperate to protect their investments that they grasped at the flimsiest of straws to try to secure a peaceful end to the war. Convinced that a meeting wasn't worth his time, Dulles finished his fish and asked Schulze-Gaevernitz to meet the men later that evening. He was going to take the train home to Bern.

The next morning, Schulze-Gaevernitz met Dulles and confirmed his suspicions of Parilli and Hausmann. Parilli's contacts with the Germans seemed to be relatively low-level officers of the SS, not the caliber of authority necessary to arrange the surrender of a meaningful number of troops. Schulze-Gaevernitz, considering the matter closed, booked a quick ski holiday at Davos. "We made a report of these meetings and dropped them into our 'Peace Feelers' file, which had been growing fat in the last few months but still seemed rather futile," Dulles wrote.

He was no more impressed when, five days later, Waibel phoned a second time. Parilli was back, this time with two SS officers in tow, Colonel Eugen Dollmann and Captain Guido Zimmer. Again Dulles decided it wasn't worth his time to meet the men himself. Instead he promised to dispatch Paul Blum, a new member of his team who was already interrogating an Italian agent near the proposed meeting place in Lugano. Dulles, still doubting this peace overture, turned his attention to more pressing matters.

Shortly after 4:00 p.m. on Saturday, March 3, 1945, Blum climbed the stairs of the Ristorante Biaggi in Lugano and entered a private dining room that Waibel had reserved. Normally used for meetings of the local Rotary Club, the room was of a classic Swiss style, with a low-timbered ceiling, a fireplace, and carved wooden furnishings. Embossed metal plates decorated the wall. Seated around a table were five men, each staring at him with a mixture of relief and annoyance.

Blum was hours late, and Professor Hausmann, a short, stocky man with a head of thick gray hair and stiff manners, had filled the time by getting on the nerves of the Germans. Earlier in the day he had delivered to the SS men a "condescending lecture" on Napoléon's exile on Saint Helena in 1815 and later took it upon himself to drive home the American demand that Germany would have to surrender unconditionally. When Dollmann said that such draconian surrender terms might be considered a "betrayal" to the German people, Hausmann launched into what Dollmann described as "dialectical pyrotechnics."

Blum surveyed the unhappy table and sized up the two SS officers. Colonel Dollmann had lived in Italy for years and was in many respects more Italian than German. Urbane, suave, and an expert on Renaissance art, he avoided wearing his SS uniform whenever he could and combed his long hair straight back. His entry into the SS had also been somewhat unusual. In 1937, he had accompanied a group of Italian youths to Germany and, at one point during the trip, stood in for Hitler's interpreter, who was ill. He so impressed Hitler and Himmler that they offered him a high SS rank and saw to it that he was stationed in Rome. "Dollmann hardly filled the bill as a blond Germanic hero," Dulles later wrote.

The other SS officer, Captain Zimmer, was obviously junior to Dollmann and struck Blum as "good looking, clean cut, not the way one pictures the typical SS officer."

Speaking in French, a language that all at the table fluently commanded, Dollmann was vague about his intentions but explained that he and his colleague were in contact with SS Obergruppenführer Karl Wolff. Blum's interest perked up. Wolff, a dynamic officer with a wide reputation, was arguably second only to Field Marshal Albert Kesselring in terms of the power he wielded on Germany's Italian front.

It sounded interesting, but Blum wanted evidence of how serious the Germans were. Dulles had given him the means to do so.

As the meeting at the restaurant was wrapping up, Blum handed Dollmann a slip of paper with two names written by Dulles. One was Ferruccio Parri, a silver-haired anti-Communist leader of the resistance whom Dulles had first met in November 1943. The other was Antonio Usmiani, a man who had been supplying military intelligence for Dulles in northern Italy. Both were then in Nazi jails.

Dulles had reason to feel responsible for Parri. In late 1944, he had arranged for a group of Italian underground leaders, including Parri, to visit Allied headquarters in Caserta, Italy. The Germans had found out about the trip and arrested Parri on his return to northern Italy. Adding to the blow, Parri had been carrying a number of papers outlining upcoming operations, forcing the resistance to cancel their plans. Then three partisans, disguised as SS men, were caught trying to rescue Parri from the Milan hotel where he was initially held. To prevent any other rescue operations, Parri had been moved to a secure SS prison in Verona, from which escape was considered impossible.

Blum explained that if Parri and Usmiani were handed over to the Allies, "the seriousness of General Wolff's intentions would be amply demonstrated."

Dollmann was stunned at the request, which reminded him of a game of "forfeits at a schoolgirls' party." Parri was possibly the most important prisoner the SS then held in Italy. What's more, the two men were incarcerated in different prisons, presenting a major logistical and security challenge. It would take a serious effort to secure their release. "I listened with no enthusiasm," Dollmann later wrote.

Dulles, too, seemed to have his doubts about where the talks would lead, and he decided for the moment to spare Washington the news of the German overture. He believed, as a general rule, that intelligence officers who ask for too many instructions end up with orders they don't like. The chance that Washington would interfere was especially large in this case, because meeting with someone like Wolff raised the possibility that the ambitious spymaster would engage in making policy—an outcome nobody in Washington, neither the OSS nor the State Department, wanted to see. "Sooner or later I would probably be faced with the decision of whether or not I should meet personally with General Wolff, but I knew that if I put this question up to headquarters in Washington they would be forced to make a high-level decision which would probably cramp my freedom of action and decision."

CHAPTER

33

"Gero, Are You Standing or Sitting?"

On March 8, Schulze-Gaevernitz was finishing a day of skiing on the slopes of the Parsenn in Davos, which was serviced by the most advanced ski lift in the world, a funicular train. He had just returned to his hotel room, still bundled in his jacket and ski pants, when the phone rang. The Swiss intelligence officer Waibel was on the line. "Gero, are you standing or sitting? Because if you're standing, you might fall over when you hear the news."

The two Italian resistance fighters had been released. "Parri and Usmiani are here," Waibel explained breathlessly. "They were delivered safe and sound a few hours ago to my man at the Swiss-Italian frontier at Chiasso. SS Captain Zimmer has driven up from Milan." Both men were now on their way to Zurich, he explained. And there was another surprise. Obergruppenführer Wolff had crossed the border not long after them.

Dressed in a business suit and accompanied by six men, Wolff was aboard a train chugging for Zurich through the Alps, so fearful of discovery that he had booked two railway cars, locked the doors, and drawn the blinds. Schulze-Gaevernitz quickly phoned Dulles, pulled off his ski gear, threw it in a suitcase, and made for the train station.

Dulles could hardly believe that Wolff had managed not only to secure the release of the two Italians, but also to plan a trip that included everything from inventing a story to cover his absence to providing security in Switzerland. "How did he do it?" Dulles wondered. "Did he regard himself as invulnerable? Was his power so great that he had nothing to fear? Was he perhaps foolhardy? How would he have survived so long and reached such high rank in the SS if that was the answer? Or did Himmler know . . . ?"

Before meeting Wolff, Dulles wanted to make sure, with his own eyes, that Parri and Usmiani were free and unhurt. Heading straight for the Klinik Hirslanden, an exclusive institution where the two had been stashed, Agent 110 found everything as Waibel had described it. "I shall never forget the scene," he later wrote. "Parri . . . was so excited that he broke into tears and threw his arms around me." Parri had assumed when SS guards removed him from his cell that he was going to be shot. When taken to a train, he concluded that he was being taken to Germany, where he would likely suffer a similar fate.

Accepting his thanks for the rescue, Dulles had one request: Would they remain in Switzerland for at least a couple of weeks? If Parri or Usmiani returned to Italy and were caught, many awkward questions would be asked about how they had escaped from a heavily guarded SS prison, questions that might derail whatever proposal Wolff had brought with him.

On the ground floor of a "rather bleak building" on the Genferstrasse in Zurich, Dulles kept a rented apartment for clandestine meetings "of the touchiest nature." To enter the building, one passed through a heavy portal that was opened with a four-inch-long key. Visitors then passed through another portal and a vestibule before getting to the front door of the flat. It was here that he planned to meet Wolff.

The meeting raised some sticky ethical questions for Dulles. Wolff's troops had committed beastly atrocities. Wolff had overseen the transportation of three hundred thousand Jews to death camps, records would later show. At one point in 1942, he had written of his "special joy" that five thousand Jews were being sent to Treblinka every day.

Wolff seemed to have anticipated that the Americans would have qualms about meeting with someone like him. In honor of the occasion, the general had prepared a dossier that painted a picture of a benevolent occupation ruler. There was a list of references featuring the names of seven or eight churchmen and Italian aristocrats, and testimonials explaining how Wolff had helped them, including a personal letter to Wolff from the cardinal of Venice, thanking him for securing the release of a nun of Jewish origin from prison.

What Agent 110 knew of Wolff's crimes is unclear, but he likely would have agreed to meet with him anyway. Dulles was above all a pragmatist, and questions of morality were not always best asked during moments like these. If Wolff could shorten the war and save American lives, then he had to be taken seriously. "After all, I reasoned, an intelligence officer should be free to talk to the Devil himself if he could gain any useful knowledge for the conduct or the termination of the war," Dulles wrote.

How much leeway Dulles felt he had in dealing with somebody like Wolff is a matter of interpretation. Roosevelt had explicitly stated that the OSS and other intelligence services should not offer any guarantees of protection to Germans after the war, no matter what they offered in return. But on February 27, Dulles received a secret communication from the OSS instructing that he could make clear that "due note" would be taken of any efforts by German officers to shorten the war. Moreover, "in the event they should become involved in future trials, reports of such activities would be introduced as evidence."

The day started poorly for Wolff. Hausmann greeted him and his small team at the border and rode with them to Zurich, lecturing the general about the upcoming negotiations, so irritating Wolff that he demanded to be left alone.

His discomfort was compounded when, near the Gotthard Pass at

Göschenen, the train's progress was blocked by an avalanche that had swept across the rail line. Though Wolff had taken every precaution to avoid being seen, he and his group were forced to leave their secured cars and board another train. While doing so, Hausmann noticed a former Italian government minister who could have recognized Wolff.

His mood did not improve in Zurich, where he spent hours waiting with growing frustration at the Zurich home of Hausmann. Over canapés and wine, Mrs. Hausmann, a former singer at the Munich Opera, sought to lighten the mood with a discussion of music. Dollmann and Zimmer were soon singing and humming some of the old standards. Wolff tried to get in the spirit to join them, but "SS generals were not accustomed to waiting," and soon he was sulking and drumming his fingers on Hausmann's table. He was finally summoned to Dulles's safe house.

Schulze-Gaevernitz greeted Wolff and his contingent when they arrived that evening, leading them inside the apartment where Dulles was waiting. Dulles had already prepared his favorite conversation starter, a crackling fire in the fireplace.

Wolff, a public-relations executive before the war, knew how to make an entrance and initially impressed the Americans. He exuded a stately and stereotypically Aryan image, with Nordic good looks, a solid build, and blond hair just starting to turn gray, combed back from a high forehead. He struck Schulze-Gaevernitz "as being a man of strong personality, determined, energetic, with a quaint mixture so typical of certain Germans, of romanticism and cold realism."

Wolff's urbane manner did not include a command of foreign languages. Summoning his heavily accented and mistake-prone German, Dulles did his best to set the group at ease, and rounds of Scotch soon circulated. Much of Dulles's personality seemed to get lost as he struggled with the endless opportunities to commit grammatical mistakes that are part of the German language. "He always struck me as a leather-faced Puritan archangel who had fled from the European sink of iniquity on the Mayflower and now returned to scourge the sinners of the old world," Dollmann later wrote of Dulles. "He was incorruptible and totally humorless."

With the fire roaring, their amber drinks in hand, Agent 110 listened. Attempting to prove his sincerity and good intentions, Wolff explained that he had sabotaged Hitler's plans to conduct a scorched-earth campaign in Italy. He had saved several hundred precious paintings from the Uffizi Gallery in Florence, various sculptures, and even the Italian king's famous coin collection. It's not clear how much he told Dulles about it, but in May 1944, Wolff had even met with Pope Pius XII to explore ways to end the war.

Exactly what Wolff sought in the meeting is still hard to fully determine. Authors Bradley F. Smith and Elena Agarossi write that Wolff, like so many Nazis before him, hoped for a deal that would unite the Western powers with Germany to fight the Soviets. He would not take such an extreme risk as meeting with Dulles otherwise.

According to the account left by Dulles, Wolff acknowledged that the war was lost and that it was time to accept the American demand for unconditional surrender. "I control the SS forces in Italy," Wolff announced, "and I am willing to place myself and my entire organization at the disposal of the Allies to terminate hostilities."

That was good news. But what really mattered was whether the regular German army could be convinced to lay down arms. Of one million German troops in northern Italy, Wolff had under his direct command only ten thousand men, as well as fifty-five thousand unreliable service and supply troops.

Wolff said that given a chance, he believed he could persuade Field Marshal Kesselring to join him in surrendering to the Americans. Kesselring was not only commander of the German army in Italy but also carried tremendous respect among other officers and his troops. Persuading him to join a surrender would deal Hitler a crushing setback. If Dulles could assure a secure line of communication to the highest levels of the Allied command, which he said he could do, Wolff might be able to persuade Kesselring or his deputy to come to Switzerland to work out the details of a mass surrender.

In fact, Wolff continued, it was possible that the surrender of troops in Italy could set off a chain reaction through the German army's command structure. As Schulze-Gaevernitz recalled, Wolff "believed that the shock emanating from an action by Kesselring and himself would be such that also in the Western theater it would hasten the end of the war, as many generals on the Western front were only waiting for someone to take the lead."

After only an hour, Dulles had heard enough. It was time to let Washington in on the scheme.

Traveling back to Bern, Dulles wondered how his bosses would take news of Wolff's proposals. The meeting might be seen at Allied command as a trick. It would be easy for a German agent to leak word of Dulles's meeting to a Soviet contact in such a way as to make it look as if Washington were about to abandon Moscow. They might also suspect that Wolff's mission was more personal. He might simply be one of the many German officers who hoped to have friends in high places when the war ended.

Yet Wolff had one ace up his sleeve. His men, he told Schulze-Gaevernitz, helped control the passes that linked Italy with the mountains of the Austrian Alps and Germany beyond.

Perhaps no corner of Europe transfixed American generals in the closing months of the war as much as southern Germany, Austria, and northern Italy. American officers from Eisenhower on down had convinced themselves that here the Nazis were preparing to make a last stand.

A possible Nazi stronghold in the Alps, known to the Allies as the National Redoubt and to the Germans as the *Alpenfestung* ("Alpine Fortress"), could not easily be conquered. American airpower was hampered in the mountains, planes unable to deliver bombs powerful enough to destroy deep caves and gun emplacements. Narrow mountain roads, often in rough condition, made it difficult for heavy armor to pass.

The Americans had already been given a taste of alpine fighting in northern Italy and had seen how difficult it was. During the winter of 1944–45, the front line of the US Fifth Army moved hardly an inch from positions it held in October. The topography was so unforgiving there that mules were called in to carry supplies to American troops. The animals were so valuable that the army established a school to train soldiers to handle them. At the same time, the Germans' skill and experience fighting in the mountains were legendary. German army manuals on the subject were translated into English and issued to American GIs.

The closer the Americans looked for justification of their fears, the more evidence they seemed to find. From neutral diplomats in Berlin, reports circulated that the families of prominent Nazis were making plans to flee to Bavaria when the war ended. Supposed eyewitnesses noted how everything from sausages, flour, and sugar to truckloads of furniture was arriving in the region and being stored in miles of tunnels deep underground, impervious to bombs from Allied aircraft.

Even the popular press back home picked up the current of fear. In November 1944, the *New York Times* ran a story about Hitler's fabled mountain retreat, the Berghof. Caves complete with air-conditioning contained huge stores of water, tools, and arms, it reported. In January 1945, *Collier's* magazine published a detailed piece about the guerrilla war that denizens of the *Alpenfestung* promised to unleash on the Americans. "Hostilities inside Germany will not end with the defeat of the German army," the author wrote. Hundreds of raiding parties, consisting mostly of hardened youth, were being trained in Bad Aussee, about fifty miles from Berchtesgaden, to conduct guerrilla attacks. Called the "Werewolves" and led by SS general Kaltenbrunner, *Collier's* reported, the guerrillas would establish themselves high in the Alps and would be armed with advanced weapons.

American generals feared it could take months, even years, to root the enemy out of a mountain fortress. As Eisenhower noted, "If the German was permitted to establish the Redoubt he might possibly force us to engage in a long-drawn-out guerrilla type of warfare, or a costly siege."

The implications of such delays were ominous. Ongoing conflict would add to casualty lists, but the political fallout worried strategists even more. Who could tell how long the precarious alliance between the Soviets and the Americans would hold? Washington feared that protracted fighting in Europe could distract the Allies from concluding the war in the Pacific.

There was just one problem with the story of the Nazi redoubt: it was almost entirely false. The Germans had, at one point, considered building *some* fortifications in the Alps. But anything other than a few construction projects had been rejected by Hitler, who considered such preparations defeatist.

Goebbels can take some of the credit for completely duping the Americans.

The German propaganda minister had initially, in December 1944, called a secret meeting of German editors and journalists and ordered them never to mention the redoubt in print. Not long after that he reconsidered his strategy. Anything that might divert the Allies in their race to Berlin was worth exploiting. So in January, Goebbels created a special unit in the Propaganda Ministry to produce stories about fortifications in the Alps, impregnable positions, massive supply caches, bombproof caves, underground factories, and elite units of troops. German security forces joined the deception game and began to leak phony blueprints of construction projects and bogus intelligence to American agents eager for any information.

From his perch in Switzerland, Dulles was ideally positioned to discover the truth of the Nazi deception. Even he was confused. "The information we get here locally seems to tend more and more to the theory of a final Nazi withdrawal into the Austrian and Bavarian Alps, with the idea of making a last stand there," Dulles wrote Washington in January 1945. Rather than trying to escape by submarine or plane, he concluded, "Hitler will probably seek a Wagnerian end, and Himmler et al. will presumably be with him." It would take him several more months before he began to grow suspicious, suggesting in March that it was more likely the Americans would find only pockets of fanatical resistance in the Alps. Few military planners in the United States, however, were willing to take that chance.

The redoubt myth gave an importance to Wolff's proposals that went well beyond ending the fighting in northern Italy. Achieving the surrender of the million or so troops so close to the Alps would also help prevent the bloody last stand that haunted the Allies. Whatever his motivation, whatever the risk to the alliance, the Obergruppenführer had to be taken seriously.

1. Allen Dulles's OSS identity card.

2. The mysterious German agent Hans Bernd Gisevius. Deeply engaged in multiple plots to overthrow Hitler, he became Dulles's main contact with the resistance movement.

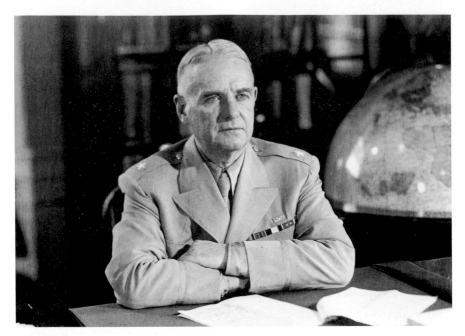

3. Dulles's boss, OSS head William Donovan, was sympathetic to Dulles's desire to support the resistance, but President Roosevelt was not.

4. Allen Dulles and Gero von Schulze-Gaevernitz. Loyal and well connected, Schulze-Gaevernitz was the invaluable number two in the OSS's Bern station.

5. American Mary Bancroft, here at Weissfluhjoch, Switzerland, worked closely with Dulles. The two became romantically involved shortly after Dulles arived in Bern.

6. Here in her youth, Dulles's wife, Clover, found life as the wife of a secret agent difficult. For Allen, the work always came first, and he would not open up to her about his missions.

7. No fancy sports cars or secret gadgets for Mary Bancroft, here in Ascona, Switzerland.

8. Famed psychiatrist Carl Gustav Jung was a trusted confidante to Bancroft. He readily provided Dulles with information about conditions inside Germany, and prepared a psychological profile of Hitler for the OSS.

9. German resistance leader General Ludwig Beck tried for years to depose Hitler, but bad luck and poor planning ultimately doomed him.

10. Wilhelm Canaris (*front left*), the head of the Abwehr (German military intelligence), near Smolensk in 1941. Canaris secretly opposed Hitler and carved out jobs in his organization for men with whom to plot the Führer's downfall.

11. Resistance leader Carl Goerdeler, here in the mid-1930s, placed great hope in striking a deal with the Western Allies. He was caught and executed by the Nazis after the July 20, 1944, attack on Hitler.

12. Was he too good to be true? German informant Fritz Kolbe, here in the late 1930s, provided Dulles with troves of high-value intelligence.

13. Claus von Stauffenberg (*far left*) with Hitler at the Wolf's Lair, July 15, 1944. Five days later he would attempt to kill Hitler and take over the German government.

14. SS General Karl Wolff contacted Dulles to arrange the surrender of German troops in Italy. He had to convince the Americans of his sincerity and his own superiors to go along with the scheme.

15. Allen Dulles and Gero von Schulze-Gaevernitz study a map of Italy. Dulles believed Operation Sunrise would thwart Soviet ambitions to expand Communist influence into the northern part of the country.

16. Mary Bancroft (*right*) and Clover Dulles in Ascona, Switzerland, scene of an Operation Sunrise secret meeting. They became lifelong friends.

17. Allen Dulles and Hans Bernd Gisevius chat in later years. Dulles looked back fondly on his time in Switzerland, a period during which many of his ideas about espionage and geopolitics were formed.

18. Allen Dulles and
his ever-present pipe.

CHAPTER

34

"I Can See How Much You and Allen Care for Each Other"

One afternoon around five o'clock in late December 1944, Dulles's wife, Clover, climbed a gangway onto an American transport ship. Stepping onto the deck of the *Joam Bele*, she was overwhelmed by the vessel's filthy condition, its unpainted fittings, a "Promenade Deck" that wasn't wide enough for a deck chair, and pipes running along its ceiling so full of holes that one could shower standing beneath them. "My heart sank a little," she confessed to her diary.

Clover had arrived late and, checking out her cabin, found the preferable lower bunks already taken. She was now forced to accept an upper berth next to a porthole, a "sort of shelf" suspended from the wall. Basics like heating, important for a winter crossing of the Atlantic, were wanting. Her cabin was like a "cold storage vault" and, lacking blankets, she would have to make do with a homemade duffel bag to keep warm.

Nor could Clover find company to share her miseries. Her three room-mates belonged to "an austere band of Mennonites" who, among other things, hated music. She had to fend off the advances of a Portuguese naval officer whom she suspected may have been using her only to impress one of her attractive cabinmates.

Still, she told herself that her suffering would all be worth it. She was finally going to see her husband. Dulles had been so busy with OSS work during his visit home a few months before that he had spent little time with her. And the family home on the Upper East Side of New York had become a lonely place. Daughter Toddy was at school in Bennington, Vermont; Joan had started at Radcliffe; and the youngest, the promising young Allen, was off to boarding school at Phillips Exeter Academy in New Hampshire.

Through friends in Washington, Clover had learned that the new American embassy in Paris needed a fleet of cars, and the government was looking for drivers to help transport the vehicles from Lisbon, where the ship would dock, to the French capital. Arriving in Europe after the ocean crossing, Clover was assigned a car and began the long drive north, traveling through the wine country of Bordeaux and, at one point, under the protection of the French resistance. She arrived, exhausted, with the gas gauge nearly on "E" in mid-January.

The streets of Paris were a familiar and no doubt exciting sight for Clover. White-shirted waiters scurried about in bistros, fashionable women went about their daily marketing, and American GIs with grinning faces and olive-drab uniforms seemed to be everywhere, most still boys thrilled by their first trip to Europe and eager to try their charms on an attractive mademoiselle.

Pulling up to the American embassy on a corner of the Place de la Concorde, Clover expected to find her husband waiting for her. He had sounded excited about the prospect of her visit. In a November letter, he wrote: "Come whenever you can. It would be grand to have you here. . . . My apartment is all ready for you and I would not have to make any changes if you don't mind a really narrow bed room." Instead, she and the other drivers were ushered to uncomfortable seats in the basement and told to wait. "We sat like mourners on a bench in the lowest depths of the chancery," Clover wrote.

A veteran State Department spouse, Clover had no tolerance for shabby treatment. She insisted on seeing the ambassador immediately. Though he didn't personally materialize, she was quickly treated as a visitor who deserved proper hospitality. An aide informed her that Dulles had made reservations at a local hotel and would visit her there as soon as he could.

For three days, Clover rattled around her hotel room wondering if every echo of approaching footsteps outside her door was her husband. When he did show up, without prior notice, he gave only ten minutes to his wife and delivered crushing news: her mother had died during her trip. Leaving her alone in her misery, he told Clover to come to his considerably nicer hotel. The next day, she smoldered for hours in the backseat of a car bound for Switzerland, her husband engrossed in a conversation with an OSS colleague on how to forge passports.

Dulles paid his wife no more attention in Bern. Life in the Swiss capital could be pleasant. Clover relaxed on the balcony at the Herrengasse and took long walks around town. But she longed to be included in his work, access that Dulles did not grant. Time and again he refused to provide the slightest hint of his activities. One morning not long after her arrival, the two were sipping coffee at a sidewalk café when a man and woman joined them. Exchanging only a few words, Allen and the man got up and walked off. After a few painful moments spent trying to make conversation with the woman who had been left behind, Clover went home. She didn't see her husband for three days, wondering the whole time if he was alive, dead, or kidnapped.

Frustrated and upset, Clover complained, "If I could only make out what Allen's *goal* is, what he wants from life, I might find it easier to understand all the sound and fury."

Part of the reason Clover may have had a hard time reconnecting with her husband was that his mind was engaged in an exciting new project with roots in Italy. For some months, Mussolini's daughter, Edda, had been hiding in Switzerland with a cache of diaries written by her husband, Italy's former foreign minister Galeazzo Ciano. Sprinkled throughout their pages were gossipy tidbits about leading Nazis and embarrassing details about relations between Berlin and Rome. In Ciano's words, they were "a bomb" waiting to explode.

Alerted to their existence by the US Army, Dulles had more than one reason to get his hands on the diaries. They offered the OSS a potentially unique glimpse into relations between the Third Reich and its allies that might be useful in a psychological campaign to discredit and embarrass the Nazis and hurt German morale.

Dulles may also have felt somewhat responsible for Edda's predicament. An American message out of Switzerland, which the Germans had intercepted and decoded, described Ciano as having doubts about the Fascists. Ciano had shortly thereafter been fired from his post as foreign minister. Though Dulles had not sent the message, he somewhat sheepishly had to acknowledge that the Americans may have outed Ciano. "I was never able to discover whether this was coincidence or whether this cable was the cause." Ciano was executed for treason in January 1944.

Persuading Edda to part with the diaries was no easy matter. She was of two minds about what to do with the materials. On the one hand, she knew her husband's last wish was to have them turned over to the Western Allies, and she hated the Nazis, Himmler and Ribbentrop in particular. "I'll be glad if I've done something to give the Bosches what they deserve," Edda said. On the other hand, she needed money, and the diaries were her most valuable asset. She could not afford to simply give them away.

Contacting Edda through intermediaries, Dulles tried to offer himself as the solution to her problems. He began by arranging for Paul Ghali, an American reporter with the *Chicago Daily News*, to buy the diaries and make the contents public. To help with her cash-flow problems, he offered Edda 3,500 Swiss francs as an advance against future royalties.

Negotiations were a pained and difficult affair, Edda often given to changing her mind. Only through perseverance and gumption, and by arranging for friends of Edda's to talk to her on his behalf, was Dulles able to persuade her to meet him face-to-face on January 7 at a small restaurant in a railway station near the village of Monthey. It was surely a fascinating meal. Edda enthralled Dulles, Ghali, and another intermediary with stories about Eva Braun, Hitler's girlfriend. She had met Braun at Hitler's "Eagles Nest" in Berchtesgaden and considered her vulgar. But by the time the group had finished their meal, Dulles was no closer to securing the diaries.

Politely asking the others to leave them alone, Dulles told Edda that the diaries were losing value every day as the war's conclusion drew nearer. She needed to let him make copies of the documents right away, or risk failing not only to fulfill her husband's wishes but also to maximize their value on the open market. Unaccustomed to such blunt talk, Edda listened with a grim face but realized that he was right. "I frankly admit she behaved with a good deal of dignity and far more reasonably than I had expected," Dulles said. "Adversity apparently has done her good." Edda agreed to let the OSS make its copies.

Eager to close the deal before Edda changed her mind, Dulles dispatched a small team to photograph the diaries, led by the handsome and athletic Captain Tracy Barnes. A product of Groton, Yale, and Harvard Law who had parachuted behind enemy lines after D-Day, Barnes possessed what Dulles considered the right qualifications for the job: "looks and charm and the willingness to use them."

The operation started well. The group was able to sneak their equipment past the Swiss guards watching Edda's room in a sanitarium where she was holed up, hiding cameras and other paraphernalia in satchels. The lights they brought, though, consumed tremendous amounts of power. When the Americans switched them on they overloaded the building's wiring and blew a fuse, killing the lights and terrifying many of the institute's psychiatric patients. When the power was restored, they resumed work, mostly under Edda's bed or in her closet so as not to be observed by the Swiss. By the next morning, they had made copies of some 1,200 documents. Yet their haste, and possibly their poor lighting, had come with a cost. Many of their photographs were so blurry and difficult to read that the men had to return days later and perform nearly the entire copying exercise again.

Another man would have kept his mistress far from the suspicious eyes of his wife. But most men lacked Dulles's cavalier approach to the vows of marriage. Bancroft, he concluded, was possibly the only person who could keep Clover occupied and out of his hair. With little apparent trepidation, he introduced the two not long after Clover's arrival.

Bancroft welcomed Clover with a warmth and openness that evidently revealed much about her evolving relationship with Agent 110. The two had by this time likely stopped sleeping with each other. As Dulles grew more absorbed in his work and continued meeting new women, the physical side of their relationship had cooled. Yet Bancroft remained genuinely fond of him. If he needed her to befriend his wife, she was up for the job.

Bancroft quickly discerned that the reserved and sensitive Clover was in some ways very different from her—Bancroft an extrovert, Clover inward looking and shy. There was something "other-worldly" about Dulles's wife, she concluded. Yet as the two spent more time together, Bancroft discovered a finely developed wit, a kindness, and a delightful cheeky side as well. Clover, Bancroft later wrote, was "relentless in her disdain of pretense and pomposity."

For her part, Clover admired the strength Bancroft demonstrated around her husband. She marveled at how Dulles, despite a frightful temper, never seemed to get angry with Bancroft. "I think that's because you are the only person who is not afraid of him," Clover told her. In her memoir, Bancroft wrote that there was something to that, but that the real reason she and Dulles got along was because she had "got his number." Dulles knew there was nothing he could say or do that would damage her deep affection for him.

What began as an awkward friendship of convenience soon blossomed into a genuine fondness for each other, strong enough to withstand Dulles himself. It didn't take Clover long to figure out that her new friend and her husband had once been more than work colleagues. At only their second or third meeting, she told Bancroft: "I want you to know I can see how much you and Allen care for each other—and I approve!" Bancroft made no comment, and the subject was never brought up again.

CHAPTER

35

"I Was Puzzled About What the Soviets Would Do with This Information"

Dulles approached the Swiss border at Annemasse from the French side in mid-March, accompanied by two soldiers in the uniforms of American enlisted men. Both, he fervently hoped, would remember their cover stories.

American major general Lyman L. Lemnitzer and British major general Terence Airey had been dispatched to help Dulles almost as soon as Washington and London heard of his contact with Wolff. Contrary to what Dulles had anticipated, Allied military leaders had jumped at the prospect of coordinating a German surrender in Italy and even gave the talks a hopeful code name: Operation Sunrise. With Dulles taking charge of the arrangements and the introductions, the two generals were to meet Wolff as soon as possible.

The team faced an immediate problem: they could not enter Switzerland without some sort of disguise. Though the Annemasse border crossing was considered one of the easier entry points, the arrival of two such senior officers would raise suspicion among Swiss guards that something curious, maybe illegal, was up. Even if they made it in, a pair of senior American officers would not go unnoticed.

Prying dog tags away from two grumpy sergeants working for the OSS (they had planned a shopping trip in Switzerland and didn't want to give up their IDs), Lemnitzer and Airey began to perfect their new identities.

The first thing the border guards would do would be to ask each man to recite his identification number, a requirement the Swiss often demanded of American soldiers entering the country. Any hesitation and they would likely be blocked from entering Switzerland. The two repeated the numbers until they were able to do so faultlessly.

Dulles suggested they begin learning more about the men they were impersonating. Adopting the life story of a Sergeant Nicholson, General Lemnitzer prepared to describe his home on Long Island and his several wonderful children. Airey, with a "most distinctive British accent," faced a more difficult task, as his ID belonged to Sergeant McNeely, a native of New York City.

Lemnitzer was the first to cross. Border officers, who had seen every trick in the book over the last few years, grilled him about his journey and, as expected, demanded he recite his dog-tag number. Nervously waiting his turn, hoping the Swiss didn't have a good ear for accents, Airey was relieved to face only a couple of questions. The two passed into Switzerland and were taken to Bern and the Herrengasse.

Anyone strolling along the sidewalks near Dulles's villa around March 15 might have noticed the unhappy faces of the two generals staring out at them. There had been a delay, Dulles learned, in the next meeting with Wolff, and rather than let the men enjoy the sights of beautiful yet spy-infested Switzerland, he decided they should remain safely indoors.

During the long hours spent rattling around the Herrengasse villa waiting for the Germans to clarify their next move, the generals had time to discuss the upcoming meeting backward and forward. One complication, they told Dulles, had emerged from an unexpected source. The Western Allies had informed the Russians of the meeting.

Dulles initially found a measure of relief in the news. "It would have been a simple matter for the Germans to let word leak to the Russians that some secret negotiations were going on in Switzerland, that the Western Allies were running out on them," Dulles later wrote. His relief was qualified. "At the same time I was puzzled about what the Soviets would do with this information."

Tensions were high between the Soviet Union and the United States in the spring of 1945. In February, Roosevelt, Stalin, and Churchill had met at the Livadia Palace at the Crimean resort of Yalta for their second summit. The trip, which required FDR to cross the Atlantic by ship, then travel by plane from Malta and finally by car for eighty miles, was exhausting. True to form, Churchill remarked that ten years of research could not have produced a worse place to hold a summit.

Trying hard to get along and present a united front, the three leaders agreed, among other things, to make the unconditional surrender of Germany a priority and hashed out zones of occupation. Dividing the country into four parts, the Americans, the British, and the French would occupy the western two-thirds of Germany. The Soviets were to take the eastern third. Berlin, surrounded by the Soviet zone, was to be divided into four sectors. New borders for Poland were discussed, as well as the formation of a democratic government there.

The harmony would be short-lived. No sooner had Roosevelt arrived back in Washington than Stalin seemed to back away from holding free elections in Poland. At the same time, reports began to surface that American POWs liberated by advancing Soviet troops were being poorly treated. When the United States suggested that American relief planes be allowed to operate in Poland, Stalin refused. "The Soviet attitude was a definite indication that they would not want any other Allies to obtain by personal inspection accurate information of conditions in Poland," Roosevelt's chief of staff, Admiral William Leahy, later wrote.

Further tearing the fabric of US-Soviet relations was a clear and insulting snub of Roosevelt's plans to launch the inaugural United Nations conference in San Francisco. The Soviet embassy in Washington notified the State Department that the Russian foreign minister would not attend. The last thing that the alliance needed was a fresh dispute sparked by the Bern OSS station chief over American-German surrender talks. Yet that's exactly what happened.

Within hours of learning from Washington of Dulles's meeting, Soviet foreign minister Vyacheslav Molotov on March 12 shot back a reply saying that he wasn't opposed to what Dulles had undertaken, but he would make two demands: that Soviet officers be included in the meetings with Dulles, and that the Americans help them enter Switzerland, a country with which Moscow did not have diplomatic relations.

Molotov's requests struck American diplomats as unwarranted and petulant, perhaps none more than W. Averell Harriman, the US ambassador to Moscow. Harriman, the son of the railroad tycoon E. H. Harriman, had earlier in his diplomatic career thought the Soviets would, despite behavior that was "crude and abhorrent to our standards," cooperate with the United States after the war was over.

By the summer of 1944, when Stalin refused to aid the Polish underground during an uprising against the Germans in Warsaw, his opinions had begun to change. Harriman cabled Washington that there was "no justification" for the Soviets to join the Bern discussions. The Soviet army had played virtually no role in Italy and had not earned a seat at the bargaining table. What's more, he worried, the Soviets would make demands on the Germans that would slow the talks and thereby prolong American fighting. Allowing them to join would set a bad precedent, leading to "even more intolerable demands from them in the future."

General John R. Deane, the head of the US military mission in the Moscow embassy, expressed similar reservations. Like Harriman, he believed that the Bern talks were purely an Anglo-American issue and no business of the Soviets. "Approving the Soviet request will be an act of appeasement which will react against us in future negotiations," he wrote.

About the time the two disguised generals waited in Switzerland, the

State Department informed Molotov that the Soviets would not be allowed to join Dulles in Bern. It was too early in what were preparatory talks. The best the Americans could offer was that the Soviets would be allowed to attend full-scale negotiations when they moved to Caserta, the Italian headquarters of Field Marshal Harold Alexander, the commander of Allied forces in the Mediterranean.

With that rebuff began days of tense and bitter recrimination and counterrecrimination between Moscow and Washington. On March 16, Molotov wrote to the Americans that the decision was "utterly unexpected and incomprehensible." Grossly exceeding his power, Molotov insisted that the talks be broken off completely.

For Harriman, the haughty and unreasonable tone was unbearable. Dashing off a message to the secretary of state, Edward Stettinius Jr., he wrote that the Soviets were testing America's backbone. "The arrogant language of Molotov's letter, I believe, brings out in the open a domineering attitude toward the United States which we have before only suspected."

Harriman was right. The Soviet Union would soon escalate the confrontation over Operation Sunrise.

Looking like something out of James Hilton's 1933 novel *Lost Horizon*, the Swiss village of Ascona clings like Shangri-La to an incongruous and wondrous landscape. Protected by snowcapped peaks, it enjoys a climate warm enough for palm trees.

Here Schulze-Gaevernitz had access to an estate that was perfectly suited for Dulles's next meeting with Wolff, a date that had finally been set. Though Kesselring's involvement remained in question, Wolff agreed to meet with the Allies on March 19. Comprising one villa, which sat directly on the shore of Lake Maggiore, and another structure up a steep hillside, the location was protected from prying eyes and large enough to handle all of Dulles's guests.

OSS headquarters in Washington had initially rejected his choice of venue, arguing that the Germans might be able to sneak up on the occupants from the lake and abduct Dulles and the two generals, as well as Wolff and his men. "It has always amazed me how desk personnel thousands of miles away seem to acquire wisdom and special knowledge about local field conditions which they assume goes deeper than that available to the man on the spot," Dulles later wrote.

After pointing out that the Germans probably were not interested in kidnapping anybody at the villa, Dulles finally got official permission to begin laying on provisions and assembled a team of guards posing as tourists. In small groups, so as not to attract too much attention, Dulles, Schulze-Gaevernitz, the two generals, and a handful of others made their way to Ascona. There was another traveler, too. Dulles took Clover with him as cover, to appear that he was taking a holiday break.

March 19 dawned bright, and Dulles prepared to greet his guests on the veranda. The gently lapping lake would provide the sort of relaxed and soothing atmosphere he believed would ease the tension of the moment. Somewhere out on the lake was Clover, dispatched in a boat by her husband to keep her out of the way.

Though Dulles and his team projected an air of confidence and warmth, they had suffered a security scare that briefly threatened to prove Washington right. Seemingly every detail had been accounted for, including the removal of German-language books from the room of General Airey so as not to offend him. (General Airey, as it turned out, enjoyed reading German poetry and asked if there were any such books in the house for him to read.) Yet Dulles and his men had forgotten about a distant cousin of Schulze-Gaevernitz's who lived nearby.

The relative chose that morning to return an ax borrowed some days earlier. Spotting the man walking down the road toward the villa, with what looked like a weapon over his shoulder, Schulze-Gaevernitz ran to warn him before nervous security guards reached for their guns.

At a little before eleven, Wolff's car turned off the main road and approached the villa complex. Settling in on the veranda, he and Dulles and a few others began to get caught up on how the negotiating landscape had changed since their first conversation. Foremost in Dulles's mind was Kesselring. In the days leading up to this meeting, Wolff had sent word that the field marshal had been made commander of the German forces in the west and would no longer have the power to surrender German troops in Italy. Trying to put a brave face on the setback, Wolff announced that the news might actually be good, as it could "open up possibilities on the western front." Kesselring's replacement in Italy, Heinrich von Vietinghoff, might be counted on to surrender. Wolff explained that he had had a "close and friendly" relationship with Vietinghoff in the past. The general was conservative, a stiff and proper aristocrat, but he might be brought around.

Wolff then made an unexpected request.

The German high command had learned that the Allies were planning a major offensive in Italy at the end of March. Could they delay the attack until Wolff could reach Kesselring? "Knowing the conservative nature of [Vietinghoff], and his military training, I doubt whether I would have, at first, much success with him unless I could assure him that both Kesselring and possibly General [Siegfried] Westphal, Kesselring's new Chief of Staff and a friend of Vietinghoff's, would back him up," he told Dulles.

While strategizing ways to persuade Vietinghoff made sense, Wolff's inquiry about the Italian offensive sounded as if he might be waffling over a peaceful surrender. "I must say that I could not help wondering at this point whether Wolff was trying to find out the date of the offensive for reasons other than those we had met to discuss," Dulles wrote. With his antenna twitching, Agent 110 proceeded with considerable caution.

After lunch, Dulles introduced Wolff to the two generals but refused to identify them or provide their actual ranks. Airey was uncomfortable with the prospect of dealing with such a senior Nazi. He tried to avoid shaking hands with Wolff, attempting to keep a large table between himself and the German when they were introduced, but the affable Wolff scuttled those efforts and managed to shake hands with Airey anyway. Airey's opinion did not improve as they chatted. He described Wolff as having "three chins and fat fingers with diamond rings," a man with "a crafty appearance" who looked nervous.

The prospect of a major surrender, not only in Italy but also on the western front, was so enticing that they decided to play out Wolff a little longer. They wouldn't give the Obergruppenführer any details about the coming offensive in Italy, but they agreed to give him some more time to reach Kesselring, five days to a week.

CHAPTER

36

"I May Be Crazy"

Bancroft possessed an uncanny knack for being in the right place at the right time. Walking through the Zurich train station eleven days earlier, she had stumbled on the arrival of Wolff and his team for their first meeting with Dulles on March 8. She might not have immediately recognized the Germans, but she could not miss Schulze-Gaevernitz, who had hurried from his ski vacation to greet the general.

Bancroft ducked into a small shop near the station to take a closer look. She decided to have a bit of fun with Dulles a few days later about the chance encounter. "I may be crazy, but I could swear that one of the men with [Schulze-Gaevernitz] was SS General Karl Wolff," she said. Dulles replied with a disingenuous ho, ho, ho. "You must be crazy. What would an SS general be doing in Zurich? And why were you hanging around the Bahnhof Enge [the area around the train station] instead of doing something useful?"

"Doing something useful" was not a problem that worried Bancroft.

After months of hiding, Gisevius was bursting with fresh ideas for his manuscript and eager to resume work with Bancroft, an enthusiasm likely stoked by word that Donovan had authorized Dulles to advance him $1,000 against his book's future proceeds. Gisevius had a long way to go. He wanted to revise the original narrative, based on the role of the resistance, and focus instead on how the failure of the putsch had been "incipient" from the very beginning.

A somewhat odd visit by Gisevius's mother, who had come to Switzerland to escape Hitler's reprisals for the July 20 attack, provided an intriguing distraction. Tiny and plump, with a bright face and a "rather kittenish manner," Mrs. Gisevius wanted to see how the book project was coming and to tour "Goethe's workroom." Leading her around the apartment, Bancroft showed her where she kept her son's manuscript and the machine for typing the translation.

Mrs. Gisevius launched into an enraptured account of her son's life. Hans, she explained, had been born to rule. He should be the one giving the orders. He had been so focused and serious as a boy that he never had time for children his own age, or for girls. By his early twenties he had acquired a collection of distinguished and respectable friends, the sort who owned large estates and enjoyed playing music. As the two chatted, Bancroft began to reappraise the woman who had seemed so grandmotherly. "I suddenly saw in that merry, kindly face the beady eyes of a crab peering at me from under a rock by the seashore, its claws quivering slightly as if waiting to grab its prey."

Bancroft was fascinated by the encounter. She still considered Gisevius an interesting case study, and she continued to discuss him with Jung. The psychologist had developed some theories about the failed July 20 attack on Hitler. Gisevius had projected his own personality onto Stauffenberg, and it may not have been such a bad thing that the putsch had failed. In Jung's view, Gisevius and Stauffenberg had been battling for one thing all along: power. "They were like a pair of lions fighting over a hunk of raw meat," he told Bancroft.

With the war coming to an end, Jung didn't expect Gisevius to achieve his dream of an important role in a new German government. The product of a solid but modest family, he would probably fall back into a rather unremarkable life. "Of course he still has rather grandiose ideas, and if he goes to the United States, he might attach himself to some current of power there that would permit him to realize at least some of them."

"And if that doesn't happen?" Bancroft asked. "If he doesn't go to the United States and clamp on to some current of power, what then?"

Jung shrugged. "Well, then frankly I don't think he will ever amount to much. He may write a book or two. But that's all. It's too bad in a way. He's really a very nice boy!"

Despite Bancroft's commitment to the translation project, Dulles still had plenty of work for her. He wanted Bancroft to study what role German women might play in the occupation. "After all," he told her, "they are credited with being Hitler's staunchest supporters. How do they feel about him now? Why? What other attitudes are they taking? What factors are influencing them? Why?" The assignment appealed to Bancroft. She had many contacts who could help, and it matched her interest in psychology.

There also was something going on in Liechtenstein, the tiny principality wedged between Switzerland and Austria, which he wanted her to investigate. With American troops approaching from the north as they drove through Bavaria, and the Soviets pushing westward, the small nation found itself in a curious predicament. Like Switzerland, Liechtenstein had declared itself neutral, and it was now a haven for the human flotsam and jetsam from both sides waiting out the political storms caused by the end of the war.

Dulles hoped to learn more about an almost forgotten group of soldiers, the so-called White Russians—Soviets who had turned on their homeland to fight with the German army. Liechtenstein was offering refuge to such men, and Dulles had learned that the Soviet secret police, the NKVD, wanted to get its hands on them. Bancroft was to investigate.

Greeted at the station on a wonderful spring day in Liechtenstein by a member of the royal household who was a good friend, Bancroft stopped by her hotel long enough to drop off her bags before setting off for the border with German-held territory.

The scene she encountered was surreal. On the other side of a small crossing had gathered a "huge mass of refugees." One of the first Bancroft spoke to through the border fence was a tall young woman in a blue silk dress with a mink stole. She wore a velvet hat with a veil and under one arm she carried a Pekingese with a pink bow on its head. Most perplexing was that the well-attired refugee was American. The woman pleaded with Bancroft to help her get across. She needed to phone her "daddy," she explained. Bancroft promised to see what she could do.

When Bancroft later inquired at the US mission in Bern, she learned the stranded American had spent the war in Germany as the girlfriend of an SS officer. With Germany's defeat at hand, she had been trying a series of border crossings to escape the crumbling Reich. The American diplomatic corps in Bern had no interest in investing time to rescue her now. "Let the SS take care of her!" an American official retorted.

As people continued to cross into Liechtenstein, Bancroft spotted her quarry: a cavalry company of White Russians. Easily allowed into the country, yet lacking any place to go, the men made their way to a nearby orchard and dismounted to rest in the spring grass. "I have seldom seen more interesting faces on a group of men," Bancroft later recalled.

Then suddenly a hush lay over the border area as a new group was allowed to pass. Seven boys, emaciated and weak, entered wearing the striped uniforms of concentration-camp inmates. All Poles, they had apparently that morning left the Dachau camp, which American soldiers had just liberated.

According to the rumor that quickly spread among people on the Liechtenstein side, the boys were all that remained of more than 1,200 who had boarded a train earlier in the day, trying to get as far from Germany as possible. Exhausted, the small group slowly walked to the same orchard where the horses of the White Russians were grazing and lay down in the grass near them. Bancroft briefly spoke with one, who showed her his grimy and torn family photographs stored in a sardine can. Eventually an ambulance arrived and took the boys to a hospital in Switzerland.

That evening, Bancroft was invited to a dinner to meet Soviet agents of the NKVD. In contrast to the miseries she had witnessed that afternoon, the Soviet meal, held at a hotel in Vaduz, the tiny capital of Liechtenstein, was happy and even a touch romantic. The Communists had had the dining room decorated with garlands of orange crepe paper, and the food and wine flowed freely. While she bathed in the atmosphere, Bancroft was approached by one of the Soviets, who introduced himself with a click of his heels and a slight bow. The top of his head barely reached her shoulder, a "little creature," yet the difference in height was more than made up for by his skill on the dance floor.

Bancroft found herself swept away in "perfect rhythm" to the "Blue Danube" waltz. She knew it was an absurd scene, an American in the employ of the OSS floating across the dance floor with a Soviet agent. The revelation that her dance partner spoke English—with a Brooklyn accent—only made the episode harder to reconcile.

That night, Bancroft went to bed a bit giddy over the memory of waltzing with her charming NKVD agent. Yet the next morning, she awoke feeling melancholy. Though she had been intimately involved in the war effort, here, at the border, she was for the first time witnessing its horrible contradictions firsthand. Not just a few nations "were in trouble" she wrote, but humanity as a whole.

Bancroft's feeling of gloom would intensify when she later learned what had happened to the White Russians she had admired for their looks, though not their politics. In a deal between the Allies and the Russians, possibly including her dance partner, they had been handed over to the Communists. None was seen again.

Inspired by her exposure to the war's end in Liechtenstein, Bancroft wanted to see more of the unraveling of wartime Germany. In late April, she and Clover, by now good friends, decided to take a self-guided tour of the border between Switzerland and the Third Reich. The two noticed how many of the Swiss shared their curiosity. From nearly every window stood someone staring across the border into Germany, the windows on the other side of the barbed wire containing white flags or Red Cross banners. Rumors swept through both sides. One Swiss soldier told them that Himmler's wife had been spotted on Lake Constance only a few days earlier.

The next day, a fog just lifting over the lake, Bancroft and Clover reached the city of Kreuzlingen, which borders the German town of Konstanz. There they noticed a couple of Swiss officers staring through binoculars at a corpse lying in a yard on the German side near some railroad cars. There had been an unfortunate incident, the officers explained to the two Americans. The previous afternoon, a German man who worked as a customs official had tried to climb the fence separating the two countries, and the Swiss customs officials, who knew and disliked him, shouted to him to turn back. As he rushed back through parked freight cars, a German soldier noticed what was happening and shot him. Now, near the corpse, which hadn't been moved, two indifferent Germans were sunning themselves. No one lifted an eye when a railway official came to investigate the body and emptied the dead man's pockets.

CHAPTER

37

"I Cannot Avoid a Feeling of Bitter Resentment Toward Your Informers"

Roosevelt, confident that the force of his personality could overcome any diplomatic crisis, concluded in late March that he could soothe the growing tension with the Soviets over Operation Sunrise by reaching out to Stalin. On Saturday, March 24, 1945, apparently before leaving on an overnight train for a few days of relaxation at Hyde Park, he wrote the Soviet leader that the Wolff affair was a misunderstanding. The Soviets must not have had all the facts accurately presented to them. Nevertheless, he would not tell Dulles to stand down "because of objection on the part of Mr. Molotov for some reason that is completely beyond my understanding."

It had been a difficult few weeks for FDR. The president had struggled for decades with polio that left him largely unable to walk, and old friends noticed that he was growing weaker. His wife, Eleanor, noted that for the first time her husband wanted her to drive his specially fitted car. Nor did he seem to enjoy the playful way that he could goad his wife into arguments. Where he had once delighted in verbal sparring, he now became upset and unable to calm himself. At the end of four days at Hyde Park, Roosevelt "had failed to erase any of the fatigue from his face." He looked, thought his personal secretary, Grace Tully, drawn and gray. The shadows under his eyes had grown darker.

Hoping to rest and regain his strength, the president set off on March 29 for his favorite retreat at Warm Springs, Georgia. Arriving at his rustic home there, he confronted the reality that his message, far from soothing Stalin's worries, had only inflamed them. Writing to the president on the twenty-ninth, Stalin claimed that the Swiss negotiations would take the pressure off the western front, allowing the Germans to shift their forces east. "This circumstance is irritating to the Soviet command and creates grounds for distrust."

Over the next several days, caustic cables between Warm Springs and Moscow slammed back and forth. On April 3, Stalin asserted that his military colleagues knew with certainty that serious negotiations had taken place, not the preliminary meetings the Americans claimed, and that Kesselring had agreed with the United States and Britain to open the western front to them.

Rapidly advancing American and English troops proved it, Stalin declared, a claim that seemed to be based on the fact that a key bridge over the Rhine River at the town of Remagen was left standing when American soldiers arrived in March. In reality, the Germans had tried to blow up the crossing just before a spearhead of the US Ninth Armored Division reached the river. The explosives they placed on the bridge structure were not powerful enough for the job.

Roosevelt, growing furious about the Soviets' attitude, served up a swift reply. "It would be one of the great tragedies of history if, at the very moment of the victory now within our grasp, such distrust, such lack of faith should prejudice the entire undertaking after the colossal losses of life, material and treasure involved," Roosevelt wrote. "Frankly, I cannot avoid a feeling of bitter resentment toward your informers, whoever they are, for such vile misrepresentations of my actions or those of my trusted subordinates."

How exactly Stalin was learning about the Sunrise talks, however misguided, vexed the Americans. One possibility was that Wolff was behind the leaks, in an effort to stir up trouble between the Allies. Another possibility is that Kim Philby, the British double agent, was leaking information to his Soviet masters.

For a time, it appeared the bickering might endanger the entire relationship. On April 4, General Deane in Moscow wrote to the Joint Chiefs about a tense meeting he had just completed with representatives of the Soviet general staff. The Soviets were cold and offered only a "terse answer" when Soviet-American military cooperation was discussed. They didn't appear willing to cooperate in allowing the Americans to use their airfields for attacks on Japan, he said. The Bern talks were clearly "a festering sore." That same day Harriman met with Molotov, who repeated his accusation that the Allies' rapid advance in the west was the product of some sort of secret deal that had been struck in Bern.

For reasons that aren't clear, Stalin finally called a truce of sorts. Whether concluding that further protest was futile or that he was seriously damaging his relationship with the West, on April 5 he held out an olive branch to Washington. Moscow denounced its neutrality pact with Japan, which had kept the two at peace since 1941 and was not to expire for another year. (The Soviets declared war on Japan in August.)

Two days later, Stalin addressed Dulles's talks directly. Though still claiming that he could not understand why the Germans were fighting so much harder in the east than in the west, he now told Roosevelt that he "never doubted" his honesty. In a letter to Churchill, Stalin said he hadn't wanted to "blacken anyone."

Roosevelt's chief of staff, Admiral Leahy, hoping to put the matter to rest, drafted a letter under Roosevelt's signature that struck a conciliatory note. In the final communication FDR had with Stalin, Leahy wrote that the Bern incident appeared to "have faded into the past without having accomplished any useful purpose." The United States looked forward to a linkup between

Soviet and Western armies and to a "fully coordinated offensive in which nazism would disintegrate."

Leaders in both capitals could breathe easier, having survived a flash point in their relations. What this meant for Operation Sunrise, however, remained an open question.

CHAPTER

38

"This Is the Most Terrible News I've Ever Had"

On April 13, Dulles and Schulze-Gaevernitz stepped out of a car at the glamorous Place Vendôme in central Paris and strode into the lobby of the Ritz. The grand hotel was almost as much of a war prize as the city itself. During their occupation the Nazis had reserved half its elegant rooms for their exclusive use.

The Ritz had suffered few ill effects from the war, but the lighting was dim and maneuvering through the labyrinth of hallways a difficult process. Searching for his room, Dulles was approached by a stranger. "I beg of you, where is 110?" Nobody outside the OSS was supposed to know his code name, and Dulles flinched. He was just forming the words "You're talking to him. I'm 110," when he grasped what was happening. In the gloomy halls, the lost man was simply looking for his room.

Dulles had come to Paris to meet Donovan to deliver an update on the latest twists in Operation Sunrise. It would be a tough day for the OSS boss, and for all Americans. That morning Donovan had been shaving in the bathroom of his suite, the same one used by Hermann Göring during the German occupation, when an OSS staffer rushed in. President Roosevelt had died on April 12 of a major cerebral hemorrhage at Warm Springs. For Donovan it was crushing news. Not only had the nation lost a beloved leader, but Donovan had also been dealt a tremendous professional setback.

The OSS had been fighting for its life almost since the day it was created. Rivals in the FBI and the branches of the military had long angled to fold the OSS into their own operations, and they had never missed a chance to criticize Donovan and his organization. According to some, the OSS operated under the thumb of British intelligence. Tales of failed secret missions and wanton wastefulness of taxpayer money circulated throughout Washington.

The loosely disciplined and disorganized OSS was culturally a world apart from the buttoned-down FBI and the G-2, the intelligence operations of the army. One officer in army intelligence, Colonel B. A. Dixon, summed up the feeling of many an OSS critic when he said: "The OSS is the most fantastic damned organization in all of our armed forces. Its people do incredible things. They seduce German spies; they parachute into Sicily one day and two days later they're dancing on the St. Regis roof. They dynamite aqueducts, urinate in Luftwaffe gas tanks, and play games with I.G. Farben and Krupp, but ninety per cent of this has not a goddamned thing to do with the war."

Donovan hoped to shed this reputation and create a new central intelligence organization with broad powers that would collect information from around the world and conduct secret operations for the government. As did the OSS, the new organization would report directly to the president.

Before leaving for Europe, Donovan had lunched with FDR at the White House in hopes of winning support for his plan. Donovan noted that the president had lost weight and hardly touched his meal, looking as if he was "on his last leg." He never managed to steer the conversation toward the future of the OSS. With the date of his departure for Europe drawing near, he arranged on April 4 for Isadore Lubin, a New Deal economist and one of his biggest supporters in the White House, to send a memo to Warm Springs extolling the virtues of the spy agency he envisioned.

Word of Roosevelt's death crippled Donovan's dreams and left him with scant protection from the OSS's most dangerous enemies. For three hours, Donovan sat on the edge of his bed, his head slumped down as other OSS officers passed through the room. "This is the most terrible news I've ever had," one heard him mutter.

After Donovan had collected himself, Dulles made his presentation on Sunrise. The operation was not going well. There had been brief hope for a quick deal after the Ascona meeting in March. Zimmer had promised Dulles that Wolff would soon return, not with half-formulated plans but with a "complete program," one with "a greater scope than had been initially contemplated."

Instead, support among the Germans for Wolff's peace plan was unraveling. On March 23, Wolff traveled to Kesselring's headquarters in hopes that the field marshal would join in a mass German surrender. Kesselring refused. He could not cut a deal with the Americans while German soldiers were still fighting the Soviets. The matter of Roosevelt's declaration at Casablanca hardened his view. "Confronted with this determination of the Allies to destroy us—proclaimed in the formula 'unconditional surrender'—we had only one reply: to sell our skins as dearly as possible, that is to fight on as long and as stubbornly as we could in hope of wearing the enemy down and so perhaps making him more willing to negotiate," Kesselring wrote.

Vietinghoff, the Wehrmacht commander in Italy, refused to go along with Operation Sunrise, telling Wolff he could not betray other German units "who were still fighting stubbornly north of the Alps." Even if he did surrender, Vietinghoff explained, German troops would likely ignore his order and fight on, leading to chaos. By the first week of April, generals Lemnitzer and Airey had seen enough. No doubt looking forward to getting out of the sergeants' uniforms that had been their cover in Switzerland, the pair flew back to Caserta.

Such tensions, and the setbacks Sunrise had suffered, did not dent

Donovan's enthusiasm for Dulles's talks. Every possibility of ending the fighting in Italy, and saving thousands of American lives, had to be pursued. That Sunrise might also show the OSS's many critics in Washington that the agency was capable of great things no doubt also figured in his thinking. Donovan, in Dulles's words, "wanted us to try everything" to make Operation Sunrise a success.

The evening of April 16, 1945, Wolff climbed into a staff car sent to collect him at an airfield outside Berlin and motored to the Hotel Adlon, Germany's finest. Exhausted from a perilous and lengthy flight from Italy conducted largely at treetop level, Wolff was given a key for a room on the fourth floor and made his way upstairs, where he collapsed onto the bed. He was so exhausted that he chose to sleep through several air raids in his room, rather than retreat to the comparative safety of the basement bomb shelter.

Berlin was the last place he wanted to be. Four days previously, Wolff had received a message from Himmler to return to the capital immediately. Though he tried to beg off, Wolff knew it was an order he could not ignore. Himmler had essentially taken his family hostage to ensure his obedience.

Himmler and Wolff had a complicated relationship, one going back many years. Wolff had once served as Himmler's chief of staff, and the Reichsführer had developed such fond feelings for him that he referred to Wolff by the familiar nickname of "Woelffchen." But there had been times of tension as well. Years before, Himmler had refused to sanction Wolff's divorce so that he could marry his beautiful blond mistress, demanding that he adhere to strict Nazi morality codes. Wolff had gone over his head and persuaded Hitler to grant him permission, an act of disloyalty that had enraged Himmler. Relations between the two had remained on edge ever since. He was furious to hear from Switzerland that his old friend was consorting with Americans.

Waking only slightly refreshed, Wolff passed through the hotel's luxurious lobby with its vaulted ceiling and grand stairway and out to the rubble-strewn street. A car was waiting to take him to Himmler.

Himmler had been suffering tremendously as the war wound down. He appeared, to one visitor, "spent and weary," and had not slept in nights. He could not long remain in one place, looking for an outlet for pent-up anxiety and tattered nerves. His relations with Hitler had also deteriorated, and he had grown suspicious of those around him. What, he now demanded to know, was Wolff doing talking to Dulles?

Wolff had had plenty of time to prepare for the interrogation and was ready to present a compelling story. He admitted to Himmler that he had seen Dulles. His goal was not to surrender himself, or his men, but to delay the Allied offensive in Italy. He could truthfully say he had even asked when the offensive would begin.

Himmler, however, had collected evidence from his agents in Switzerland suggesting that Wolff was being less than honest. If Wolff wouldn't tell him the truth, perhaps his security chief, Kaltenbrunner, could get to the bottom of Wolff's activities. Arriving later in the day, the SS general and Himmler presented sheaves of paper prepared by German agents, some of which painted a fairly accurate picture of what Wolff was up to.

No matter what was written in the reports, Wolff maintained that he was secretly playing the Americans for fools. Around and around the questioning went until finally, at midnight, Wolff decided to take a gamble. He wanted to go back to Berlin, he said, to see Hitler. And he wanted Himmler and Kaltenbrunner to come with him.

Himmler, not surprisingly, found a reason to decline a meeting with the man he was coming to fear. But Kaltenbrunner decided to call Wolff's bluff. He would go. Without returning to his hotel, Wolff took a chauffeur-driven car back into the city and headed straight to the Führer.

Located beneath the garden in the Reich Chancellery in the heart of Berlin, the Führerbunker had originally been constructed as an air-raid shelter for Hitler and his inner circle. As the bombing had become more severe, the subterranean structure had been expanded into a labyrinth of tiny rooms and hallways that served as both Hitler's home and the nerve center of the German war effort. Some of its rooms located thirty feet underground, the complex was self-contained, a diesel motor providing heating, lighting, and water. Living conditions were terrible. The air was foul, and the space was crowded and sparsely appointed, considering it served a head of state. Bare wires provided dim lighting, and the walls were largely unadorned save for a few paintings that had been brought in to give it the appearance of a home.

Shortly before 4:00 a.m., Wolff and Kaltenbrunner were led down two flights of stairs to Hitler's private quarters, a red carpet on the floor the only reminder of his former glory. Arriving in a tiny anteroom, they were told to wait until Hitler was ready for them. Grim-faced and haggard staff and guards shuffled to and fro in the halls, adding to a sense of pending doom.

Hitler burst from his quarters and for a moment seemed surprised to see Wolff. "Ah, you're here, Wolff," he said. "Good! Please wait until the briefing is over."

The Führer, Wolff noticed, was a shadow of the man he had long known. Normally carrying himself with stiff military carriage, he was now "bent, shaky and flabby, his features sunken. He dragged his body around heavily and slowly." His right hand trembled constantly, and he seemed to have trouble standing, able to walk only a few steps before he would appear to lose his balance and have to be made to sit down. His mouth dripped with saliva that he didn't seem to notice.

Ushered into the conference room, Wolff steadied himself for what was to come. Hitler stepped in close and fixed his eyes on his visitor. "Kaltenbrunner and Himmler have informed me of your negotiations in Switzerland with Mr. Dulles.

"What made you disregard my authority so flagrantly? In your duties as commander of the SS in Italy you are familiar with only a small section of the overall military and political situation. I do not have the time nor the opportunity to tell every individual commander what is happening on the other battle fronts or even on the political level. Is it clear to you just what an enormous responsibility you have thus taken on your shoulders?"

"Yes, my Führer."

"What made you do this?"

Speaking rapidly so that he could not be interrupted and locking his eyes with Hitler's, Wolff reminded him of an earlier meeting on February 6 that had included Foreign Minister Ribbentrop. Wolff had indicated that he was planning to reach out to the Allies, and Hitler had not then protested. Wolff went on to describe his first meeting with Dulles on March 8, explaining that it had happened too fast for him to receive instructions from Berlin.

"Now I am happy to report to you, my Führer, that I have succeeded in opening doors, through Mr. Dulles, to the President, Prime Minister Churchill and Field-Marshal Alexander. I request instructions for the future."

Hitler stared at Wolff for a long moment before replying. "Good. I accept your presentation. You're fantastically lucky." But before he could reach a final judgment, Hitler went on, he would have to get some rest. With that, he asked Wolff to return the next afternoon at five o'clock.

Though tempted to flee the capital, Wolff reported to the Führerbunker the next day as ordered, to find the atmosphere even more desperate. There would be no miracle rescue. The Russians would seal Berlin off in a matter of days. Hitler, most knew, would likely remain in the bunker to the end. As if to drive home the verdict, an Allied bombing mission appeared over the capital while Wolff waited. Even deep underground, the explosions were so powerful that the earth shook beneath Wolff's feet.

The strange collection of men, women, and children who sheltered in the bunker complex knew that such attacks came in waves. When the bombing subsided there was usually time to relax for a moment or two, even to emerge from the bunker for a breath of fresh air. Hitler enjoyed these brief strolls aboveground, and he invited Wolff to join him in what was left of the chancellery garden.

Bundled in a warm coat, Hitler led Kaltenbrunner, Wolff, and another officer upstairs and outside. The scent of scorched timber filled the air and the grounds were torn up, but they still found a usable path. Hitler, to Wolff's surprise, had not given up, arguing that his defenses could hold out for six, maybe eight weeks. During that time, he was sure the alliance between the Americans and the Soviets would collapse. He would then decide which side to join. Wolff, Hitler ordered, must therefore hold out in Italy as long as possible.

Wolff replied, "My Führer, isn't it clear which side you would take in such a conflict?"

Hitler stared back. "I will decide in favor of the side which offers me the most. Or the side which establishes contact with me first."

Hitler then seemed to drift off into his thoughts, calmly explaining that it had always been his ambition to withdraw from leadership of Germany and watch the development of the German people from a distance. "I shall soon turn my power over to the most competent of my associates."

Feeling emboldened, Wolff asked Hitler about heavy German losses. "That is of no concern at all. I have just detailed to you the further course of events, and I will await them calmly. Don't lose your nerve, man. I need my nerves for other things; I cannot allow myself to be softened by these reports. For the man who is to make the final decision must not let himself be moved by the misery and horror that the war brings to every individual on the front and in the homeland. So do what I say. Fly back, and give my regards to Vietinghoff."

As they strolled, Hitler continued: "Go back to Italy; maintain your contacts with the Americans, but see that you get better terms. Stall a bit, because to capitulate unconditionally on the basis of such vague promises would be preposterous. Before we come to an agreement with the Americans, we've got to get much better conditions."

On April 20, Wolff arrived at his headquarters in Italy exhausted mentally and physically. With Parilli and Dollmann, he broke out a bottle of champagne and drank to the fact "that his head was still attached to his shoulders."

CHAPTER
39

"In View of Complications Which Have Arisen with Russians"

Dulles returned to the Herrengasse from his meeting with Donovan in Paris with a renewed sense of mission. He had a better grasp of the political forces arrayed against him and fired off a cable to General Lemnitzer explaining his theories about why the Soviets had been so opposed to Operation Sunrise. They were more concerned about grabbing real estate than the prospect of the Americans cutting a deal behind their backs. Moscow, he wrote, wanted to "get [its] hands on Trieste and North Italy" before the Allies did. The Soviets had placed a higher priority on taking Trieste than even Berlin itself.

Nestled in the extreme northeast corner of Italy, Trieste and its environs were a knotty mixture of history and ethnic loyalties. Ruled by Italy only since the end of World War I, and over the objections of Yugoslavia, the region was composed of Italians along the western coastal areas and mostly ethnic Slovenians and Croatians to the east.

So complicated was the region that no serious discussion about its future had been held among the Soviets, the Yugoslavs, and the Western powers. Even the British and the Americans, normally close allies, could not agree between themselves about their aims there, other than the short-term objective that the area serve as an important military supply and communications link to Austria.

That all meant that gaining military control of the region around Trieste was of vital importance. If Sunrise was a success, Dulles said, it likely would mean that Allied forces would be the first to occupy the city. If Sunrise failed and the fighting continued, the Germans would likely eventually fall back west of Venice and toward the foothills of the Alps. That would allow either Soviet troops, or Yugoslav and Italian pro-Communist partisans, to occupy the area. Ultimately, whoever arrived first would likely dictate the "zones of postwar influence, or even occupation."

By about the time Dulles made his report, the dispute over the future of the region was coming to a head. On April 20, Tito's forces reached the 1939 Italy-Yugoslavia border and began moving toward Trieste. Three days later, the Anglo-American forces crossed the Po River, and the Fifteenth Army Group under the command of General Mark Clark began a drive toward the city. No less a figure than Churchill was concerned, proclaiming that it was important to reach Trieste first. "The actual status can be determined at leisure . . . possession is nine points of the law."

It was thus with particular frustration that Dulles received a cable from Washington dated April 20, 1945, a memo that like so many others from Washington was marked "Urgent—Top Secret." The Combined Joint Chiefs of Staff, which was composed of British and American military leaders, ordered Agent 110 to terminate contact with German emissaries on Operation Sunrise. It had become clear to them that the German commander in chief in Italy did not intend to surrender his forces on acceptable terms. Continuing such a hopeless mission was no longer worth the cost, "especially in view of complications which have arisen with Russians." Though the tension surrounding Sunrise had subsided, President Harry Truman had concluded that it was no longer worth the risk of antagonizing the Soviets anew.

The complexities and risks of the Sunrise talks, even Dulles acknowledged, must have given the new president reason for pause, and he took the news with a healthy measure of resignation. "It was true that the negotiations had dragged on interminably," Dulles admitted. "Very possibly our Joint Chiefs felt that there was little to be gained then by pressing the Italian surrender issue with the Soviets."

Monday morning, April 23, 1945, the Swiss intelligence officer Max Waibel, still blissfully unaware of Truman's decision, phoned Dulles. The Germans were suddenly ready to get serious about the Sunrise talks. Though Wolff had returned from Berlin badly shaken and unsure how to proceed, the advance of American troops up the Italian peninsula had convinced him, Vietinghoff, and others to end the fighting.

Three officers, Waibel excitedly told Dulles, had entered Switzerland from Italy—Major Eugen Wenner, Lieutenant Colonel Victor von Schweinitz, and Wolff. Schweinitz, he added, had full powers to sign a peace accord on behalf of the German army in Italy. Wolff and Schweinitz were now ready to fly to Allied headquarters at Caserta, Italy, to arrange the final details. The three now wanted to see Dulles in Lucerne.

Whatever happiness Dulles felt at the news was overshadowed by his awkward political position. "To say that I was in a predicament would put it mildly," Dulles later wrote. "Treating with the Germans now would be a clear violation of instructions."

Waibel could hardly believe his ears as Dulles explained the problem. "Here are German delegates to sign an unconditional surrender and the Allies just don't want to see them! It looks as if you want to end the war by killing people," Waibel complained to Dulles. Dulles agreed. The Combined Joint Chiefs would never have ordered him to break off contact with Wolff had they known about the new attitude of the Germans. He drafted a cable to Field Marshal Alexander in Italy, requesting that he be allowed to resume "contact" with Wolff.

While Dulles waited for a reply, the German delegation set up camp at Waibel's house, a steeply roofed three-story abode with a patio that overlooked a garden. Hoping to hear something in a matter of hours, the men grew more anxious and worried as the delay lasted first overnight and then into a new day. Several times they sent notes to Waibel asking for updates.

Wolff endured the vigil with increasing irritation. With chaos erupting behind German lines, he was desperately needed back in Italy to organize the German defenses. Not only did he have a duty to his men, but his absence would soon become so glaring that Berlin was bound to find out where he was. Having heard nothing from the Allies, on the afternoon of April 25, he sent word to Dulles that if the Combined Chiefs acceded to restarting talks, they could deal with Schweinitz and Wenner, who were going to remain behind. He was returning to his post.

Wolff's car made it only about six miles past the Swiss border before he realized how quickly things had deteriorated for the German army. The roads were teeming with partisans hunting down anyone associated with the years of fascism. Few targets would have been as juicy as the head of the SS in their part of the country, and Wolff could not expect to survive long in their hands. Desperate to link up with other Germans and find refuge, he and his men remembered that the SS border police were billeted not far away in a sumptuous estate at Cernobbio, near the western shore of Lake Como.

Known locally as Villa Locatelli, the SS building belonged to a maker of Italian cheese before the war and suited Wolff's taste for fine living and refinement, as well as his more pressing need for safety. Dreading the sight of a checkpoint or groups of partisans, Wolff directed his driver to get to Cernobbio as quickly as possible. Incredibly, he made it to safety that night, though barely ahead of partisans who surrounded the building. Escape was impossible.

On the morning of April 26, Schulze-Gaevernitz met Dulles in his office in Bern and described Wolff's misadventures. How Schulze-Gaevernitz had learned what had happened to the SS general spoke to the shortcomings of the Italian resistance. Though partisans had surrounded Wolff's estate, they either had been unable to find the telephone lines or had forgotten about them, because Wolff's men had been on the phone several times over the night, first trying to arrange a rescue party and then, when they learned that other German forces in the area were in as much trouble as they were, reaching the Swiss, who in turn had gotten word to Schulze-Gaevernitz.

Schulze-Gaevernitz now chose his words carefully. Dulles's loyal number two knew of the orders from the Combined Joint Chiefs of Staff and was determined not to put his boss in an awkward position. He announced that he would like to "go on a little trip for a few days." Dulles quickly understood the game, formally reminding his colleague that they were to break off contact with Wolff, but just as quickly adding that there was no ban on eliciting information about the German. "I realized, of course, what he was going to do, and that he intended to do it on his own responsibility," Dulles later confessed.

CHAPTER

40

An Overloaded Mercedes-Benz

The final months of the war had been miserable for Kolbe. Immensely proud of the work he was doing, he grew increasingly frustrated that the US military wasn't making use of the intelligence he had provided them. Factories that produced war-related goods had not been bombed, and his work didn't seem to be appreciated. What was the point of risking his life to collect so much information, he wondered, if nobody was acting on it?

On the return from his last visit to Bern in February, he had been forced to ride home in a drafty boxcar, using his backpack for a pillow. In Berlin, his mother had lost her apartment to bombing raids. His sanctuary—the Charité Hospital, where he had performed so much work for Dulles—had also been hit and badly damaged. Adding to his misery was that he had been drafted into a militia to defend the Foreign Ministry, a job that looked like a suicide mission.

Kolbe was nothing if not an opportunist and, in a bizarre assignment from Karl Ritter, he saw his chance to escape. Kolbe's boss needed someone to drive his car, his mistress, her two-year-old child, and a small mountain of personal belongings to the comparative safety of Bavaria. Though Kolbe had to swear he would return to Berlin, he knew nobody could stop him from continuing on to Switzerland.

The car that Ritter provided was poorly suited for the job, a two-door convertible Mercedes built for cruising summer country lanes. Packing the car seemed to require an engineering degree. Every nook and cranny of the backseat was filled with belongings, and the baby's stroller was lashed to the roof. The passengers—Ritter's mistress, the baby, and in a last-minute addition, the wife of Professor Sauerbruch—wedged themselves into the front seats. The four were so tightly crammed that Kolbe would have to ask them to adjust their legs every time he shifted gears. Staying up half the night copying materials for Dulles, Kolbe said good-bye to his fiancée and prepared for his journey south. Ahead lay 350 miles of discomfort and danger.

Problems quickly surfaced. Hardly had the car gotten outside the city limits of Berlin than it broke down. For nearly the entire journey, they would have to be pulled by an SS tow truck, a charcoal-burning beast that could muster less than twenty miles an hour and had to frequently stop to clean its fouled pipes.

Traveling early in the morning and late in the day to avoid Allied aircraft, Kolbe and his passengers passed countless refugees and burned-out cars along the roadside. Fields were filled with dead animals, and trees were covered with aluminum strips dropped by Allied airplanes to jam German radar.

For almost four days, the Mercedes and the soot-belching tow truck rolled south until finally the group spotted the sign welcoming them to Kempten, their destination. His joints surely aching, Kolbe was able to rid himself of Ritter's ersatz family.

Over the next several days, Kolbe and Mrs. Sauerbruch moved deeper into southern Germany, sheltering for a time at a Benedictine monastery in

Ottobeuren, where, for the first time in some while, they ate as much as they wished. For the last leg of his trip, Kolbe traveled alone, on a bicycle loaned him by an Iranian student who had been stranded in Germany since the war started. On April 3, 1945, he arrived in Bern, and the following night, still recovering from his ordeal, he met with Dulles.

CHAPTER

41

"I Will Never Forget What You Have Done for Me"

A little after 10:00 p.m. on April 26, three cars passed through the Swiss border into Italy: Schulze-Gaevernitz's hastily assembled mission to rescue General Wolff. In the lead car, adorned with white flags, were two SS officers who had once worked at the border and could hopefully deal with the German soldiers the convoy might encounter. Following in the second car were Don James of the OSS and three Swiss known to the partisans in the border area for having helped exchange sick, wounded, and captured fighters in recent months. That car's headlights would illuminate the white flags of the lead vehicle. The third car carried partisans who happened to be at the border and had agreed to join the group. Schulze-Gaevernitz, providing himself a fig leaf of deniability about the mission, remained in Switzerland. The team was to be led by James, who knew nothing about Dulles's orders forbidding contact with Wolff.

The OSS agent's first move was to avoid heading directly for Wolff, as that was probably too dangerous. James decided he needed a higher authority to check off on his mission and ordered the small convoy to Como, where partisan leaders had set up a headquarters of sorts. Hoping to obtain an explanatory note they could show at possible roadblocks, they would then set off for Cernobbio.

The rescue mission quickly learned how volatile northern Italy had become. The three cars had barely made any progress into the country when they met trouble. Partisans watching motorways for Germans opened fire. Rather than trying to outrun the ambush, James ordered the convoy to stop. He was pretty sure who was shooting at him and decided it was safest to announce himself. Alighting from his car, James stepped in front of the headlights so that all might see his face. The Italian leading the shooting party turned out to be a friend. Running to James, he threw his arms around the American in a joyful greeting. One crisis averted, the rescue team raced through the night to Como.

Again James's planning paid dividends. Arriving in the city, one of the many wonderful enclaves perched on the shore of the Italian lakes, the group made contact with partisan leaders. As he had hoped, James persuaded them to help, and armed with papers of introduction, the convoy motored out of town and around the far side of Lake Como. The papers they had obtained, though, were of value only if anybody read them, and the partisans along their route were not interested. The convoy was fired on, and at one point it was the target of a poorly thrown hand grenade. All failed to inflict any damage, and the group reached Villa Locatelli in good condition.

Wolff, in full-dress SS uniform, greeted his saviors with delirious gratitude and offered some of the most prized gifts to be had in wartime Italy: Scotch and Lucky Strike cigarettes, captured by Rommel's men in North Africa. James tactfully suggested that it might be safer for Wolff to travel in less conspicuous attire. Once he had been persuaded to change into a business suit, Wolff was hurried outside and instructed to take a place in the backseat of the middle car of the convoy.

In a small, dimly lit restaurant near the Chiasso train station that looked like "a Mexican tavern during the days of the gold rush," the Swiss intelligence officer Waibel and Schulze-Gaevernitz waited. The pair had spent the evening doing their best to pass the time watching a steady stream of dubious-looking characters. Some were agents of various intelligence services, others partisans, still others black marketers looking to deal currency. Perhaps most unsavory of all was a collection of reporters from Swiss and foreign newspapers.

When they couldn't stand the tedium or the proximity of the reporters any longer, the two went to the border-control post less than a mile away to see if they could find out anything of the rescue mission.

Finally, after ninety minutes, James's team arrived. It had been a difficult ride. Partisan checkpoints had halted the convoy's progress time after time as it motored back to Switzerland, but again the OSS man's plans worked to perfection, and each car had successfully navigated through without anyone thinking to take a peek into the backseat where Wolff hid.

Schulze-Gaevernitz, still concerned about maintaining a modicum of deniability about the operation, attempted to remain out of view from the rescue team in a car parked at a corner of the customs house. Apparently he didn't hide well enough, because it wasn't long before Wolff spotted him and bolted to the car. With a hearty handshake, he exclaimed, "I will never forget what you have done for me." After a night in a local hotel, Wolff headed to the new German headquarters in Italy.

Tucked in a broad valley surrounded by snowcapped mountains in northern Italy, the city of Bolzano was nearly as Germanic as Italian. Along its narrow cobblestoned streets, several languages including German were spoken. In its pretty squares stood statues of Teutonic heroes. The German army headquarters had been tunneled into a nearby mountain.

It was to this seemingly welcoming destination that Wolff raced in hopes of winning support for the surrender of German forces in Italy. The trip started auspiciously. The morning of April 27, Dulles received a triple-priority message from the Combined Joint Chiefs instructing that the

Sunrise talks were to be resumed. Wasting no time, Agent 110 arranged for a radio expert, Vaclav Hradecky, a Czech who had escaped from the Dachau concentration camp and now worked with the OSS, to travel disguised as an SS officer to Wolff's headquarters. There he set up a transmitter to pass messages, which hopefully would include one from Wolff telling the Allies that the Germans were ready to raise the white flag.

There were no such happy reports from the German headquarters. The surrender team was running into problems. Though old friends were there, Wolff found that some of the German officers he met wanted nothing to do with Sunrise. One quickly phoned Kesselring and Kaltenbrunner, telling them what he had learned of Wolff's activities. Kesselring was incensed. He refused to consider negotiating, and German officers who Berlin feared might agree with Wolff were quickly relieved.

Things were only marginally better for Schweinitz and Wenner, who had traveled to Italy to sign the surrender. The twenty-page capitulation document the Allies had prepared, titled "Instrument of Local Surrender of German Forces in Italy," left key questions vague and undefined. What was to become of the German forces that surrendered? Would they be declared prisoners of war and accorded protection? Would they remain in Italy, as a group, or be broken up and sent to camps in the United States, England, and, of special concern, to the Soviet Union? Relatively low ranking, neither officer felt comfortable putting his name to a document until such issues were clarified.

Only after considerable arm-twisting by Schulze-Gaevernitz and the Allied negotiators did the pair through clenched teeth sign the document on the afternoon of April 29, agreeing that German forces in Italy would surrender at noon, GMT, on May 2. While the newsreel photographers captured the signing in an elaborately staged ceremony, the two Germans could have been forgiven for wondering if anything about the document they were now signing would come to pass.

With the help of Dulles, the two immediately departed for Bolzano in what would be a journey of almost comic misadventures. The trials began when it was discovered that the OSS had failed to make arrangements to get them back into Switzerland, to pass safely through to Bolzano. By the time their papers were sorted out, they had missed the last train out of Geneva and were stuck, with the surrender document in their briefcases, waiting in a chilly outdoor restaurant while a frantic effort was made to track down the OSS man in Geneva who had a car but was out for the evening.

When the two, along with Schulze-Gaevernitz, arrived in Bern late that night, they discovered that another plan was being cooked up to get the surrender document to Wolff. One of Dulles's men, Tracy Barnes, had volunteered to be flown in a private plane as close to Bolzano as was safe and to bail out. He planned to somehow deliver the document by hand, a fast but potentially deadly exercise. To Dulles's relief, the weather was too bad for flying, and the mission was scrubbed. The two Germans, fortified by coffee and sandwiches, would have to continue on by car.

The next morning, they found they could not leave Switzerland, once again lacking the correct travel documents. With the clock ticking toward the ceasefire deadline, Dulles phoned Switzerland's acting foreign minister and explained the history of Sunrise and what it meant for Switzerland. The man agreed, and soon the Germans were allowed to pass. Finally, on the morning of April 30, Schweinitz and Wenner entered northern Italy and raced along icy mountain roads to German headquarters. There they discovered that their adventures were not yet over. A new turn of events would change the entire landscape of the peace mission they had undertaken.

That same day, shortly after lunch, with his secretaries deep in his bunker, a stooped and frail Hitler asked that members of his inner circle be assembled. Wearing his uniform jacket and black trousers, he wanted to say good-bye. Hitler had finally recognized that all was lost. The Soviet army was now at the doorstep of his bunker. And, reacting with a fit of rage, Hitler had learned on April 28 that the Reuters news agency was reporting that Himmler was seeking contact with the West in order to offer Germany's unconditional surrender.

Accompanied by Eva Braun, whom he had married the day before, Hitler moved down the line of his most trusted confidants: Martin Bormann; Goebbels and his wife, Magda; several generals; his secretaries Traudl Junge and Gerda Christian; and others.

Holding out his hand to each, he muttered a few words.

His farewells complete, and accompanied by Braun, Hitler disappeared into his study. Throughout the bunker, all was deathly quiet, only the drone of the diesel ventilator breaking the silence. Upstairs, Traudl Junge chatted softly with the six Goebbels children as they played after their lunch, unaware that their mother and father would soon poison them before committing their own suicides.

Together, Hitler and Braun seated themselves on a sofa positioned near a portrait of Frederick the Great. Shortly before 3:30, Braun, her legs pulled up, opened her mouth and inserted a brass-cased capsule containing prussic acid, the same method of suicide that Hitler had tested on his beloved Alsatian, Blondi, the previous afternoon, killing the dog instantly. Braun slumped over on the armrest of the couch, dead.

Hitler lifted a Walther pistol. In front of him was a photograph of his mother as a young woman. He fit the barrel of the weapon in his mouth and pulled the trigger.

In most any other country, in most any other war, word that the nation's commander in chief had committed suicide would probably have been enough for his senior generals to surrender to an enemy that was about to defeat them anyway. But not Kesselring and the others like him.

Shortly after midnight on May 2, with only hours to go before the surrender was to take effect, orders arrived from the Luftwaffe High Command and Kesselring to arrest a number of officers trying to arrange the Italian surrender. Around Bolzano, everything descended into chaos. Wolff ordered seven police tanks under his command be drawn up to protect his headquarters. He then asked the radio operator Dulles had sent with him to dispatch a distress call to General Alexander in Italy. Allied paratroopers must be immediately sent to the German headquarters to protect him and others working on Sunrise. "Thus, around two in the morning, preparations were made for a small war among the Germans themselves over the issue of the surrender," Dulles wrote.

The sun shone wonderfully in Bern on May 2. It was a market day, and farmers' carts rumbled noisily over the cobblestone streets. At the Herrengasse, Dulles and Schulze-Gaevernitz huddled around a radio. Though they were the prime architects of a possible deal, they could not be included in radio traffic with headquarters at Caserta, Italy, and had to rely on the same commercial news broadcasts as anybody else. Hours of tense waiting passed, Dulles staring outside at the red geraniums in the window boxes.

Shortly after 5:00 p.m., a Swiss radio station relayed a news flash. There was little detail, just the simple announcement that the Germans in Italy had surrendered. The duo quickly reset the dial to the BBC broadcast from London. Churchill, they learned, had announced the surrender to the House of Commons.

Dulles didn't know the details yet, but the fight over Sunrise had gone down to the wire, culminating in a bitter telephone exchange between Wolff and Kesselring. Shouting at each other until they were exhausted, the two went over familiar arguments, Wolff attempting to appeal to Kesselring's known distaste for the Soviets. "A cease-fire now will give the Anglo-Americans the possibility of stopping the advance of the Russians into the West, of countering the threat of the Tito forces to take Trieste, and of a Communist uprising which will seek to establish a Soviet republic in Northern Italy." Only with the sun about to rise on the morning of May 2 had Kesselring given in.

Dulles could hardly contain his excitement. It had taken longer than expected, and it had lost much of its impact, but the peace deal he had set out to broker months before was finally done. "With a tremendous sigh of relief and joy we stood up and all but danced around the room," Dulles later wrote. Bottles of champagne were soon found and the entire Bern staff rounded up for a triumphant toast.

CHAPTER

42

"Countless Thousands of Parents Would Bless You"

At Eisenhower's headquarters in Reims, France, Dulles suffered an attack of gout that ensured he would not be kicking up his heels. Several days after the Sunrise deal, he hobbled on crutches throughout the building, known somewhat romantically to Americans as the little red schoolhouse.

Despite his affliction, his mood was ebullient. The months of talks, slow and tortured as they had been, had helped ensure Wolff's cooperation. Contrary to Allied fears, the Germans had not set torch to Italian artworks and other treasures, and had treated prisoners from the Italian underground more humanely than they might otherwise have. Telegrams were arriving from General Lemnitzer and Brigadier General John Magruder at the OSS, congratulating Dulles. "Countless thousands of parents would bless you were they privileged to know what you have done," Magruder wrote on May 3.

The race for Trieste had ended in a dead heat that prevented the

Communists from gaining control. On the morning of May 1, advance troops belonging to Tito's Fourth Army entered the city but had been unable to force the Germans to surrender. Fearing brutal treatment from Tito's men, most of the Germans there waited to give themselves up to the New Zealand troops of Bernard Freyberg. The two forces jointly held portions of Trieste and the surrounding area, uneasily waiting for directions.

Dulles had traveled to Reims to witness a historic event. In the early hours of the morning of May 7, three German officers led by Colonel General Alfred Gustav Jodl arrived "erect and expressionless," according to the *Stars and Stripes* correspondent, to meet with representatives of the Allied powers and sign Germany's complete, global surrender. In a room lined floor-to-ceiling with maps of Europe, journalists scribbled in their notebooks, and photographers and newsreel operators jostled for a view. The transaction lasted a quarter of an hour from beginning to end. All hostilities, the surrender document said, were to cease at 23:01 Central European Time, May 8, 1945. The Soviet Union demanded a second surrender ceremony the next day, on its own turf in Berlin.

Now that the war in Europe was over, Dulles cast an eye toward his own future. Although the OSS seemed precarious, he hungered after a job as the head of its European operation in London, the premier overseas post in the OSS. Though he had been passed over once before, Agent 110 hoped that things had changed. J. Russell Forgan, the OSS commander there who had resigned to return to civilian life as a New York financier, supported his candidacy.

Dulles had options outside government. His brother Foster, who was then working in San Francisco as an adviser to the conference establishing the United Nations, tempted him with a lucrative opportunity to come back to Sullivan & Cromwell. "We'll clean up together. An awful lot of things are opening up. We'll clean up."

Going back to work with his brother was not without complications. He would again have to play the junior member in the relationship. Bancroft strenuously opposed any job that tied Allen too closely to Foster, after learning that when their father lay dying, he had named Foster the new head of the family. "His relationship to Foster was the one sore point between us—the one subject that, after one knockdown, drag-out fight, I never mentioned again," Bancroft later wrote.

Eager to sort out his next step, Dulles packed a bag for the flight over the Atlantic and a visit to Washington.

Dulles arrived at OSS headquarters in May to find the spy agency shrouded in despair. Shortly after Roosevelt's death, Truman had received a damning report about the OSS prepared by Colonel Richard Park, who served in the White House as an assistant to Edwin "Pa" Watson, a military adviser to Roosevelt.

Caustic and accusatory, the fifty-nine-page document contained an exhaustive list, some items true, some not, of OSS shortcomings, failures, and wastefulness. No rumor or half-truth was missed, no matter the source. OSS officers, Park wrote, were poorly trained, and British intelligence regarded their American counterparts as "putty in their hands." German spies had penetrated OSS operations throughout Europe and Asia. Bad intelligence provided by the OSS after the fall of Rome had led thousands of French troops into a Nazi trap.

Compounding the Park report were indications that Donovan and Truman did not get along. A star football player and a graduate of Columbia Law School, Donovan was also a creature of Wall Street. The president had worked in a haberdashery that had gone out of business. He had begun his political career as a county judge.

A meeting on May 14 to discuss the future of American espionage portended the worst. Truman did not give Donovan enough time to deliver his main points, wrapping their talk up after a scant fifteen minutes. In his diary entry for the day, Truman wrote with disdain that Donovan had "come in to tell how important the Secret Service [sic] is and how much he could do to run the government on an even basis."

In the midst of all the anxiety, Donovan delivered more disappointing news: He was going to eliminate the job of European intelligence chief. Instead, he was restructuring European OSS operations around country stations, and the head of each would report to him. Donovan cushioned the blow somewhat, announcing that he was ready to offer Dulles the best of the lot—head of the German operation.

Dulles surely saw compelling reasons to pursue either course in front of him. Earning a Wall Street lawyer's salary while advancing his career at home would allow him to reconnect with old friends. On the other hand, Dulles had believed that the months immediately after the war would be decisive for Germany's future and for the future of Europe. He left no record of his thoughts, but after a short period of deliberation, he chose to stay with the OSS and return to Europe.

Dulles's first order of business was to find a home for the new OSS German station within the American zone of occupation. Never one to shortchange himself, he selected the Henkell sparkling wine works near Wiesbaden, not far down the Rhine River from the headquarters of US forces in the sprawling I. G. Farben office complex in Frankfurt. Centered on "the most beautiful mansion you can imagine," in the words of one who worked there, the Henkell facilities offered ample office space that included conference rooms, private offices, even laboratories, all in the airy luxury that Dulles had known in Switzerland. The facility was surrounded by a spacious garden. A short walk away stood an impressive collection of private villas popular among wealthy, retired Germans before the war.

The OSS took over one such villa that was "well-staffed and comfortable—verging on plush," though the choice of decor was typical German bourgeois. Wandering its halls and rooms, OSS agents were struck by wall decorations consisting largely of trophies of game. One stuffed specimen in particular caught their attention, a rabbit head on which a taxidermist with a sense of humor had mounted a small set of horns. From the day of this discovery on, the villa was known among the Americans as the "Horned Rabbit Club."

With impressive ingenuity, they found ways to provide themselves with creature comforts. Frank Rositzke, an OSS officer transferred from London, was charged with the "great responsibility" of having hot cinnamon red wine ready each evening. The men also discovered that a "particularly vile Spanish brandy" sold at the PX could be rendered a "relatively potable drink" by mixing it with canned grapefruit juice, a concoction they called "Franco's Revenge."

Despite such creativity, Agent 110 understandably arrived at his office each morning feeling wistful for his days in Switzerland, and missing his team. He offered Bancroft a job in Germany, and the opportunity seemed to make sense. She had asked Rufenacht for a divorce, and her daughter was away at boarding school. When she discussed it with Gisevius, he "yammered . . . incessantly" that her going represented the logical next step in a "very interesting career."

But Bancroft had plenty of reasons to disagree. She had big plans to write a novel or do some film work writing dialogue for documentaries. She was close to landing a job with the Associated Press, and one of her first assignments would be a profile of Jung. After two and a half years of spying for Dulles, she was "exhausted emotionally, physically, psychically. I never wanted to hear the words *intelligence work* again." Most telling, whenever Dulles brought the subject up, she fell victim to the sneezing attacks that had plagued her in the 1930s before she worked with Jung. "No, Germany was not for me," she concluded.

Nor would Dulles be spending much time with Gisevius. "Tiny" did travel to Germany for a time, but projects in Switzerland beckoned. His book, he believed, was more important than ever, and he worked tirelessly to get it published as quickly as possible. Also consuming his attention was a Swiss police investigation into Martha Rigling and Johann Wüst, the two who had brought Eduard Schulte's plans for a new Germany to the attention of the Nazi security services.

There were other reasons for Dulles to feel ill at ease in his new post. He had loved the life of the lone wolf in Bern, operating until the autumn of 1944 by his own rules and without anybody looking over his shoulder. "I think in a sense I was lucky. . . . I didn't get cluttered up with the bureaucracy of a large organization." In Germany, he discovered that management, never his strong suit, would become a much larger part of the job, as his staff quickly ramped up to around one hundred people. The steady stream of OSS agents departing government work for their old, high-paying jobs on Wall Street or comfortable lives in academia left Dulles with a "revolving door" at the Henkell works. An office that was fully staffed on Monday might find itself at half power on Friday.

The number of open positions vastly outstripped the number of qualified candidates, and some staff members who were sent to Germany should not have been in a place with so many temptations. The deprivation of Berlin presented countless opportunities for black-market trading—two dozen cartons of Camel cigarettes could be swapped for a 1939 Mercedes-Benz. Once, OSS agents were caught trading on the black market. The illicit activity cast a cloud over Dulles's operation. Noted the deputy American military governor of Germany, General Lucius D. Clay, "How the hell can you expect those guys to catch spies when they can't smell the stink under their own noses?"

On any given day, the OSS team was called on to round up war criminals, retrieve valuable works of stolen art, gather evidence for the upcoming war crimes trials to be held in Nuremberg, or help historians research the final days of the Reich. For a time, Dulles even attempted to broker a peace deal in the Pacific, working with Japanese diplomats and military officers in Switzerland who wanted to surrender to the United States. To Dulles's disappointment, President Truman ordered the atomic bomb dropped on Japan before he could complete his diplomatic effort to end the war. "There were so many, often conflicting, demands for information that it was almost impossible to sort out the priority objectives," the OSS officer Richard Helms wrote.

CHAPTER

43

The Crown Jewels

From the chaos that was the OSS German station, Dulles was able to carve out time to tackle jobs that he considered important. Most urgent was the care and feeding of what became known as the "crown jewels"—members of the resistance who deserved American aid for what they had done against Hitler, "good Germans" who could play an important role in rebuilding Germany's shattered economy.

OSS agents accustomed to cloak-and-dagger assignments now spent their days chauffeuring or delivering meals to the "middle-aged men Dulles hoped would eventually play a role in rebuilding a democratic Germany," Helms wrote. These men and women were scattered around Germany and suffered twin hardships. Though they had fought an evil regime, many were unwelcomed members of the community, viewed by ordinary Germans as having been party to military defeats that had taken their loved ones. At the same time, many had a hard time convincing the Americans of their wartime contributions, even some of Dulles's most loyal colleagues. The State Department questioned the political leanings of Schulze-Gaevernitz when his sister married into a prominent German family, some of whom had at one time supported Hitler. And Waetjen was accused of supporting Hitler, even though he had worked with Dulles in the run-up to the July 20 assassination attempt.

Still, Dulles's team fought to protect the crown jewels. One of those aided was Fabian von Schlabrendorff, the German officer who had bravely tried to blow up Hitler's plane on the eastern front in the spring of 1943 and had participated in the July 20 plot as well. That Schlabrendorff was alive was a miracle. Around noon on February 3, 1945, he had been standing handcuffed in the dock at the infamous "People's Court" that meted out kangaroo justice and death penalties to the July 20 plotters when an air raid began. Though members of the court had taken refuge, one bomb scored a direct hit on the courtroom, causing a heavy beam to fall on the head of the judge, killing him with Schlabrendorff's files still in his hand. His trial never restarted, and he spent the last months of the war bouncing between one German prison and another.

American troops eventually found Schlabrendorff and put him in prison on the island of Capri. He might have languished there—American camp staff had heard plenty of tales claiming heroics against the Nazis—had it not been for Dulles and his team. Schulze-Gaevernitz discovered Schlabrendorff and arranged for him to be set free, even providing him with a car to return to Germany to search for his wife.

Dulles was also able to help Kolbe. At the end of the war he lived at the Herrengasse villa, where he continued to carry out small assignments for Dulles. He had, for instance, agreed to seek out Otto Köcher, a German diplomat, to find out if the Nazis were transporting gold to Switzerland. When Köcher refused to cooperate, the Americans made sure that the Swiss deported him back to Germany, where an American prison cell was waiting. (Köcher committed suicide while in American custody.)

Dulles then put Kolbe to work on a number of projects in Germany.

Provided with an American jeep and a driver, Kolbe traveled to Bavaria in June to try to track down his old boss Ritter and possibly even Ribbentrop, both of whom had gone into hiding. Kolbe soon discovered that conducting a manhunt required a different set of skills than smuggling documents. In the search for Nazi leaders of the Foreign Ministry, Kolbe not only failed to find anybody but was also duped by bogus information that complicated the OSS hunt.

Kolbe then went to Wiesbaden to be near Dulles and to help American prosecutors prepare for upcoming war crimes trials, telling all he knew about the inner workings of the Foreign Ministry. There he met Gisevius, and left none too impressed, distrustful of anyone who had ever worked in the Gestapo.

Later, Dulles arranged for Kolbe to return to Berlin, where he was given a cushy job helping the American occupation authorities with translation and other tasks; he was also able to recover from a severe car accident. Considered a "person of reference," Kolbe was well looked after by Dulles's men. He received food packages that were the envy of other Germans and even the use of a car, an almost unimaginable luxury in the months after Germany's surrender. Though he was generous about sharing his good fortune with other Germans, providing food and arranging jobs for friends, many harbored distaste for a man who had spied for the Allies.

Dulles inadvertently helped secure the future of Fritz Molden, the Austrian who had worked for him in 1944 and 1945. After meeting Dulles several times, Molden had gone on to serve as the liaison officer between the Austrian resistance and the American military and made numerous visits to Austria to coordinate the work of the resistance and to prepare for the Allied invasion. Dulles now thought that Molden might help him with a personal problem. His daughter, Joan, then twenty-two, had arrived in Switzerland with two of his nieces, and she needed help reaching Vienna—a difficult journey considering the war damage in Austria. Dulles asked the ex-soldier and resistance fighter to travel with the small group and make sure they arrived safely. As a father, even an absentee one as he had been most of his life, Dulles might have known better than to put his attractive daughter in close contact with this handsome, dark-haired hero. Molden and Joan soon fell deeply in love, and eventually married.

Dulles likewise felt compelled to help the families of martyred resistance fighters. He soon found Freya von Moltke, wife of the Kreisau Circle leader, living in miserable conditions on the family estate. Army rations were delivered to her home, as was a monthly stipend. With the Soviets tightening their grip on the area, Dulles arranged for her and her children to move to the American sector and eventually to the United States.

It did not take long for Dulles to see in defeated Germany the horror that he had feared since the earliest days of his assignment in Switzerland. German society was crumbling.

Even just a short journey outside his OSS headquarters revealed broken bridges, factories that had been reduced to twisted mounds of steel, and, in major cities, block after block of rubble. Walking down a street in cities like Frankfurt and Berlin, people could casually peer into the lives of neighbors whose apartments were missing walls.

Most normal functions of a settled society had ceased. Water mains were crushed, electricity was sporadic, there was no mail service, and trains were destroyed or couldn't run for lack of track. In July, less than 10 percent of the industrial plants in areas occupied by the United States were functioning.

Hannover, the scene of some of the most severe bombing, was virtually destitute. Half of all businesses and 80 percent of public buildings had been destroyed. Of the city's eighty-seven school buildings, only four were still standing. One American who witnessed the scene observed that the population "moved like ghosts—pale, silent, sullen, their spirits broken, their hopes shattered." Everywhere were the women who tried to clean up their neighborhoods and who became known as the *Trümmerfrauen,* or "rubble women."

Hunger soon swept across Germany. While two thousand calories per person per day was believed to be the minimum level needed to prevent disease and civic unrest, caloric intake in some urban areas was half that. Food shortages were especially acute in the American and British zones of occupation. The most populated areas, they had never produced enough food to feed themselves. People there also had to compete with the rivers of refugees, carrying their meager belongings in pushcarts and wagons, fleeing not just eastern Germany but eastern European nations as well. The deputy American military governor of Germany, General Lucius Clay, noted that "hunger was to be seen everywhere and even the refuse pails from our messes, from which everything of value had been removed, were gone over time and time again in a search for the last scrap of nourishment."

Girls and boys in tattered clothes grew thinner. Their mothers traded family treasures such as furniture, jewelry, and record players for potatoes and small cuts of meat. During a tour of Berlin, the US assistant secretary of war, John McCloy, saw women and children ripping at the flesh of a dead horse with their bare hands. "It is all a very depressing sight and gives evidence of the crazy character of man," he wrote. In the summer of 1945, more than half of the babies born in Berlin died as infants.

Dulles found daily life eerily similar to what he had seen in Germany after World War I, and just the sort of environment that seemed tailor-made for the Soviets and the spread of communism. Getting the right people into critical jobs to rebuild the economy was vital.

He had begun preparing for this moment not long after his arrival in Switzerland, building a lengthy list of Germans whom the Americans could rely on during the occupation. It was an eclectic group. Businessmen made up a good share. There were also churchmen, labor leaders, and political figures, even left-leaning ones. Other than hardened pro-Soviet Communists, Dulles paid scant attention to the political views of those whom he thought could help. "We should not be disturbed at, in fact, we should welcome, a liberal and leftist-oriented Germany," Dulles wrote around this time. Socialists in Germany, he maintained, were really not much different from Democrats in the United States.

One who fit Dulles's vision was the former Reichstag member Wilhelm Hoegner. He had opposed the Nazis from the earliest days of the party and had fled to Switzerland to work with a group of German exiles. Hoegner met Dulles there in November 1943, and Agent 110 had asked him, as he had other Germans he met, to prepare a paper on his thoughts about postwar Germany. The result apparently met Dulles's standards, because the two, often accompanied by Schulze-Gaevernitz, met often throughout 1944 and 1945 to discuss politics, especially regarding Bavaria, an area that the Munich-born Hoegner knew well.

With the war over, Dulles wasted no time in getting Hoegner to Germany. On June 6, a member of his team drove Hoegner in an American jeep from Switzerland to Munich, where he began working out a detailed plan for Germany's political rebirth. A few months later, US occupation authorities named him minister president of Bavaria, and he proved himself to be a staunch opponent of the Communists and the Soviet Union.

Yet for every German whom Dulles was able to help, there were scores who were prevented from taking jobs with the Americans.

American policy toward Germany was enshrined under an officious-sounding document known as Joint Chiefs of Staff Directive 1067. Though an intergovernmental policy, JCS 1067 was heavily influenced by the secretary of the treasury, Henry Morgenthau Jr., a pugnacious and determined advocate of imposing a severe peace on Germany. One of Roosevelt's longtime friends, Morgenthau enjoyed a level of intimacy with Roosevelt that was the envy of many in Washington and had helped shape American postwar policy before the president's death. Morgenthau was also Jewish, a fact not missed by his many enemies, who accused him of seeking revenge for the Holocaust. Known as the "Morgenthau Plan," his proposals for postwar Germany were harsh. He wanted to transform the nation into a land of simple farmers. The great mines of the Ruhr, home to much of Europe's steel production, were to be flooded, and severe limits placed on German industrial output. And no ounce of leniency was to be accorded to any German who had been involved with the Nazi Party.

According to JCS 1067's wording, Nazi Party members who had "been more than nominal participants in its activities" were to be prevented from holding any meaningful jobs in postwar Germany. In the weeks and months that followed, American occupation authorities sought to clarify that vague definition, providing detailed descriptions of what Nazi Party involvement could be tolerated by American occupiers. By early July, a US Forces European Theater directive established no fewer than 136 categories of involvement in Hitler's regime that could get a German barred from a job.

Morgenthau and his allies did everything they could to implement the rules strictly. Detention centers in the American zones soon were filled to overflowing with Germans linked to the party. The United States, Dulles wrote about this time, had been forced into "the concentration camp business" because of the vast numbers of Germans that they had incarcerated, some one hundred thousand in all.

Derisively known among army officers as the "Morgenthau Boys," a group of 140 men led by Bernard Bernstein, a former Treasury official and Morgenthau ally, were among the most determined hunters of civilians with links to the Nazi Party. Employing what they called "flying visits," ten-man investigation teams descended on banks and financial institutions in search of those whom they believed had helped the German war effort, arresting them on the spot. By September 1945, they had rounded up 9,500—proof, Bernstein claimed, of the guilt of members of Germany's financial system.

One celebrated target was Hermann Abs, a director at Germany's largest bank, Deutsche Bank. Abs had never joined the Nazi Party, and when the British discovered him in Berlin shortly after the war, they put him to work reestablishing the banking system. Abs, however, had also been a loyal member of the bank that directly funded German companies that employed slave labor and drove thousands to their deaths. He was just the sort of man Bernstein wanted to arrest. Employing considerable political pressure, he eventually succeeded in having the banker turned over to the Americans, much to the scorn of their ally. As one British official present during the American interrogation of Abs put it, "The Americans wanted to get their eye-for-an-eye revenge."

Dulles feared the strict American policy would trap many who weren't really Nazis and who were needed to rebuild Germany. Since the 1930s, many of the most important jobs in Germany—utility workers, police

officers, bankers, factory foremen, firemen, municipal administrators—had
been doled out largely to party members. Many had joined simply to have
a job. The Germans had a word for such people, *Muss-Nazi*, or "Nazi by
necessity."

Further complicating the issue was the sheer number of party members.
By the end of the war, about eight million Germans belonged to the party, or
about 10 percent of the total population, and that figure swelled by several
factors when one counted affiliated organizations such as the German Labor
Front, the League of German Women, and the National Socialist People's
Welfare. "We have already found out that you can't run railroads without
taking in some Party members," Dulles declared.

Eduard Schulte, the German industrialist who was one of the first to in-
form the West of the Nazi extermination camps, was another casualty. Dulles
had arranged for Schulte to return to Germany immediately after the Nazis
surrendered, intent on seeing him assume a place in helping the occupation
authorities, and ultimately possibly becoming a minister of economics or
finance. Yet in the eyes of the American occupation government, Schulte
was suspect. In 1941, he had received a Nazi decoration, and the American
Justice Department fretted over what role his company had played in supplying Germany's armaments industry. Despite Dulles's best efforts, Schulte
was barred from working with the Americans. He returned to Switzerland
in bitter frustration.

CHAPTER

44

"It Was Three Allies and One Enemy"

On September 18, 1945, Donovan cabled Dulles with a grave message. He had tried everything he could think of to save the OSS, including a publicity campaign that provided details of Dulles's Operation Sunrise to the *Saturday Evening Post*. Yet he now had to tell Dulles that he had lost his battle and had been forced to implement a "liquidation budget." The OSS's Research and Analysis branch was to be taken over by the State Department. And the intelligence and special operations work, reformed as the Strategic Services Unit, would go to the War Department, where it would be run by Brigadier General John Magruder. By executive order, the OSS would cease to exist on October 1, 1945.

For the second time in only a few months, Dulles had a life-changing decision to make. Though the OSS was gone, there was still an opportunity to continue intelligence work in Europe. One of the first messages that Magruder sent to Germany pleaded with Dulles and the rest of his staff to remain at their posts.

OSS officer Helms, who lived with Dulles in Germany, knew that Agent 110 was none too thrilled about staying on in a "jerry-built and transient SSU organization." Agents were quitting in droves. During the autumn of 1945, the number of staff fell from ten thousand to fewer than two thousand. Nearly all the officers in stations around Europe—London, Paris, Rome, Vienna, Madrid, Lisbon, and Stockholm—left the service. Of the twenty-three stations in Asia, fifteen closed.

It was also becoming clear that the nature of the mission was rapidly changing. The behavior of the Soviets seemed to prove Dulles right about their ambitions. At first, Moscow had allowed political and other freedoms in its zone of occupation. But by later in the summer, once postwar agreements had been arranged between Truman and Stalin at the Potsdam Conference in July and August, the Soviets became confrontational.

American troops, once able to pass freely into the Soviet zone, now found barriers installed on major streets. Several of Dulles's men, attempting to arrest a German general wanted for war crimes, were attacked and beaten by Soviet soldiers, who took the German away. Rivalries quickly emerged over attempts by both countries to secure top German scientists to work for them. Reports circulated that the Soviets had erected loudspeakers on their side of the Elbe River to broadcast messages urging German technical experts to leave the American zone and emigrate to the Soviet Union to continue their work.

Most worrying were signs that the Soviets were moving to institute a government loyal to Moscow. As Dulles had long warned, members of the Free Germany Committee began to appear. In April 1945, one of the committee's most important members, Walter Ulbricht, returned to Germany with a group of German Communists, including former POWs, with orders to help get the German Communist Party around Berlin on its feet. Not long thereafter, two groups led by members of the Free Germany Committee fanned out around the Soviet zone of occupation with similar briefs.

"It was three Allies and one enemy," OSS officer Helms later wrote. "What were the Russians doing with their troops in their zone? It didn't take long to figure out they weren't going to tell you a damn thing. In fact, they were going to keep you out of there, and they were going to be very hostile."

The Americans had scored one major coup when German army general Reinhard Gehlen turned over to them a trove of valuable Nazi intelligence about the Soviets, which he had buried for safekeeping in metal drums in the Alps. But the United States was woefully late in gearing up an intelligence arm to tackle the Soviets and knew little about what was going on in Moscow. They began by recruiting German police officers and politicians who could tell them what was happening in the Soviet zones of occupation, but the results were meager. Operations as mundane as monitoring the comings and goings of Soviet troop transports in Berlin were undertaken primarily to give the Pentagon "a sense that someone was trying to keep an eye on the Red Army."

All this was too much for Dulles. "It had been apparent for some weeks that his personal objectives went well beyond managing an organization scattered across occupied Germany, under the thumb, if not fist, of the military occupation authorities, and with a most uncertain line of command to Washington," Helms later wrote.

That autumn, Dulles announced that he, too, was leaving Germany and the government.

CHAPTER
45

"Most of My Time Is Spent Reliving Those Exciting Days"

New York City department stores were just hanging their Christmas decorations as Dulles arrived home and began to rebuild his old life. The familiar bells rung by Salvation Army volunteers pierced the cold air. Men in smart suits gathered in bars to discuss a disappointing season of football for the New York Giants. Newspaper headlines trumpeted steady gains in the Dow Jones Industrial Average. It all seemed a world away from his life in Europe.

The legal projects that awaited him at Sullivan & Cromwell contrasted markedly with the life he had known the last three years—the intrigue of Bern, the intoxication of northern Italy, the deprivation of Germany. It was a life that Dulles found himself unable to let go of. "I must admit that these days I find it hard to concentrate on my profession of the law," he said. "Most of my time is spent reliving those exciting days when the war was slowly dying."

Friends would note how Dulles bent the ears of visitors for hours at a time, most of them happy to comply as he recounted his spy stories. Soon streams of former colleagues flowed through his office. Tracy Barnes, who had helped retrieve the Ciano diaries, called on Dulles, as did Richard Helms. A number of contacts in Germany continued to feed him information about the conditions there. Schulze-Gaevernitz, still worried about the care and feeding of "good Germans," warned that the democratic forces in Germany could easily fall again under the control of totalitarian elements, "entailing disastrous consequences for the whole of Europe."

Searching to regain some of his former life, Dulles began to frequent his old haunt, the Council on Foreign Relations at the Harold Pratt House on Sixty-Eighth Street, just a quick walk from his home. In short order he was elected the council president and named chair of Western European Affairs, a key study group that brought together the leading lights of American foreign policy—members of the State Department, business leaders, and influential academics. The future of Germany, and the threat of the Soviet Union, soon came to preoccupy him.

Dulles's first major contact in Switzerland was similarly consumed by the aftermath of the war. In addition to his other projects, Gisevius had been preparing to finally exact justice from old enemies. That spring of 1946, he left Switzerland to testify in Germany at the Allies' war crimes trials. He traveled with a friend.

When Bancroft declined Dulles's offer of a job with the OSS in Berlin, he had offered her the chance to select another "reward" for her years of service to him and the OSS. Now she had made up her mind. She wanted to go with Gisevius to Nuremberg.

The journey from the Swiss border to the Bavarian town, roughly 270 miles, was an uncomfortable one for the pair. As with most Americans traveling through Germany in the months after the war, they were struck by the magnitude of the wartime destruction. Würzburg, one city in northern Bavaria through which they passed, had been bombed on the night of

March 16, 1945, only weeks before the end of the war, and a horrific fire-storm had swept through the city, killing several thousand.

During a stop in the town, Bancroft struck up a conversation with a woman who was sitting on a wooden chair in front of a pile of ruins that had been her home. A cat, Bancroft remembered, nestled nearby, keeping the woman company. Like many Germans, the woman didn't blame the Americans or the British for the destruction. But neither did she hold herself or her fellow Germans responsible. "We have our Führer to thank for this!"

Nuremberg was a quintessential Bavarian city, famed for its timbered buildings, its scientists, its contributions to printing, and its Christmas market. From the late 1930s, however, the city had become well-known as the site of the Nazi Party's boisterous outdoor rallies. On the outskirts of town on a massive parade ground, Hitler had delivered speeches to crowds that numbered upward of seven hundred thousand. The 1934 Nazi Party Congress there had been the subject of a well-known film by the acclaimed director Leni Riefenstahl. *Triumph of the Will* was a propaganda masterpiece that incorporated then-novel techniques such as moving cameras and aerial photography. Partly because the city had served as something of a spiritual home for the Nazis, and also because its courthouse, the Palace of Justice, had survived the war in usable condition, the Allies chose Nuremberg to stage the trials of suspected war criminals.

Bancroft and Gisevius checked into a villa that was owned by a countess, a slim young woman with blond hair that fell about her shoulders. She was a pleasant hostess and doted on her guests, who were mostly there to testify at the trials and constituted an intriguing group.

Around every corner, behind every door, was someone with a fascinating story. Bancroft met Hitler's personal photographer, Heinrich Hoffmann, and listened closely as he conducted a monologue about a variety of topics, including his claim that he had been the one to introduce Hitler to Eva Braun. Diaries purportedly written by Braun that were then surfacing, Hoffman said, were fakes. Extracts of the books he had seen were written too crudely and simply to have been by Hitler's mistress. "Eva had a fine literary style," he assured Bancroft.

It's doubtful that Gisevius listened patiently to such stories. His distaste for the Nazis left little room for romanticized assessments of Eva Braun's writing skills. More important was his coming role on the witness stand. Hjalmar Schacht, an old friend from the resistance, was on trial for his work with Hitler, and Gisevius hoped his testimony would help his case.

Schacht was undeniably linked to the Nazis. Early on, he had contributed money to the party and had backed Hitler's takeover of Germany. In 1933, he had been reappointed head of the German central bank, the Reichsbank, and a year later Hitler named him minister of economics. The more he saw of Hitler and his policies, however, the more Schacht began to pull back, and he later openly expressed disdain for the Nazis' anti-Semitic attitudes. By 1938, he felt strongly enough to join the Beck coup attempt. Schacht had later aided the Breakers on July 20 and had been arrested by the Gestapo. He had spent time in concentration camps.

At the same time, Gisevius hoped to contribute to the testimony against Hermann Göring, the commander of the German air force and a Nazi Party leader, who was accused of war crimes. Gisevius did not have much insight into Göring's crimes late in the war, but he had intimate knowledge of his activities as Prussian minister of the interior, a period during which Gisevius believed Göring had engaged in a series of plots to advance the Nazi Party.

On the afternoon of April 24, 1946, Gisevius was called to the witness stand for the first time. Wearing a dark suit and a headset that translated questions from the American prosecutors into German, Gisevius testified a few yards away from Göring and other defendants, who sat together, some wearing sunglasses to protect their eyes from the bright lights of photographic equipment.

His testimony, which spanned three days, revolved around the history of the German resistance. The court, he said, should not be preoccupied with the fact that Schacht had served in senior positions in the Nazi regime. Schacht had, in fact, agonized over those duties and what he should do. Part of him wanted to quit, but he would only be replaced with a radical Nazi. "I can testify that many men, who later became members of the opposition, implored Schacht to take that line and to keep at least one foot in," Gisevius told the court.

Göring, on the other hand, had been a ruthless and lawless rogue since the early 1930s, he argued.

As Gisevius's time in the witness box drew to a close, the American prosecutor, Robert Jackson, asked him to summarize what drove the resistance. His reply could well serve as an epitaph for all who had died to defeat the Nazi regime: "It was a fight for human rights. From the very first moment on, among all classes of people, in all professional circles, and in all age groups, there were people who were ready to fight, to suffer, and to die for that idea."

Postscript

The morning of Tuesday, March 5, 1946, a motorcade carrying former prime minister Churchill and President Truman rolled down the redbrick main thoroughfare of Fulton, Missouri. It was a wonderful spring day in the Midwest, with temperatures in the upper sixties, and thousands had turned out—many waving American and British flags—to see the two. Truman, born about two hundred miles away, was rightfully proud of the reception and was confident that he had suitably impressed Churchill the night before over a card game that had lasted into the wee hours of the morning.

After lunch with Frank McClure, the president of Westminster College, a Presbyterian men's school, Truman and Churchill marched in an academic procession to the college gymnasium, where an eager crowd had gathered to hear Churchill speak on world events. Introduced by Truman, Churchill stepped to the rostrum. Gazing out over the sea of spectators, he began to speak in the grave tones that so many immediately recognized from radio broadcasts. He had, Churchill said, great respect for the Russian people and for Stalin. Still, it was his duty to present "certain facts." He then launched into the heart of one of the most important and memorable speeches of the twentieth century.

"From Stettin in the Baltic to Trieste in the Adriatic, an Iron Curtain has descended across the Continent. Behind that line lie all the capitals of the ancient states of Central and Eastern Europe. Warsaw, Berlin, Prague, Vienna, Budapest, Belgrade, Bucharest and Sofia, all these famous cities and populations around them lie in what I must call a Soviet sphere, and all are subject in one form or another, not only to Soviet influence but to a very high and, in many cases, increasing measure of control from Moscow."

The Soviets, Churchill told the enraptured audience, did not want war. Rather, they wanted the fruits of war and the continuous expansion of their power. What was needed now was for a union of the English-speaking peoples—by which he largely meant Great Britain and the United States—to stand up to them.

Only through resolute action could the advance of Soviet communism be stopped, because, Churchill said, he understood the Russian mind. There was nothing they so admired as strength and nothing for which they had less respect than weakness.

Later known as the Iron Curtain speech, the address was for Dulles a gratifying yet worrying indication that the course of history was unfolding exactly as he had foreseen.

The Soviets were proving ever more combative with the Americans. Disagreements over implementing reparations had poisoned relations between the two "allies." The Soviet "policy of Communist world domination which had been checked by war was brought out of moth balls and clearly formed the basis of their day-to-day planning," General Clay of the US occupation wrote. At the same time, the Soviets backtracked on political and personal freedoms in Germany. Where they had initially permitted the formation of several political parties within their zone of occupation, they now forced the merger of the powerful Social Democratic Party and the German Communist Party. The new party, the Socialist Unity Party (SED), soon showed itself loyal to Moscow.

In the Soviet zone, a brutal crackdown began. In 1946, US occupation authorities were distressed to learn that two judges who had recently rendered decisions unfavorable to German Communist leaders were arrested by unknown police in their homes in their western sector of Berlin. When Clay sought information about the pair, the Soviets promised an investigation but never revealed what happened to the men. "It was an early indication of Soviet effort to intimidate Germans opposed to communism, which was to lead later to many additional arrests," Clay later wrote.

Causing a sensation in Washington at the same time was a paper of more than five thousand words prepared by George Kennan at the American embassy in Moscow. Known as the "Long Telegram," the report argued that the United States had been naive to think it could look forward to harmonious relations with Moscow. The Kremlin held a neurotic view of the world that was based in a history of insecurity and was not always governed by logic or reason. Like Churchill, Kennan concluded that the Soviets were sensitive "to the logic of force." The State Department lauded the piece, and the secretary of the navy, James Forrestal, had it copied and distributed to upper-level officers.

Evidence that appeared to support such an assessment was emerging around the globe. In Iran, Moscow seemed to be angling to gain control over northern areas of the oil-rich country. In Turkey, the Soviets maneuvered for dominance over the Black Sea straits and territory near the border.

President Truman, who for months had sought accommodation, was losing his patience and beginning to acknowledge publicly that the relationship had changed. Soviet expansion, Truman now promised, would be met "with an iron fist and strong language." In what would become one of his famous one-liners, Truman wrote, "I'm tired of babysitting the Soviets."

Using his position as the head of the Council on Foreign Relations as a platform, Dulles gave speeches and wrote articles on the problems that Germany faced. The centerpiece of the effort was to be a book on the Breakers and the July 20 Valkyrie plot to murder Hitler. The story, Dulles hoped, would introduce to Americans the brave Germans who were worth helping, especially considering Germany's place on the front line in the looming confrontation with the Soviet Union.

Not all his efforts were successful. Dulles could display a tin ear when it came to prose. For *Collier's* magazine, he wrote a somewhat odd piece, two full pages that took readers on a lengthy and tedious tour of Berlin's history that few likely finished. Finally arriving at the last couple of paragraphs, Dulles offered up some useful opinion. A half-mile radius of destruction around Hitler's chancellery should be preserved as it then stood, as a "perpetual memorial to the Nazis and Prussia." But there was no reason for further harsh punishment. Berlin, he wrote, "need not share the fate of Carthage or the retribution which Jehovah visited upon Sodom and Gomorrah."

Slowly, supporters began to emerge. A Chicago lawyer, Laird Bell, had seen American policy and the work of the Morgenthau Boys as deputy director of the Economic Division of the Office of Military Government. He believed that the punitive JCS 1067 had long been overtaken by events, and began, in his own words, a "one-man crusade" against it.

American policy, Bell told members of the council, was still guided by "war hysteria with vengeance as its principal ingredient." After one meeting in New York in February 1946, Bell and other council members decided to get together to try to "get the right slant to public opinion on Germany." Over these weeks Bell met with the famed economist John Kenneth Galbraith and luminaries from the State Department such as Charles Kindleberger. For the moment, however, such men advised that it was counterproductive to make a major issue out of 1067, as doing so would energize the "residual power of the Morgenthau group."

Dulles also began to develop new ideas about how to deal with the growing Soviet threat. In a letter to his brother in May, he outlined thinking that was remarkably similar to what would become the prevailing American policy toward the Soviets in the decades to follow. Echoing the containment policy, Dulles wrote that he doubted the Soviets and his own country would soon live happily together. Nor did he think that an immediate confrontation was inevitable. The West, he wrote, should attempt to buy time until the Soviets developed the sort of liberties existing in the West. In the meantime, the United States should seek a measure of "insulation" from Russia.

One of the few of Germany's magnificent performing arts centers to survive the war was Stuttgart's Opera House. Built in a Romanesque style with a row of columns and situated before a reflecting pond, the building, which could seat more than one thousand people, had hosted musical performances since 1912.

On Friday evening, September 6, 1946, Secretary of State James F. Byrnes, flanked by a small group of American dignitaries, including American army officers wearing their green uniforms, strode onstage and looked out on a crowd of members of the occupation government, and an unusually large number of Germans.

In a reedy voice, Byrnes spoke into a large microphone that carried his address on the radio throughout the western zones of Germany with simultaneous German translation.

Things, he said, were about to change for Germany. The United States now hoped to aid in the economic reconstruction of the country. What's more, the United States was ready to return the government of Germany to the Germans. The American people would support efforts by Germans "to win their way back to an honorable place among the free and peace-loving nations of the world."

Lest the German people think the United States was abandoning Germany, he went on to stress that US troops would remain "as long as there is an occupation army in Germany."

The event marked a repudiation of the Morgenthau Plan and the culmination of what Dulles had sought since first arriving in Switzerland. The Soviets were now seen as America's adversary, and Germany had become an important ally in that confrontation. In the months that followed, Secretary of State George Marshall began to develop plans for a major European recovery program. Dulles was a passionate supporter of the Marshall Plan and drafted a book-length manuscript that he hoped would generate support for the rebuilding effort.

Officially unveiled in 1947 and known as the European Recovery Program (ERP), the four-year project provided $13 billion in economic support to help rebuild European economies in order to prevent the spread of communism. At the same time, Marshall moved quickly to scrap JCS 1067 and replace it with JCS 1779, a policy aimed at rebuilding Germany because it was vital to the reconstruction of all of Europe. In the years that followed, Europe's economy achieved rapid growth as the output of agricultural and industrial goods surged.

The Characters

MARY BANCROFT

Bancroft and Rufenacht divorced in 1947. In the early summer of 1953, she returned to the United States with her daughter and resumed her close relationships with both Allen and Clover. Clover even became good friends with Bancroft's first husband, Sherwin, and looked after him following a serious auto accident.

During the rest of her life, Bancroft delivered numerous lectures on international topics; wrote two novels, *Upside Down in the Magnolia Tree* (1952), and *The Inseparables* (1958); and drafted several more. Her memoir, *Autobiography of a Spy*, was published in 1983.

Settling in New York, Bancroft got involved in local politics and kept up her interest in psychology. She was a consultant and book reviewer for *Psychological Perspectives* and served on its editorial board. Bancroft died on January 10, 1997.

HANS BERND GISEVIUS

Gisevius earned some notoriety as one of the star witnesses for the Nuremberg trials. His testimony helped convict Hermann Göring, who was able to cheat the hangman's noose with a suicide tablet that was smuggled into his cell. Gisevius also testified against Wilhelm Keitel and Wilhelm Kaltenbrunner.

The book that he worked on with Bancroft during the war was published in 1946 under the German title *Bis zum bitteren Ende*, and two years later an English translation appeared, *To the Bitter End*.

After the war crimes trials, Gisevius's life unfolded as Jung had predicted. He got married and spent some time in Texas. "Tiny" then moved back to Germany, wrote, and eventually settled near Lake Geneva, where he lived in relative anonymity. Gisevius died in 1974.

FRITZ KOLBE

Dulles's agent Wood moved to Berlin shortly after the war and performed a number of jobs for the OSS, nursing dreams of one day getting a job in a new, reformed German Foreign Ministry. Yet life was difficult. His work for the OSS left him a controversial figure among his own countrymen, and he would for the rest of his life wrestle with accusations of treason for the help he provided the Allies.

Unable to advance himself in Germany, he and his wife, Maria, traveled to the United States in 1949. With funding arranged by members of the OSS, he attempted to establish a business selling asbestos. He was bilked out of his investment by his business partner and found that he didn't much like the United States and its culture of consumption. After only a few months, he returned to Germany and got a job at a magazine operated by a concentration camp survivor. Thwarted from his ambition of returning to the Foreign Ministry, he accepted a job as the European sales rep for an American power tool company, based in Switzerland. He died in Bern in 1971. Twelve people attended the funeral. Kolbe was finally honored by the German Foreign

Ministry in 2004 when a brass plaque bearing his name was affixed to the door of a conference room there. Joschka Fischer, the German foreign minister, called the recognition "long overdue."

WILLIAM DONOVAN

In the immediate months after the OSS was dissolved, Donovan traveled to Nuremberg, where he served as special assistant to chief prosecutor Robert Jackson. Among his personal interests were tracking down and gathering evidence about Nazi crimes against his captured agents.

Donovan returned to his job as a Wall Street lawyer and continued to urge Congress to create a centralized intelligence agency. In 1949, he became chairman of the American Committee on United Europe, which opposed communism.

In 1953, Eisenhower appointed Donovan as ambassador to Thailand. Donovan died in 1959.

GENERAL KARL WOLFF

Wolff was arrested immediately after the war and imprisoned by the Allies for several years for his membership in the SS. Throughout much of the 1950s, Wolff worked in advertising. Rumors persisted that he was in the employ of the CIA and that Dulles was protecting him as part of the payback for the role he played in Operation Sunrise.

But Wolff could not escape his own country's legal system. In 1964, after new evidence of his involvement in deporting some three hundred thousand Italian Jews to death camps surfaced, he was sentenced to fifteen years in prison.

Wolff served only part of his sentence and was released in 1969 due to ill health. Later in life, Wolff frequently appeared in the media to discuss the war. A popular commentator, Wolff claimed that Hitler had at one point ordered him to occupy the Vatican and kidnap the pope, an assertion some historians question. He died in 1984.

GERO VON SCHULZE-GAEVERNITZ

In the months immediately after the war, Schulze-Gaevernitz worked with Dulles in Germany to help locate Germans with anti-Nazi credentials who could assist in the occupation. He was awarded the US Presidential Medal of Freedom in 1945 for his work with Dulles on Operation Sunrise.

In 1946, Schulze-Gaevernitz returned to private life and helped Schlabrendorff finish his book on the resistance. It was published in 1947 under the title *They Almost Killed Hitler.* In the years that followed he pursued business interests in Europe and South America.

Throughout his life, Schulze-Gaevernitz maintained contact with colleagues from the war years. He closely followed Wolff's trial and presented to a German court a full account of the general's efforts to end the war in Italy. "Wolff began to see the light in 1943, and tried not to extricate himself but to extricate the nation out of its tragic situation," Schulze-Gaevernitz wrote. In 1965, he proposed a reunion of those involved in Operation Sunrise in Ascona, which many of the participants attended. Schulze-Gaevernitz died in 1970.

ALLEN DULLES

In 1947, Dulles served as an adviser to government bodies working on the creation of a central intelligence agency. Early in that year he prepared a nine-page memo for the Senate Armed Services Committee focused largely on portraying intelligence gathering as a lot of routine but hard work, far from the glamorous reputation that it sometimes had. He also laid out the qualifications for the head of a future central intelligence body as those very similar to his own. In June that year, another committee dealing with espionage, the House Committee on Expenditures in the Executive Departments, invited Dulles to testify.

Dulles had hoped that he might be tapped to lead the CIA when it was created later that year. His candidacy, however, suffered several flaws. The military still possessed a loud voice in American espionage and was opposed to a civilian leading an intelligence operation. What's more, he was a Republican, the wrong party as far as Truman was concerned. Rear Admiral Roscoe H. Hillenkoetter was named director.

In 1951, Dulles was offered a job within the CIA overseeing the agency's covert activities as deputy director for plans, and not long thereafter was promoted to deputy director of central intelligence, second in the intelligence hierarchy. In 1953, the recently elected Republican president Eisenhower finally offered Dulles the post he had so long desired, naming him director of the CIA.

Working with Foster, who was named secretary of state in January 1953, Dulles became a central figure in a new kind of warfare.

Coordinating espionage and diplomacy, the pair aimed to counter Soviet expansion, perceived or real, wherever they found it, and in ways that would have been unthinkable before World War II.

The strategy initially produced results. Fearful of Communist influence (or, as critics would say, to aid American business interests) in Iran and Guatemala, the Dulles brothers orchestrated clandestine coups that deposed governments in both nations and replaced them with friendly regimes.

In the months and years that followed, American secret operations expanded greatly. In 1958, confronted with yet another perceived Communist threat—this time from Indonesia—Dulles prepared a clandestine effort to topple President Sukarno, who was warmly greeted on a visit to the United States. Again employing and arming rebels who were helped by American air power, the CIA felt that the coup's prospects were bright. The agency, however, failed to realize the strength of Sukarno's domestic position, and the mission was scrubbed shortly after a CIA pilot was shot down and interrogated by Sukarno's forces.

Despite that setback, the pace of the CIA's anti-Communist activities increased. In Vietnam, the CIA propped up the shaky regime of Prime Minister Ngo Dinh Diem. In the Congo, plans were drawn up to depose or even kill Prime Minister Patrice Lumumba. His domestic opponents, aided by the Belgians, ultimately assassinated him.

Of all Dulles's operations at the CIA, his effort to topple Fidel Castro gained the most notoriety. The basic plan was much the same as others the CIA had employed elsewhere—training and arming revolutionaries who would overthrow the government and pave the way for a pro-American regime. In the case of Cuba, the CIA recruited anti-Castro Cubans from around Miami, who formed the backbone of a small invasion force, 1,400 men in total. At the same time, the CIA borrowed a number of B-26 bombers from the Alabama National Guard and repainted them with the insignia of the Cuban air force.

As planning for the operation progressed, those around Dulles began to notice how tired he looked. In 1952, his son, Allen Macy Dulles, a bright and promising young man, suffered critical head wounds while serving as a lieutenant in the Marines in the Korean War. For years, the family spent a small fortune on treatments that produced little results. In May 1959, after a long and a painful fight with colon cancer, Foster died. A year later, unwelcome attention was turned on Dulles and the CIA when an American spy plane flown by Francis Gary Powers was shot down over the Soviet Union. The incident was embarrassing for President Eisenhower, who first denied that the United States engaged in such espionage, but later had to admit he'd lied.

By 1961, Dulles seemed to withdraw from some of his duties, turning important jobs over to subordinates. When the invasion of Cuba took place in April, Dulles wasn't even in the United States.

On the seventeenth of that month, the American-backed force landed at a beach on the south coast of Cuba known as the Bay of Pigs. It was a fiasco. Castro had learned of the attack and ordered roughly twenty thousand of his men to advance toward the rebels' landing area. After suffering heavy casualties, the invasion force reloaded its survivors on transport ships and evacuated.

Dulles was allowed to remain on the job, in order to dedicate a new CIA headquarters in Langley, Virginia, but all knew his days were numbered. In the autumn of 1961, President Kennedy fired him.

In the years that followed, his legacy in espionage came under increasing scrutiny. The "with us or against us" philosophy he shared with his brother, the tendency to view nationalist movements as a sign of creeping communism, and the way that smaller countries were bullied, was increasingly questioned. Dulles would parry such accusatory inquiries by stating that the United States was engaged in a new kind of war, one that required new kinds of strategies.

Dulles would receive a vote of confidence in November 1963 when President Lyndon Johnson named him one of seven members of the Warren Commission to investigate the assassination of President John F. Kennedy.

As his health deteriorated in the late 1960s, Dulles frequently looked back on his years in Switzerland with fondness. He wrote several books, *The Craft of Intelligence* (1963), *The Secret Surrender* (1966), and *Great True Spy Stories* (1968). He often reminisced about his posting in Bern. It marked a time when the enemy was clear-cut, and nobody was looking over his shoulder. Dulles died in 1969 in Georgetown, in Washington, DC.

Acknowledgments

This book would not have come to life without the support of my wife, Karen. As my best friend, she indulged my impossibly illogical "method" and daily shared my enthusiasm over small discoveries. Equally important was her help with the manuscript as my first reader. A former bureau chief for *Newsweek* magazine, she brought the skilled eye and ear of a veteran journalist, helping with everything from shaping the narrative to proofing the copy.

I also owe my two daughters, Elisabeth and Anna, huge thanks for their understanding and support. Many an evening over the dinner table they patiently listened and asked smart questions about the project that often took over the household.

This manuscript would not have been possible without the guidance of my editor, Alice Mayhew. One of the giants of her profession, Alice helped direct the project from its earliest stages, asking penetrating questions and disciplining my writing. Most important, Alice identified a thread to the story that was key to making the narrative more powerful. Someone who shares my passion for history, she was a constant inspiration and an honor to work with.

Almut Schoenfeld, a former colleague from *The Wall Street Journal,* made an invaluable contribution to the book by searching the German National Archives and German Foreign Ministry archives in Berlin. Always enthusiastic, Almut is a self-starter and offered many fresh ideas about sources of material.

In Bern, Michael Hischier dived into the Swiss National Archives and unearthed documents about characters in the book that shed fresh light on the dangers they faced.

Especially fascinating was meeting with Peter Sichel, a former OSS agent who came to know Dulles in the closing months of the war and had worked for him. Mr. Sichel was most generous with his time and helped fill in some of the gaps left in the archival files and books.

The starting point for my archival research on Dulles in the United States was the Seeley G. Mudd Manuscript Library at Princeton, home to his vast collection of papers. There Daniel Linke provided considerable help in navigating boxes of personal letters, unpublished versions of Dulles's books, newspaper clippings, photographs, and other Dulles memorabilia.

Librarians at the US National Archives in College Park, Maryland, were likewise of tremendous help. More than a few are history junkies who contributed their own valuable thoughts to this book.

Equally supportive were the librarians of the Radcliffe Institute for Advanced Study at Harvard University, who overcame a record-setting snowstorm during my visit to provide unfailingly cheerful assistance with the papers of Mary Bancroft.

Lucas Delattre, the author of *A Spy at the Heart of the Third Reich*, helped me track down papers relating to Fritz Kolbe. Gudrun Fritsch generously provided access to several fascinating photos of Kolbe.

Paul Barron at the George C. Marshall Foundation in Lexington, Virginia, was a terrific help on OSS cables flowing from Washington to Bern. Doug Miller at the Pan Am Historical Foundation assisted with details of Dulles's travels. The author Gordon Thomas helped me better understand Kim Philby's work as a double agent. Maria Ferrari aided with Italian translation.

I would like to mention several books that were of considerable help. The first was Neal H. Petersen's *From Hitler's Doorstep: The Wartime Intelligence Reports of Allen Dulles, 1942–1945*. Published in 1996, the book is a collection of Dulles's cables from Bern to Washington, each transmission set up with a brief contextual summary, including the correspondence of code names and numbers with actual people.

I should also mention three excellent biographies of Dulles that influenced my thinking, especially in the early days of my research: *Allen Dulles: Master of Spies* by James Srodes, *Gentleman Spy: The Life of Allen Dulles* by Peter Grose, and, most recently, Stephen Kinzer's *The Brothers*.

Finally, I would like to give special thanks to my friend and agent, Michael V. Carlisle at InkWell Management, who first steered me toward the subject of this book and shepherded the project into the nurturing home of Alice and the ever-supportive Stuart Roberts at Simon & Schuster.

Bibliography

ARCHIVES AND ABBREVIATIONS

Arthur and Elizabeth Schlesinger Library on the History of Women in America, Radcliffe Institute for Advanced Study, Harvard University (Bancroft Papers)

Central Intelligence Agency archives

C. G. Jung Institute of Los Angeles

Columbia University—Oral History Research Office

Deutsches Bundesarchiv (German National Archives)

Franklin D. Roosevelt Presidential Library and Museum

Gedenkstätte Deutscher Widerstand (German Resistance Memorial Center)

George C. Marshall Foundation, James Srodes Collection (GCMF)

Harry S. Truman Library and Museum

Hoover Institution Archives, Stanford University

Library of Congress

National Archives at College Park, Maryland (NACP)

Politisches Archiv des Auswärtiges Amt (Diplomatic Archive of the German Ministry for Foreign Affairs)

Schweizerisches Bundesarchiv (Federal Archives of Switzerland)

Seeley G. Mudd Manuscript Library, Princeton University, personal papers of Allen Welsh Dulles (AWD Papers)

University of Wisconsin Digital Collections—Foreign Relations of the United States

JOURNALS AND PUBLICATIONS

Collier's
Der Spiegel
Foreign Affairs
Foreign Policy
Frankfurter Allgemeine Zeitung
Intelligence and National Security
International Journal of Intelligence and Counterintelligence
Journal of Central European Affairs
Journal of Contemporary History
The Journal of Military History
New York History
The New York Times
Prologue Magazine
Psychological Perspectives
The Saturday Evening Post
Studies in Intelligence
Sydney Morning Herald
The Washington Post

BOOKS, ARTICLES, AND GOVERNMENT REPORTS

Agarossi, Elena. *A Nation Collapses: The Italian Surrender of September 1943*. Translated by Harvey Fergusson II. Cambridge: Cambridge University Press, 2000.

Agarossi, Elena, and Victor Zaslavsky. *Stalin and Togliatti: Italy and the Origins of the Cold War*. Stanford, CA: Stanford University Press, 2011.

Agosti, Aldo. *Palmiro Togliatti: A Biography*. London: I. B. Tauris, 2008.

Allen, Roy. *The Pan Am Clipper—The History of Pan American's Flying-Boats, 1931 to 1946*. New York: Barnes & Noble, 2000.

Ambrose, Stephen E. *Ike's Spies: Eisenhower and the Espionage Establishment*. Reprint edition. New York: Anchor, 2012.

Armstrong, Anne. *Unconditional Surrender: The Impact of the Casablanca Policy upon World War II*. New Brunswick, NJ: Rutgers University Press, 1963.

Backer, John H. *Priming the German Economy: American Occupational Policies, 1945–1948*. Durham, NC: Duke University Press, 1971.

Baedeker, Karl. *Switzerland, Together with Chamonix and the Italian Lakes*. Leipzig: Karl Baedeker, 1938.

Bair, Deirdre. *Jung*. Boston: Little, Brown, 2004.

Balfour, Michael, and Julian Frisby. *Helmuth von Moltke: A Leader against Hitler*. London: Macmillan London, 1972.

Bancroft, Mary. *Autobiography of a Spy*. New York: William Morrow, 1983.

Beevor, Antony. *Stalingrad*. New York: Penguin Books, 1998.

Bell, D. S., and Byron Criddle. *The French Communist Party in the Fifth Republic*. Oxford: Oxford University Press, 1994.

Beschloss, Michael R. *The Conquerors: Roosevelt, Truman, and the Destruction of Hitler's Germany, 1941–1945*. New York: Simon & Schuster, 2002.

Blum, John Morton. *Roosevelt and Morgenthau*. Boston: Houghton Mifflin, 1970.

———. *Years of War, 1941–1945*. Boston: Houghton Mifflin, 1967.

Boehm, Eric H. *We Survived: Fourteen Histories of the Hidden and Hunted in Nazi Germany*. Revised and updated edition. New York: Basic Books, 2009.

Bower, Thomas M. *The Pledge Betrayed: America and Britain and the Denazification of Postwar Germany*. Garden City, NY: Doubleday, 1982.

Bradley, Omar. *A Soldier's Story*. New York: Holt, 1951.

Bradsher, Greg. "A Time to Act: The Beginning of the Fritz Kolbe Story, 1900–1943." *Prologue Magazine*, Spring 2002.

Breuer, William B. *Daring Missions of World War II*. New York: Wiley, 2001.

Brown, Anthony Cave. *The Secret War Report of the OSS*. New York: Berkeley, 1976.

———. *Wild Bill Donovan: The Last Hero*. New York: Times Books, 1982.

Bruce, David K. E. *OSS against the Reich: The World War II Diaries of Colonel David K. E. Bruce*. Edited by Nelson D. Lankford. Kent, Ohio: Kent State University Press, 1991.

Butow, Robert J. C. *Japan's Decision to Surrender*. Stanford, CA: Stanford University Press, 1954.

Casey, William. *The Secret War against Hitler*. Washington, DC: Regnery, 1988.

Churchill, Winston. *The Hinge of Fate*. Boston: Houghton Mifflin, 1950.

Clay, Lucius Du Bignon. *Decision in Germany*. Westport, CT: Greenwood, 1950.

———. *The Papers of General Lucius D. Clay: Germany, 1945–1949*. Volume 1. Bloomington: Indiana University Press, 1974.

Colvin, Ian. *Master Spy: The Incredible Story of Admiral Wilhelm Canaris, Who, While Hitler's Chief of Intelligence, Was a Secret Ally of the British*. New York: McGraw-Hill, 1952.

Cookridge, E. H. *Gehlen: Spy of the Century*. New York: Random House, 1972.

Critchfield, James H. *Partners at the Creation: The Men Behind Postwar Germany's Defense and Intelligence Establishments*. Annapolis, MD: US Naval Institute Press, 2003.

Dallek, Robert. *Franklin D. Roosevelt and American Foreign Policy, 1932–1945*. New York: Oxford University Press, 1979.

Delattre, Lucas. *A Spy at the Heart of the Third Reich: The Extraordinary Story of Fritz Kolbe, America's Most Important Spy in World War II*. New York: Atlantic Monthly Press, 2005.

Delzell, Charles F. *Mussolini's Enemies: The Italian Anti-Fascist Resistance*. Princeton, NJ: Princeton University Press, 1961.

Dietrich, John. *The Morgenthau Plan: Soviet Influence on American Postwar Policy*. New York: Algora Publishing, 2003.

Dollmann, Eugen. *Call Me Coward*. London: William Kimber, 1956.

Dorrill, Stephen. *MI6: Inside the Covert World of Her Majesty's Secret Intelligence Service*. New York: Free Press, 2002.

Dorwart, Jeffrey. "The Roosevelt-Astor Espionage Ring." *New York History* 62, no. 3 (July 1981): 307–22.

Dulles, Allen. *Germany's Underground: The Anti-Nazi Resistance*. New York: Da Capo Press, 2000.

———. *The Secret Surrender*. New York: Harper & Row, 1966.

Dulles, Allen, ed. *Great True Spy Stories*. New York: Ballantine Books, 1982.

Dulles, Allen, and Hamilton Fish Armstrong. *Can We Be Neutral?* New York: Harper & Brothers, 1936.

Dulles, Eleanor Lansing. *Eleanor Lansing Dulles, Chances of a Lifetime: A Memoir*. Englewood Cliffs, NJ: Prentice-Hall, 1980.

Eisenberg, Carolyn Woods. *Drawing the Line: The American Decision to Divide Germany, 1944–1949*. Cambridge, UK: Cambridge University Press, 1998.

Eisenhower, Dwight D. *Crusade in Europe*. Garden City, NY: Doubleday, 1948.

Feis, Herbert. *Churchill-Roosevelt-Stalin: The War They Waged and the Peace They Sought*. 2nd edition. Princeton, NJ: Princeton University Press, 1966.

Fest, Joachim. *Plotting Hitler's Death: The Story of German Resistance*. Translated by Bruce Little. New York: Metropolitan Books, 1996.

Fisher, Ernest F., Jr. *Cassino to the Alps*. Washington, DC: Center of Military History, 1977.

FitzGibbon, Constantine. *Denazification*. London: Joseph, 1969.

FitzGibbon, Constantine, Rudolf Hoess, Joachim Neugroschel, Rudolph Hoess, and Primo Levi. *Commandant of Auschwitz: The Autobiography of Rudolf Hoess*. London: Phoenix, 2000.

Friedrich, Carl J. *American Experiences in Military Government in World War II*. New York: Rinehart, 1948.

Galante, Pierre. *Operation Valkyrie: The German Generals' Plot against Hitler*. New York: Cooper Square Press, 2002.

Garland, Albert N., and Howard McGaw Smyth. *Sicily and the Surrender of Italy*. Washington, DC: Office of the Chief of Military History, Department of the Army, 1965.

Gellately, Robert. *Stalin's Curse: Battling for Communism in War and Cold War*. New York: Vintage, 2013.

Gimbel, John. *The American Occupation of Germany: Politics and the Military, 1945–1949*. Stanford, CA: Stanford University Press, 1968.

Ginsborg, Paul. *A History of Contemporary Italy: Society and Politics, 1943–1988*. New York: Palgrave Macmillan, 2003.

Gisevius, Hans Bernd. *To The Bitter End*. New York: Da Capo Press, 1998.

Goodwin, Doris Kearns. *No Ordinary Time: Franklin and Eleanor Roosevelt: The Home Front in World War II*. New York: Simon & Schuster, 1995.

Groscurth, Helmuth, Helmut Krausnick, and Harold C. Deutsch. *Tagebücher eines Abwehroffiziers 1938–1940; Mit weiteren Dokumenten zur Militäropposition gegen Hitler*. Stuttgart: Deutsches Verlags-Anstalt, 1970.

Grose, Peter. *Gentleman Spy: The Life of Allen Dulles*. Boston: Houghton Mifflin, 1994.

Halbrook, Stephen P. *The Swiss & the Nazis: How the Alpine Republic Survived in the Shadow of the Third Reich*. Havertown, PA: Casemate, 2010.

Harriman, William Averell. *Special Envoy to Churchill and Stalin, 1941–1946*. New York: Random House, 1975.

Hassell, Agostino von, Sigrid MacRae, and Simone Ameskamp. *Alliance of Enemies: The Untold Story of the Secret American and German Collaboration to End World War II*. New York: Thomas Dunne Books, 2006.

Hassell, Ulrich von. *Ulrich von Hassell Diaries, 1938–1944: The Story of the Forces against Hitler inside Germany*. Garden City, NY: Doubleday, 1947.

Hayden, Sterling. *Wanderer*. New York: Knopf, 1963.

Heideking, Jürgen, and Christoph Mauch, eds. *American Intelligence and the German Resistance to Hitler: A Documentary History*. With the assistance of Marc Frey. Boulder, CO: Westview Press, 1996.

Helms, Richard. *A Look over My Shoulder: A Life in the Central Intelligence Agency*. New York: Random House, 2003.

Herring, George C. *Aid to Russia, 1941–1946: Strategy, Diplomacy, the Origins of the Cold War*. New York: Columbia University Press, 1973.

Hersh, Burton. *The Old Boys: The American Elite and the Origins of the CIA*. New York: Scribner's, 1992.

Hill, Russell. *Struggle for Germany*. London: Gollancz, 1947.

Hoegner, Wilhelm. *Der Schwierige Aussenseiter; Erinnerungen eines Abgeordneten, Emigranten und Ministerpräsidenten*. Munich: Isar Verlag, 1959.

Höttl, Wilhelm. *The Secret Front: Nazi Political Espionage, 1938–1945*. New York: Enigma Books, 2003.

Hoffmann, Peter. *The History of the German Resistance, 1933–1945*. Translated by Richard Barry. 3rd edition. Montreal: McGill-Queen's University Press, 1996.

Hoffmann, Peter, ed. *Behind Valkyrie: German Resistance to Hitler: Documents*. Montreal: McGill-Queen's University Press, 2011.

Hooft, W. A. Visser't. *Memoirs*. 2nd edition. Geneva: World Council of Churches, 1987.

Hopf, Ted. *Reconstructing the Cold War: The Early Years, 1945–1958*. Reprint edition. New York: Oxford University Press, 2014.

Hull, Cordell. *The Memoirs of Cordell Hull*. Volume 2, part 1. Whitefish, MT: Kessinger Publishing, 2010.

Isaacson, Walter, and Evan Thomas. *The Wise Men: Six Friends and the World They Made: Acheson, Bohlen, Harriman, Kennan, Lovett, McCloy*. New York: Simon & Schuster, 1986.

Jacobsson, Per. *The Per Jacobsson Mediation*. Basel Centre for Economic and Financial Research, series C, no. 4, 1967.

Kauffman, Sanford B. *Pan Am Pioneer: A Manager's Memoir*. Edited by George Hopkins. Lubbock: Texas Tech University Press, 1996.

Kecskemeti, Paul. *Strategic Surrender*. 2nd edition. New York: Atheneum, 1964.

Kennan, George F. *Memoirs, 1925–1950*. New York: Pantheon, 1983.

Kershaw, Ian. *Hitler, 1936–1945: Nemesis*. New York: W. W. Norton, 2001.

Kesselring, Albert. *The Memoirs of Field-Marshal Kesselring*. 2nd edition. London: William Kimber, 1954.

Kinzer, Stephen. *The Brothers: John Foster Dulles, Allen Dulles, and Their Secret World War*. Reprint edition. New York: St. Martin's Griffin, 2014.

Kleist, Peter. *Zwischen Hitler und Stalin 1939–1945 Aufzeichnungen*. Bonn: Athenaum, 1950.

Klemperer, Klemens von. *German Resistance against Hitler: The Search for Allies Abroad, 1938–1945.* Oxford, UK: Clarendon Press, 1992.

Knightley, Phillip. *The Master Spy: The Story of Kim Philby.* New York: Knopf, 1989.

Koch, H. W. "The Specter of a Spate Peace in the East: The Russo German Peace Feelers, 1942 to 1944." *Journal of Contemporary History* 10, no. 3 (1975): 531–49.

Kramarz, Joachim. *Stauffenberg.* New York: MacMillan, 1967.

Laqueur, Walter, and Richard Breitman. *Breaking the Silence.* New York: Simon & Schuster, 1986.

Larson, Erik. *In the Garden of Beasts: Love, Terror, and an American Family in Hitler's Berlin.* New York: Crown, 2011.

Lasby, Clarence G. *Project Paperclip: German Scientists and the Cold War.* New York: Atheneum, 1971.

Leahy, William D., and Harry S. Truman. *I Was There: The Personal Story of the Chief of Staff to Presidents Roosevelt and Truman, Based on His Notes and Diaries Made at the Time.* New York: Whittlesey House, 1950.

Leffler, Melvyn. *A Preponderance of Power: National Security, the Truman Administration, and the Cold War.* Stanford, CA: Stanford University Press, 1993.

Lindbergh, Charles A. *The Wartime Journals of Charles A. Lindbergh.* New York: Harcourt Brace Jovanovich, Inc., 1970.

Lovell, Stanley. *Of Spies & Stratagems.* Englewood Cliffs, NJ: Prentice-Hall, 1963.

von der Lühe, Irmgard. *Elisabeth von Thadden: Ein Schicksal unserer Zeit.* Dusseldorf: Eugen Diederichs Verlag, 1966.

Macintyre, Ben, and John Le Carre. *A Spy among Friends: Kim Philby and the Great Betrayal.* New York: Crown, 2014.

Manvell, Roger, and Heinrich Fraenkel. *The Canaris Conspiracy: The Secret Resistance to Hitler in the German Army.* New York: McKay, 1969.

———. *Heinrich Himmler.* New York: Putnam, 1965.

———. *The July Plot.* London: Pan, 1966.

Manvell, Roger, Heinrich Fraenkel, and Roger Moorhouse. *The Men Who Tried to Kill Hitler.* New York: Skyhorse Publishing, 2008.

Mastny, Vojtech. *Russia's Road to the Cold War: Diplomacy, Warfare, and the Politics of Communism, 1941–1945.* New York: Columbia University Press, 1979.

McIntosh, Elizabeth P. *Undercover Girl.* New York: Macmillan Company, 1947.

McCullough, David. *Truman.* New York: Simon & Schuster, 1993.

Medoff, Rafael. *Blowing the Whistle on Genocide: Josiah E. DuBois, Jr. and the Struggle for a U.S. Response to the Holocaust.* West Lafayette, IN: Purdue University Press, 2008.

Merritt, Richard L. *Democracy Imposed: U.S. Occupation Policy and the German Public, 1945–1949*. New Haven, CT: Yale University Press, 1995.

Messer, Robert L. *The End of an Alliance: James F. Byrnes, Roosevelt, Truman, and the Origins of the Cold War*. Chapel Hill: University of North Carolina Press, 1982.

Meyer, Winfried. *Unternehmen Sieben: Eine Rettungsaktion fur vom Holocaust Bedrohte aus dem Amt Ausland/Abwehr im Oberkommando der Wehrmacht*. Frankfurt am Main: Hain, 1993.

Minott, Rodney G. *The Fortress That Never Was: The Myth of Hitler's Bavarian Stronghold*. New York: Holt, Rinehart and Winston, 1964.

Molden, Fritz. *Exploding Star: A Young Austrian against Hitler*. New York: Morrow, 1979.

Moorhouse, Roger. *Killing Hitler: The Plots, the Assassins, and the Dictator Who Cheated Death*. New York: Bantam Books, 2006.

Morgenthau, Henry. *Mostly Morgenthau: A Family History*. New York: Ticknor & Fields, 1991.

Moseley, Ray. *Mussolini's Shadow: The Double Life of Count Galeazzo Ciano*. New Haven, CT: Yale University Press, 2000.

Mosley, Leonard. *Dulles: A Biography of Eleanor, Allen, and John Foster Dulles and Their Family Network*. New York: Doubleday, 1978.

Moyzisch, Ludwig Carl. *Operation Cicero*. London: Wingate, 1950.

Murphy, Mark. "The Exploits of Agent 110." *Studies in Intelligence* 37, no 1 (1994): 63–70.

Murphy, Robert. *Diplomat among Warriors: The Unique World of a Foreign Service Expert*. Garden City, NY: Doubleday, 1964.

Naimark, Norman M. *Revolution and Counterrevolution in the Soviet Occupied Zone of Germany, 1945–46*. Washington, DC: National Council for Soviet and East European Research, 1991.

Nordmeyer, Helmut. *Hurra, wir leben noch: Frankfurt a. M. nach 1945: Fotografien, 1945–1948*. Gudensberg-Gleichen: Wartberg, 2000.

O'Connor, Raymond G. *Diplomacy for Victory: FDR and Unconditional Surrender*. New York: W. W. Norton, 1971.

Painter, David. *The Cold War: An International History*. London, New York: Routledge, 1999.

Paterson, Thomas G. *On Every Front: The Making and Unmaking of the Cold War*. Revised Edition. New York: W. W. Norton, 1993.

Persico, Joseph E. *Roosevelt's Secret War: FDR and World War II Espionage*. New York: Random House Trade Paperbacks, 2002.

Petersen, Neal H. *From Hitler's Doorstep: The Wartime Intelligence Reports of Allen Dulles, 1942–1945*. University Park: Penn State University Press, 2008.

Petrov, Professor Vladimir. *Money and Conquest: Allied Occupation Currencies in World War II*. Baltimore: Johns Hopkins University Press, 1967.

Philby, Kim. *My Silent War: The Soviet Master Spy's Own Story*. New York: Grove, 1968.

Powers, Thomas. *The Man Who Kept the Secrets: Richard Helms & the CIA*. New York: Knopf, 1979.

Project, United States War Dept Strategic Services Unit History. *War Report of the OSS*. New York: Walker & Co, 1976.

Rauch, Basil. *Roosevelt: From Munich to Pearl Harbor; A Study in the Creation of a Foreign Policy*. New York: Creative Age Press, 1950.

Read, Anthony, and David Fisher. *Operation Lucy: The Most Secret Spy Ring of the Second World War*. New York: Coward-McCann, 1981.

Rees, David. *Harry Dexter White: A Study in Paradox*. New York: Coward, Mc-Cann & Geoghegan, 1973.

van Roon, Ger. *German Resistance to Hitler: Count von Moltke and the Kreisau Circle*. Translated by Peter Ludlow. New York: Van Nostrand Reinhold, 1971.

Roosevelt, Elliott. *As He Saw It*. Reprint edition. Westport, CT: Greenwood Press, 1974.

Sandford, Gregory W. *From Hitler to Ulbricht: The Communist Reconstruction of East Germany, 1945–1946*. Princeton, NJ: Princeton University Press, 1983.

Sassoon, Donald. *The Strategy of the Italian Communist Party*. New York: Palgrave Macmillan, 1981.

Schellenberg, Walter, and Alan Bullock. *The Labyrinth: Memoirs of Walter Schellenberg, Hitler's Chief of Counterintelligence*. Translated by Louis Hagen. Boulder, CO: Da Capo Press, 2000.

Scheurig, Bodo. *"Free Germany": The National Committee and the League of German Officers*. Translated by Herbert Arnold. Middletown, CT: Wesleyan University Press, 1969.

Schlabrendorff, Fabian von. *The Secret War against Hitler*. Translated by Hilda Simon. New York: Pitman, 1965.

Schoenhals, Kai P. *The Free Germany Movement: A Case of Patriotism or Treason?* New York: Greenwood Press, 1989.

Scholl, Inge, and Dorothee Sölle. *The White Rose: Munich, 1942–1943*. Middletown, CT: Wesleyan University Press, 1983.

Senarclens, Pierre de. *From Yalta to the Iron Curtain: The Great Powers and the Origins of the Cold War*. Oxford: Berg, 1995.

Shirer, William L., and Ron Rosenbaum. *The Rise and Fall of the Third Reich: A History of Nazi Germany*. Reissue edition. New York: Simon & Schuster, 2011.

Simpson, Christopher. *By Christopher Simpson Blowback: America's Recruitment of Nazis and Its Effects on the Cold War*. London: Weidenfeld & Nicolson, 1988.

Smith, Bradley F., and Elena Agarossi. *Operation Sunrise: The Secret Surrender*. New York: Basic Books, 1979.

Smith, Richard. *OSS: The Secret History of America's First Central Intelligence Agency*. Berkeley: University of California Press, 1972.

Smith, Walter Bedell. *Eisenhower's Six Great Decisions: Europe, 1944–1945*. New York: Longmans, Green, 1956.

Smyth, Howard McGaw. *Secrets of the Fascist Era: How Uncle Sam Obtained Some of the Top-Level Documents of Mussolini's Period*. Carbondale: Southern Illinois University Press, 1975.

Srodes, James. *Allen Dulles: Master of Spies*. Washington, DC: Regnery Publishing, 1999.

Stein, Harold, ed. *American Civil-Military Decisions: A Book of Case Studies*. Tuscaloosa: University of Alabama Press, 1963.

Stern, Fritz, and Elisabeth Sifton. *No Ordinary Men: Dietrich Bonhoeffer and Hans von Dohnanyi, Resisters Against Hitler in Church and State*. New York: New York Review Books, 2013.

Stimson, Henry L., and McGeorge Bundy. *On Active Service in Peace and War*. New York: Harper and Brothers, 1948.

Strong, Kenneth. *Men of Intelligence: A Study of the Roles and Decisions of Chiefs of Intelligence from World War I to the Present Day*. London: Cassell & Company, 1970.

Taylor, Frederick. *Exorcising Hitler: The Occupation and Denazification of Germany*. New York: Bloomsbury Press, 2013.

Thomas, Gordon. *Secret Wars: One Hundred Years of British Intelligence Inside MI5 and MI6*. New York: St. Martin's Griffin, 2010.

Toland, John. *The Last 100 Days: The Tumultuous and Controversial Story of the Final Days of World War II in Europe*. New York: Modern Library, 2003.

Ulam, Adam B. *Stalin: The Man and His Era*. Boston: Beacon Press, 1987.

Volkman, Ernest. *Spies: The Secret Agents Who Changed the Course of History*. New York: Wiley, 1994.

Waibel, Max. *1945—Kapitulation in Norditalien—Operation Sunrise: Originalbericht des Vermittlers Max Waibel*. Basel: Novalis Schaffhausen, 2002.

Wala, Michael. *The Council on Foreign Relations and American Foreign Policy in the Early Cold War*. Providence, RI: Berghahn Books, 1994.

Waller, Douglas. *Wild Bill Donovan: The Spymaster Who Created the OSS and Modern American Espionage*. New York: Free Press, 2012.

Waller, John H. *The Unseen War in Europe: Espionage and Conspiracy in the Second World War*. New York: Random House, 1996.

Ward, Geoffrey C. *Before the Trumpet: Young Franklin Roosevelt*. New York: Konecky & Konecky, 1985.

Watt, Richard M. *The Kings Depart: The Tragedy of Germany: Versailles and the German Revolution*. New York: Dorset Press, 2001.

Weiner, Tim. *Legacy of Ashes: The History of the CIA*. New York: Anchor Books, 2008.

West, Nigel. *The Circus: MI5 Operations, 1945–1972*. New York: Select Magazines, 1984.

———. "Fritz Kolbe and Allen Dulles: Masterspies?" Review of *Betraying Hitler: The Story of Fritz Kolbe* by Lucas Delattre. *International Journal of Intelligence and Counterintelligence* 19, no. 4 (2006): 756–61.

———. *MI6: British Secret Intelligence Service Operations, 1909–1945*. New York: Random House, 1983.

Whalen, Robert Weldon. *Assassinating Hitler: Ethics and Resistance in Nazi Germany*. Selinsgrove, PA: Susquehanna University Press, 1993.

Whitcomb, Claire, and John Whitcomb. *Real Life at the White House: 200 Years of Daily Life at America's Most Famous Residence*. New York: Routledge, 2002.

Wilhelm, Maria de Blasio. *The Other Italy: The Italian Resistance in World War II*. New York: W. W. Norton, 1988.

Wires, Richard. *The Cicero Spy Affair: German Access to British Secrets in World War II*. Westport, CT: Praeger, 1999.

Wiskemann, Elizabeth. *The Europe I Saw*. New York: St. Martin's, 1968.

Woods, Randall B., and Howard Jones. *Dawning of the Cold War: The United States' Quest for Order*. Chicago: Ivan R. Dee, 1994.

Yergin, Daniel. *Shattered Peace*. New York: Penguin Books, 1990.

Zimmerman, Jonathan. *Small Wonder: The Little Red Schoolhouse in History and Memory*. New Haven, CT: Yale University Press, 2009.

Zink, Harold. *The United States in Germany, 1944–1955*. Princeton, NJ: Van Nostrand, 1957.

MULTIMEDIA WORKS

Jung Institute of Los Angeles. *Remembering Jung: A Conversation about C. G. Jung and His Work with Mary Bancroft*. DVD. 2011.

Notes

PREFACE

xiii *"Long live our Sacred Germany!"*: Roger Manvell and Heinrich Fraenkel, *The July Plot* (London: Pan, 1966), 151.

xiv *In the words of a British intelligence officer*: Kenneth Strong, *Men of Intelligence: A Study of the Roles and Decisions of Chiefs of Intelligence from World War I to the Present Day* (London: Cassell, 1970), 135.

xv *"But which of the victors?"*: Allen Welsh Dulles, *Germany's Underground: The Anti-Nazi Resistance* (New York: Da Capo Press, 2000), 166.

CHAPTER 1: PORTAL ON THE REICH

3 *"Our countries were at war"*: Dulles, *Germany's Underground*, 128.

3 *"the tall one"*: Hans Bernd Gisevius, *To the Bitter End* (New York: Da Capo Press, 1998), 500.

3 *"learned professor of Latin or Greek"*: Dulles, *Germany's Underground*, 129.

3 *Overthrowing their Fascist dictator without such assurances*: "Burns" to "Victor" (Dulles to Washington), telegram, January 13, 1943, in Neal H. Petersen, *From Hitler's Doorstep: The Wartime Intelligence Reports of Allen Dulles, 1942–1945* (University Park: Penn State University Press, 2008), 29–30. Dulles does not name Gisevius in this transmission, but he almost surely is referring to a conversation with him.

CHAPTER 2: "I HAVE NEVER BELIEVED IN TURNING BACK"

5   *At about three in the afternoon*: AWD Papers, series 1, Correspondence, box 41, folder 8.

5   *President Roosevelt wanted Donovan*: Douglas Waller, *Wild Bill Donovan: The Spymaster Who Created the OSS and Modern American Espionage* (New York: Free Press, 2012), 83.

6   *In one report, Dulles's team*: NACP, RG 226, entry 210 A1, box 62, folder WN 3005.

6   *Even in the late 1930s*: Tim Weiner, *Legacy of Ashes: The History of the CIA* (New York: Anchor Books, 2008), 6.

7   *"rather dumpy, corpulent figure"*: Stanley Lovell, *Of Spies & Stratagems* (Englewood Cliffs, NJ: Prentice-Hall, 1963), 210.

7   *"enthusiastic amateurs"*: Waller, *Wild Bill Donovan*, 93.

7   *For a few weeks*: Ibid., 73.

7   *From his laboratories emerged*: Lovell, *Of Spies & Stratagems*, 46.

8   *"Switzerland is now, as it was in the last war"*: NACP, RG 226, entry 216 A1, box 4, file 26834.

8   *What the post really demanded*: Ibid.

8   *"I guess the best thing for you to do"*: Mark Murphy, "The Exploits of Agent 110," *Studies in Intelligence* 37, no 1 (1994): 63–70.

8   *"I cannot tell you much about what I do"*: Ibid.

9   *"I never heard what happened to her"*: Leonard Mosley, *Dulles: A Biography of Eleanor, Allen, and John Foster Dulles and Their Family Network* (New York: Doubleday, 1978), 46.

9   *There he learned that an American naval vessel*: NACP, Constantinople post files, RG 84, vol. 16, March 9 and 12, 1921. Also see vol. 17, July 26, 1921.

9   *A few years later, practicing law in New York*: Jeffrey Dorwart, "The Roosevelt-Astor Espionage Ring," *New York History* 62, no. 3 (July 1981): 307–22. Also see James Srodes, *Allen Dulles: Master of Spies* (Washington, DC: Regnery Publishing), 152.

10 *Once, visiting Donovan in his room*: Waller, *Wild Bill Donovan*, 118.

10 *Once that happened, analysts in Washington figured*: Allen Dulles, *The Secret Surrender* (New York: Harper & Row, 1966), 12.

11 *Dulles now faced an anxious decision*: Peter Grose, *Gentleman Spy: The Life of Allen Dulles* (Boston: Houghton Mifflin, 1994), 150. There are several accounts of this story with slightly different details.

12 *"If I were picked up by the Nazis in Vichy France"*: AWD papers, box 74, folder 5, series 2.

13 *"It wouldn't have been easy"*: Dulles, *The Secret Surrender*, 14.

13 *From their late teens*: Stephen P. Halbrook, *The Swiss & the Nazis: How the Alpine Republic Survived in the Shadow of the Third Reich* (Havertown, PA: Casemate, 2010), 137. The number of Swiss called up for national defense would swell considerably as the war went on.

13 *Demolition experts placed charges*: Dulles, *The Secret Surrender*, 25.

14 *Medieval shopping arcades*: Karl Baedeker, *Switzerland, Together with Chamonix and the Italian Lakes* (Leipzig: Karl Baedeker, 1938), 174.

14 *Harrison, a product of Harvard*: "Leland Harrison, Ex-Diplomat, Dies," *New York Times*, June 8, 1951.

15 *"Where did you have dinner"*: Srodes, *Allen Dulles*, 227.

CHAPTER 3: THE "ETERNAL PLOTTER"

17 *"We were living in a den of murderers"*: Gisevius, *To the Bitter End*, 29.

17 *They would sometimes meet in a rowboat*: Ibid., 145.

18 *"whose main characteristic"*: Fabian von Schlabrendorff, *The Secret War against Hitler*, trans. Hilda Simon (New York: Pitman, 1965), 149.

19 *"Though they themselves"*: Gisevius, *To the Bitter End*, 179.

19 *He had once installed Halina Szymańska*: John H. Waller, *The Unseen War in Europe: Espionage and Conspiracy in the Second World War* (New York: Random House, 1996), 92.

20 *Gisevius helped by driving*: Gisevius, *To the Bitter End*, 320.

20 *Desperately, the conspirators passed word*: Ibid., 319.

20 *When the prime minister returned*: Roger Moorhouse, *Killing Hitler: The Plots, the Assassins, and the Dictator Who Cheated Death* (New York: Bantam Books, 2006), 101–4.

20 *"We spent the rest of the evening meditating"*: Agostino von Hassell, Sigrid MacRae, and Simone Ameskamp, *Alliance of Enemies: The Untold Story of the Secret American and German Collaboration to End World War II* (New York: Thomas Dunne Books, 2006), 49–50.

21 *Before employees arrived*: Moorhouse, *Killing Hitler*, 58.

21 *There he was found carrying*: Peter Hoffmann, *The History of the German Resistance, 1933–1945*, trans. Richard Barry, 3rd ed. (Montreal: McGill-Queen's University Press, 1996), 257–58.

22   *"Self-taught in planting bombs"*: Gisevius, *To the Bitter End*, 406.

22   *"An assassination without a simultaneous* Putsch*"*: Ibid., 404.

CHAPTER 4: "ROOSEVELT'S EMISSARY"

23   *The public rooms were particularly*: Walter Laqueur and Richard Breitman, *Breaking the Silence* (New York: Simon & Schuster, 1986), 120.

24   *It didn't hurt that the villa*: Greg Bradsher, "Allen Dulles and No. 23 Herrengasse, Bern, Switzerland, 1942–1945," *The Text Message Blog*, National Archives, November 9, 2012, http://blogs.archives.gov/TextMessage/2012/11/09/allen-dulles-and-no-23-herrengasse-bern-switzerland-1942-1945/.

24   *Writing to his wife, Clover*: Allen Dulles to Clover Dulles, November 28, 1942, AWD Papers, box 18, folder 10.

24   *Armed with a lengthy list*: NACP, RG 226, entry 214 A1, box 7, file 25826.

24   *And an Austrian lawyer, Kurt Grimm*: Srodes, *Allen Dulles*, 220, 227.

25   *"He was a handsome, polished"*: Letter from Edwin C. Lee, February 22, 1977, GVG Papers, Hoover Institution.

25   *Schulze-Gaevernitz was also a confirmed opponent*: AWD Papers, box 74, file 5, p. 8.

27   *A daughter of Hugh Bancroft*: Mary divorced her Swiss husband, Jean Rufenacht, not long after the war, and is universally referred to by her maiden name, Bancroft.

27   *"What I did not realize"*: Jung Institute of Los Angeles, *Remembering Jung: A Conversation about C. G. Jung and His Work with Mary Bancroft*, DVD, 2011.

27   *She was also smart*: Mary Bancroft, *Autobiography of a Spy* (New York: William Morrow, 1983), 106–7.

27   *"At that instant"*: AWD Papers, series 1, correspondence, box 7, folder 3.

28   *Several newspapers, including the* Washington Post*"*: "To Help the Boers. Why an Eight-Year-Old Boy Wrote a History," *Washington Post*, April 6, 1902.

29   *By 1935, he was describing the "sinister impression"*: Grose, *Gentleman Spy*, 121.

29   *"that the intelligent Germans had allowed"*: Ibid., 127.

29   *Dulles authored a book*: Allen Welsh Dulles and Hamilton Fish Armstrong, *Can We Be Neutral?* (New York: Harper & Brothers, 1936).

30   *"Well I thought my career there was fixed"*: "A *Redbook* Dialogue: A. W. Dulles and Ian Fleming," June 1964, AWD Papers, box 62, folder 8, series 2, writings.

30   *The article enshrined him*: Signature R 58/441, Bundesarchiv.

30   *"As a result, to my network flocked"*: Laqueur and Breitman, *Breaking the Silence*, 167.

CHAPTER 5: UNCONDITIONAL SURRENDER

32   *mansion-like Schloss*: Ger van Roon, *German Resistance to Hitler: Count von Moltke and the Kreisau Circle*, trans. Peter Ludlow (New York: Van Nostrand Reinhold, 1971), 16.

33   *an absolutely secure location*: Ibid., 115.

33   *But around eleven o'clock, after "a few sallies"*: Peter Hoffmann, ed., *Behind Valkyrie: German Resistance to Hitler: Documents* (Montreal: McGill-Queen's University Press, 2011), 66–68.

33   *"They would not renounce their oath to Hitler"*: Gisevius, *To the Bitter End*, 466.

34   *"thus making me the object of the curiosity"*: Ibid., 465.

34   *"Russians at the entrance"*: Antony Beevor, *Stalingrad* (New York: Penguin Books, 1998), 383.

34   *Graffiti appeared challenging Hitler*: Ian Kershaw, *Hitler, 1936–1945: Nemesis* (New York: W. W. Norton, 2001), 552.

35   *"The failure of the 'Stalingrad putsch,'"*: Dulles, *Germany's Underground*, 66.

35   *A coded American report*: Ibid., 130.

36   *including identifying Sicily*: Hanson W. Baldwin, "Offensive Strategy Laid Down at Casablanca," *New York Times*, January 31, 1943.

36   *"The elimination of German, Japanese and Italian"*: US Department of State, *Foreign Relations of the United States: The Conferences at Washington, 1941–1942, and Casablanca, 1943* (Washington, DC: US Government Printing Office, 1968), 727.

37   *Churchill wrote that it was "with some feeling of surprise"*: For a discussion of the debate over Roosevelt's announcement, see Winston Churchill, *The Hinge of Fate* (Boston: Houghton Mifflin, 1950), 686, and Anne Armstrong, *Unconditional Surrender: The Impact of the Casablanca Policy upon World War II* (New Bunswick, NJ: Rutgers University Press, 1963), 11–12.

37   *One opponent of the Nazis, Ewald von Kleist-Schmenzin*: Joachim Fest, *Plotting Hitler's Death: The Story of German Resistance*, trans. Bruce Little (New York: Metropolitan Books, 1996), 211.

CHAPTER 6: "BECAUSE YOU'RE YOU"

38 *"cheery, extroverted man"*: Bancroft, *Autobiography of a Spy*, 129–30.

39 *"attractive woman with wavy hair"*: Ibid., 130.

39 *She loved the outdoors*: Grose, *Gentleman Spy*, 73–74.

39 *"My husband doesn't converse with me"*: Ibid., 246–47.

39 *Over the years, their relationship*: Burton Hersh, *The Old Boys: The American Elite and the Origins of the CIA* (New York: Scribner's, 1992), 92.

39 *"There were at least a hundred women"*: Mosley, *Dulles*, 125.

40 *"He struck me at first"*: Bancroft, *Autobiography of a Spy*, 131.

40 *"at the height of my sexual prowess"*: Deirdre Bair, *Jung: A Biography* (Boston: Little, Brown, 2004), 487–88.

40 *"Where did you ever hear such a story?"*: Bancroft, *Autobiography of a Spy*, 133.

40 *As a teenager, she had idolized*: Ibid., 7.

41 *Though she admitted to herself*: Ibid., 60–64.

41 *"one hell of an attractive man"*: *Remembering Jung*.

41 *Opinionated and outgoing*: Mary Bancroft, "Jung and his Circle," *Psychological Perspectives* 6, no. 2, Jung Centenary Issue II (Fall 1975): 116.

43 *Feeling like a character in a play*: Bancroft, *Autobiography of a Spy*, 137.

CHAPTER 7: "A YANKEE DOODLE-DANDY"

45 *"grew in time into a virtual center"*: Gisevius, *To the Bitter End*, 481.

45 *the two even concluded they had met*: Laqueur and Breitman, *Breaking the Silence*, 170.

45 *Schulte had met many of the party's leading lights*: Ibid., 40, 41, 52.

45 *had until recently housed little more*: Ibid., 12–15.

46 *Among the others were Gisevius*: Lucas Delattre, *A Spy at the Heart of the Third Reich: The Extraordinary Story of Fritz Kolbe, America's Most Important Spy in World War II* (New York: Atlantic Monthly Press, 2005), 160.

46 *"There is some subtle influence in a wood fire"*: Dulles, *The Secret Surrender*, 95.

47 *"a Yankee doodle-dandy blow-in"*: Gordon Thomas, *Secret Wars: One Hundred Years of British Intelligence Inside MI5 and MI6* (New York: St. Martin's Griffin, 2010), 96.

47 *"was like a man with a big bell"*: Anthony Read and David Fisher, *Operation Lucy: The Most Secret Spy Ring of the Second World War* (New York: Coward-McCann, 1981), 112.

47 *No Brit was more disgusted*: Ernest Volkman, *Spies: The Secret Agents Who Changed the Course of History* (New York: Wiley, 1994), 189.

47 *"an utter shit"*: Moorhouse, *Killing Hitler*, 193.

47 *"fierce proprietary obsession"*: Kim Philby, *My Silent War: The Soviet Master Spy's Own Story* (New York: Grove, 1968), 103.

47 *"He resented the installation"*: Ibid.

47 *It didn't take long*: Auswärtiges Amt archives, R 901/61140.

CHAPTER 8: "UTTERLY WITHOUT SCRUPLES"

49 *Prince Max Egon zu Hohenlohe-Langenburg slid into the seat*: Mosley, *Dulles*, 144–45.

50 *"utterly without scruples"*: Von Hassell, MacRae, and Ameskamp, *Alliance of Enemies*, 151.

50 *Walter Schellenberg, head of the SS's foreign intelligence*: Walter Schellenberg and Alan Bullock, *The Labyrinth: Memoirs of Walter Schellenberg, Hitler's Chief of Counterintelligence*, trans. Louis Hagen (Boulder, CO: Da Capo Press, 2000), 310. For the debate about Dulles's reply, see Richard Smith, *OSS: The Secret History of America's First Central Intelligence Agency* (Berkeley: University of California Press, 1972), 214–15, and Klemens von Klemperer, *German Resistance against Hitler: The Search for Allies Abroad, 1938–1945* (Oxford, UK: Clarendon Press, 1992), 324. See also Srodes, *Allen Dulles*, 261.

51 *"If you make a serious error in your preparations"*: Schellenberg and Bullock, *The Labyrinth*, 315.

51 *The logic behind an argument to tilt East*: Dulles to Washington, telegram, April 7, 1943, in Petersen, *From Hitler's Doorstep*, 56.

51 *In his official communiqués to Washington*: How Dulles responded to Prince Max is the subject of some dispute. According to a highly dubious German account, Dulles spoke in ways the Germans would have loved to hear—repudiating Roosevelt's unconditional surrender demand, making anti-Semitic remarks, and saying that Germany should never again be forced to go through a peace like the one imposed on it after World War I. A number of historians consider this account to be the product of German wishful thinking.

Certainly, elements of it are inconsistent with Dulles's attitudes, especially at this point in the war. There may have also been an effort on the part of Germans at the meeting to make Dulles look like a promising negotiating partner. See Von Hassell, MacRae, and Ameskamp, *Alliance of Enemies*, 151.

51 *writing that he was likely driven*: Dulles to Washington, telegram, April 7, 1943, in Petersen, *From Hitler's Doorstep*, 56.

CHAPTER 9: "IMPOSING THEIR BRAND OF DOMINATION"

52 *Germany, highly industrialized with*: Vojtech Mastny, *Russia's Road to the Cold War: Diplomacy, Warfare, and the Politics of Communism, 1941–1945* (New York: Columbia University Press, 1979), 12.

52 *"The revolution will not stop at Russia"*: Richard M. Watt, *The Kings Depart: The Tragedy of Germany: Versailles and the German Revolution* (New York: Dorset Press, 2001), 173–74.

52 *"beguiled by the autocratic methods"*: Dulles, *Germany's Underground*, 165.

53 *In 1925, the Soviets provided*: Waller, *The Unseen War in Europe*, 29–30.

53 *"The experience of history shows"*: Adam B. Ulam, *Stalin: The Man and His Era* (Boston: Beacon Press, 1987), 584–85.

53 *Heinrich Müller, the head of the Gestapo*: Schellenberg and Bullock, *The Laby-rinth*, 318–20.

54 *Then in Turkey, when eavesdropping*: NACP, RG 84, vol. 441, Records of For-eign Service Posts, Diplomatic Posts, Turkey, Bolsheviks, July 21, 1921.

54 *Driving with a US Army colonel*: Grose, *Gentleman Spy*, 70–71.

55 *"imposing their brand of domination"*: Dulles to OSS, William Donovan, and David Bruce, telegram, December 6, 1942, in Petersen, *From Hitler's Door-step*, 25.

55 *On February 13, he reported to Washington*: Telegram, February 13, 1943, in Petersen, *From Hitler's Doorstep*, 40.

55 *"It is considered possible in responsible German circles"*: Telegram, February 23, 1943, in Petersen, *From Hitler's Doorstep*, 42.

CHAPTER 10: TWO BOTTLES OF COINTREAU

57 *They would have to seize*: Fest, *Plotting Hitler's Death*, 192.

57 *"most revolting spectacle"*: Von Schlabrendorff, *The Secret War against Hitler*, 234.

58 *"The failure of our attempt"*: Ibid., 236.

58 *The next day, Schlabrendorff flew*: Ibid., 237.

59 *As if he sensed danger*: Fest, *Plotting Hitler's Death*, 196.

59 *Operation Seven, a scheme to smuggle Jews*: Waller, *The Unseen War in Europe*, 307.

60 *Proceeding first to Wilhelm Canaris's wood-paneled*: Fest, *Plotting Hitler's Death*, 203.

60 *The group pushed passed Oster*: Gisevius, *To the Bitter End*, 477.

60 *"Should he ignore those pleas"*: Ibid.

61 *"lost its managing director"*: Fest, *Plotting Hitler's Death*, 203.

61 *"conspiratorial vacuum"*: Ibid.

CHAPTER 11: "WHO, ME? JEALOUS?"

62 *"It certainly was not my idea of romance"*: Bancroft Papers, box 17, file 220.

62 *"namely an opportunity to work"*: Ibid.

63 *And again on December 29, he wrote*: Bancroft Papers, box 26, file 219.

64 *Briner's husband had just returned*: Bancroft, *Autobiography of a Spy*, 145.

64 *and cautioned herself*: Ibid., 89.

64 *"nasty little man with shifty eyes"*: Ibid. Bancroft doesn't mention Dulles by name here, but the text seems to refer to him.

65 *On one occasion, the couple was interrupted*: Ibid., 152.

65 *"I can't marry you"*: Ibid., 138.

66 *"I continued managing"*: Ibid.

66 *"You are out of your cotton-picking mind"*: Remembering Jung.

66 *"The incident of the broken code"*: Dulles, *Germany's Underground*, 131.

67 Time *magazine reported that Stalin*: George C. Herring, *Aid to Russia, 1941–1946: Strategy, Diplomacy, the Origins of the Cold War* (New York: Columbia University Press, 1973), 22.

67 *Congress had financed with a $1 billion*: Ibid., 21.

67 *The Russians, Roosevelt now told an adviser*: Robert Gellately, *Stalin's Curse: Battling for Communism in War and Cold War* (New York: Vintage, 2013), 23.

68 *In 1938, he had told an American journalist*: Deirdre Bair, *Jung*, 483.

68 *Among other things, Jung predicted*: Dulles to OSS London, telegram, February 3, 1943, in Petersen, *From Hitler's Doorstep*, 36.

68 *"[a]lthough probably only the prospect of five thousand corpses"*: Bancroft, *Autobiography of a Spy*, 163.

69   *From that moment on, Bancroft later wrote*: Bair, *Jung*, 492.

69   *"There was scarcely a subject"*: Bancroft, *Autobiography of a Spy*, 164.

70   *"My God! I don't know if that's so good!"*: Ibid., 166.

CHAPTER 12: "THERE IS JUST THE GLIMMER OF A CHANCE THAT THIS MAN IS ON THE SQUARE"

71   *Gerald Mayer, the War Information officer*: Edward P. Morgan, "The Spy the Nazis Missed" in *Great True Spy Stories*, ed. Allen Dulles (New York: Ballantine Books, 1982), 15–16. There are slightly different details and dates for the first meeting between Kolbe and Dulles. See Delattre, *A Spy at the Heart of the Third Reich*, 95.

72   *"he'll undoubtedly turn up at your shop in due course"*: Anthony Quibble, "Alias George Wood," *Studies in Intelligence* 10, no. 1 (Winter 1966): 69–90.

72   *"There is just the glimmer"*: Dulles, *Great True Spy Stories*, 17.

73   *"Prussian-Slavic features," his blue-gray eyes*: Quibble, "Alias George Wood."

74   *"We have no way of knowing"*: Morgan, "The Spy the Nazis Missed," 21.

75   *His son, Peter, was still in Africa*: Quibble, "Alias George Wood."

75   *"Do not instill in him hatred"*: Delattre, *A Spy at the Heart of the Third Reich*, 102.

76   *This informant would be known as "George Wood"*: Quibble, "Alias George Wood."

76   *"Did those selfless fighters"*: German Foreign Ministry Archives, Nachlass Fritz Kolbe, Band 11, Dok 11, p. 1.

76   *"Every existing security safeguard"*: Cable from Bern to OSS Washington, August 21, 1943, CIA archives.

CHAPTER 13: "YOU COULD HAVE PEACE IN EIGHT DAYS"

77   *A wide veranda offered pleasing views*: Michael Balfour and Julian Frisby, *Helmuth von Moltke: A Leader against Hitler* (London: Macmillan London Ltd., 1972), 9.

77   *the holiday weekend offered*: Van Roon, *German Resistance to Hitler*, 147.

78   *"bewilderingly brilliant creature"*: Elizabeth Wiskemann, *The Europe I Saw* (New York: St. Martin's, 1968), 168.

78   *he was secretly followed*: Van Roon, *German Resistance to Hitler*, 184.

78   *"could never bring himself"*: Wiskemann, *The Europe I Saw*, 168–69.

78 *"What worried me"*: W. A. Visser't Hooft, *Memoirs*, 2nd ed. (Geneva: World Council of Churches, 1987), 159.

79 *"more reasonable"*: Van Roon, *German Resistance to Hitler*, 147.

79 *Kleist found his way*: Peter Kleist, *Zwischen Hitler und Stalin 1939–1945 Aufzeichnungen* (Bonn: Athenaum, 1950), 240.

79 *Clauss had no position*: H. W. Koch, "The Spectre of a Seperate Peace in the East: Russo-German 'Peace Feelers,' 1942–44," *Journal of Contemprary History* 10, no. 3 (July 1975): 531–49.

79 *"I guarantee you"*: Kleist, *Zwischen Hitler und Stalin*, 241.

79 *Neutral Turkey was home*: Waller, *Wild Bill Donovan*, 156.

80 *"a touch of my old and best-loved Chinese homeland"*: Van Roon, *German Resistance to Hitler*, 196.

80 *He would famously enter Istanbul*: Waller, *Wild Bill Donovan*, 156.

80 *a Czech engineer*: Ibid.

81 *The western front, Moltke proposed*: Balfour and Frisby, *Helmuth von Moltke*, 270.

81 *He was also in no way a spy*: David K. E. Bruce, *OSS against the Reich. The World War II Diaries of Colonel David K. E. Bruce*, ed. Nelson D. Lankford (Kent, OH: Kent State University Press, 1991), 30.

81 *the gathering was a reminder of better times*: Irmgard von der Lühe, *Elisabeth von Thadden: Ein Schicksal unserer Zeit* (Dusseldorf: Eugen Diederichs Verlag, 1966), 200.

CHAPTER 14: "I WOULDN'T TELL DULLES"

84 *Her imagination racing*: Bancroft, *Autobiography of a Spy*, 168.

84 *"Tiny" kept a fund in Switzerland*: Gisevius, *To the Bitter End*, x.

84 *On May 12, Gisevius listened*: Ibid., 478.

84 *Rather than appearing to hide*: Winfried Meyer, *Unternehmen Sieben: Eine Rettungsaktion fur vom Holocaust Bedrohte aus dem Amt Ausland/Abwehr im Oberkommando der Wehrmacht* (Frankfurt am Main: Hain, 1993), 385.

85 *Months would pass*: Gisevius, *To the Bitter End*, 478.

85 *"and discussed from every possible angle"*: Bancroft Papers, box 6, file 78.

85 *He had seldom met anyone with "such inner restlessness"*: Ibid.

85 *he wouldn't want anything on record*: Bancroft Papers, box 1, file 13.

86 *One summer afternoon she invited*: Bancroft, *Autobiography of a Spy*, 192–94.

86   *"Never. No sheet of paper exists"*: Ibid., 194.

87   *The speech, he told one source, was a "masterpiece"*: Bundesarchiv, Signature—R 58/441.

87   *the total mobilization of all the vital forces*: Armstrong, *Unconditional Surrender*, 214.

87   *"The unconditional surrender of the Axis Powers"*: "Burns" to "Victor," telegram, February 11, 1943, in Petersen, *From Hitler's Doorstep*, 40.

88   *This might entice younger officers, whom he called "the captains"*: Bancroft Papers, box 1, file 13.

88   *"What am I—and my friends—"*: Bancroft Papers, box 1, file 13.

89   *"How dare they upset me like this"*: Bancroft, *Autobiography of a Spy*, 199–200.

90   *"Thanks. That's just what I needed"*: Ibid., 152–61.

90   *Dulles, as with Bancroft, had seized*: NACP, RG 226, entry 211 A1, box 35, file 20037 and RG 226, entry 123, box 13, folder 147. Also see Grose, *Gentleman Spy*, 198.

90   *"an American friend of mine"*: Bancroft Papers, box 14, file 196.

90   *"Am I supposed to have a romance"*: Ibid., 141. Bancroft doesn't specifically refer to the countess, but the Italian is evidently the woman she was referring to.

91   *"still drunk on revolution"*: Bair, *Jung*, 494.

91   *Jung's analysis also judged*: Ibid., 495.

91   *"Sometimes I think any personal unhappiness"*: Bancroft Papers, box 1, file 13. Underlines are Bancroft's.

CHAPTER 15: THE COMMITTEE FOR A FREE GERMANY

93   *the hotel's La Terrasse restaurant*: "Die Geschichte des Bellevue Palace in Bern," Bellevue Place Bern, accessed May 11, 2016, https://bellevue-palace.ch/MediaFolder/_pdfbe/Geschichte_BP_d.pdf.

94   *Why, Kleist wanted to know*: Peter Kleist, *Zwischen Hitler und Stalin*, 244–45.

94   *Dulles wrote Washington on August 26 quoting several sources*: Bern to Washington, telegram, August 26, 1943, in Petersen, *From Hitler's Doorstep*, 110–11.

94   *"Free Germany Committee"*: Bern to Washington, telegram, August 29, 1943, in Petersen, *From Hitler's Doorstep*, 115.

94   *Outwardly, the group was nothing more*: Bodo Scheurig, *"Free Germany": The National Committee and the League of German Officers*, trans. Herbert Arnold (Middletown, CT: Wesleyan University Press, 1969), 32–77.

95 *Some in Dulles's circle of informants*: Bern to Washington, telegram, October 1, 1943, in Petersen, *From Hitler's Doorstep*, 137.

95 *Born in India and nicknamed "Kim"*: Volkman, *Spies*, 8–11.

96 *"It is calculated by Russia"*: Dulles to Donovan, telegram, February 10, 1943, in Petersen, *From Hitler's Doorstep*, 39.

96 *So convincing were Philby's assertions*: Thomas, *Secret Wars*, 96–97.

96 *"political warfare" was lagging behind "military warfare"*: Dulles to OSS headquarters, telegram, August 19, 1943, in Petersen, *From Hitler's Doorstep*, 105.

CHAPTER 16: "TWENTY PERCENT FOR LIBERATION AND EIGHTY PERCENT FOR RUSSIA"

98 *"might at least cause"*: Dulles to OSS headquarters, telegram, May 8, 1943, in Petersen, *From Hitler's Doorstep*, 62–63.

99 *"berating me for the way"*: Bancroft, *Autobiography of a Spy*, 187.

99 *The psychological damage*: Ibid.

99 *led by none other than Mussolini*: Paul Ginsborg, *A History of Contemporary Italy: Society and Politics, 1943–1988* (New York: Palgrave Macmillan, 2003), 16–17. At the end of 1943, there were about nine thousand partisans. The figure would climb to between twenty and thirty thousand by the spring of 1944.

100 *By some estimates*: Donald Sassoon, *The Strategy of the Italian Communist Party* (New York: Palgrave Macmillan, 1981), 29.

100 *Helping lead the units*: Charles F. Delzell, *Mussolini's Enemies: The Italian Anti-Fascist Resistance* (Princeton, NJ: Princeton University Press), 290.

100 *Italian Communists worked closely*: Elena Agarossi and Victor Zaslavsky, *Stalin and Togliatti: Italy and the Origins of the Cold War* (Stanford, CA: Stanford University Press, 2011), 97.

100 *As one OSS officer remarked*: Smith, *OSS*, 112.

100 *Moscow had instructed*: Agarossi and Zaslavsky, *Stalin and Togliatti*, 98.

100 *Soviet influence*: Smith and Agarossi, *Operation Sunrise*, 37.

101 *"And I am very wet"*: Mosley, *Dulles*, 141.

101 *Among them was Ferruccio Parri*: Dulles, *The Secret Surrender*, 21.

101 *Campione had been a mecca*: Mosley, *Dulles*, 142.

102 *One was a bomb detonator*: Lovell, *Of Spies & Stratagems*, 88.

102 *The town was "defended" by six police officers*: Dulles, *The Secret Surrender*, 19.

102 *one a former journalist named Donald Jones*: Ibid., 186–89.

102 *Loading rifles for twenty men*: AWD Papers, box 74, folder 5, pp. 9–11.

103 *The surprised police, as expected, surrendered*: Mosley, *Dulles*, 143.

103 *"Enough were sold"*: AWD Papers, box 74, folder 5, pp. 9–11.

CHAPTER 17: "A HIGH-TENSION POWER LINE"

104 *"a high-tension power line"*: Bancroft, *Autobiography of a Spy*, 190.

105 *"Why the hell didn't you go?"*: Ibid., 190–91.

105 *the two enjoyed a relatively frank relationship*: Joachim Fest, *Plotting Hitler's Death: The Story of German Resistance*, trans. Bruce Little (New York: Metropolitan Books, 1996), 229.

106 *Popitz believed the country*: Dulles, *Germany's Underground*, 155.

106 *Gingerly, Popitz explained*: Waller, *The Unseen War in Europe*, 296.

106 *"pure intentions but few sure political instincts"*: Fest, *Plotting Hitler's Death*, 229.

106 *Who exactly Langbehn met*: Dulles, *Germany's Underground*, 162. Dulles makes no mention of seeing or hearing about Langbehn in his account of the story.

107 *He denied any knowledge*: Waller, *The Unseen War in Europe*, 296.

107 *Wüst immediately understood*: Dossier: Johann Wüst, 1894. E4320B#1990/133 #519, Swiss National Archives, Bern.

107 *Gisevius devised a compelling plan*: Dossier: Johann Wüst, 1894. E4320B#1990/133#519, Swiss National Archives, Bern. Also, E/27/10005—10024, Swiss National Archives, Bern.

108 *The only way to do that, he reasoned*: Laqueur and Breitman, *Breaking the Silence*, 191.

108 *He added that Gisevius*: Ibid., 192.

108 *Normally extroverted, he had been in a glum mood*: Ibid., 179–80. See these pages for a complete transcript of the warning that alerted Schulte that he needed to escape to Switzerland.

109 *For the next several days, Schulte raced*: Ibid., 181.

110 *"My whole temperament"*: Gisevius, *To the Bitter End*, 479. Gisevius doesn't say exactly when Canaris visited him other than to mention that "a few weeks" later, Canaris was removed as head of the Abwehr. That occurred in February 1944.

CHAPTER 18: "THE QUALITIES OF A GENIUS"

111   *"the qualities of a genius"*: Roger Manvell, Heinrich Fraenkel, and Roger Moorhouse, *The Men Who Tried to Kill Hitler* (New York: Skyhorse Publishing, 2008), 62.

112   *"I picked this one"*: Robert Weldon Whalen, *Assassinating Hitler: Ethics and Resistance in Nazi Germany* (Selinsgrove, PA: Susquehanna University Press, 1993), 23.

112   *The man of accomplishment had to relearn*: Joachim Kramarz, *Stauffenberg* (New York: MacMillan, 1967), 120.

112   *Eliminating Hitler, Stauffenberg concluded*: Klemperer, *German Resistance against Hitler*, 350–51.

113   *"dubious political course"*: Manvell and Fraenkel, *The July Plot*, 77.

CHAPTER 19: "OBVIOUSLY A PLANT"

114   *The lights of a Triumph sports car*: Morgan, "The Spy the Nazis Missed," 26.

115   *"I'll rejoin you up there"*: Delattre, *A Spy at the Heart of the Third Reich*, 123.

115   *They had planned to blow up*: German Foreign Ministry Archives, Nachlass, Fritz Kolbe, Band 11, Dok 11, pp. 9–16.

116   *"The sight of the Berlin papers"*: Philby, *My Silent War*, 104.

116   *"Kolbe was obviously an instrument"*: Richard Helms, *A Look over My Shoulder: A Life in the Central Intelligence Agency* (New York: Random House, 2003), 33.

117   *"it will have been far and away"*: Delattre, *A Spy at the Heart of the Third Reich*, 130.

117   *He was well thought of*: Ibid., 116.

118   *"I now firmly believe"*: Dulles to Washington, telegram, December 29, 1943, in Petersen, *From Hitler's Doorstep*, 186.

119   *Barely managing to extinguish*: German Foreign Ministry Archives, Nachlass Fritz Kolbe, Band 11, Dok 11, p. 31.

119   *And one evening, he spent a couple of hours*: Ibid., 28.

119   *"But take care"*: Morgan, "The Spy the Nazis Missed," 23.

120   *"He was an action guy"*: Peter M. F. Sichel, author interview, November 19, 2013, New York.

CHAPTER 20: "NOW ALL IS LOST"

121 *A more skilled group of revolutionaries*: Balfour and Frisby, *Helmuth von Moltke*, 297.

122 *"We began to breathe more easily"*: Eric H. Boehm, *We Survived: Fourteen Histories of the Hidden and Hunted in Nazi Germany*, revised and updated edition (New York: Basic Books, 2009), 135.

122 *From January 10 to 12, 1944, Gestapo cars*: Balfour and Frisby, *Helmuth von Moltke*, 297–98.

123 *Vermehren had, after only a couple*: Ben Macintyre and John Le Carre, *A Spy among Friends: Kim Philby and the Great Betrayal* (New York: Crown, 2014), 79–81.

124 *When Vermehren did not report*: Von Hassell, MacRae, and Ameskamp, *Alliance of Enemies*, 178.

125 *his father had been*: Waller, *The Unseen War in Europe*, 310.

126 *Gisevius acknowledged that he had dined*: Mosley, *Dulles*, 140.

126 *"Two more charming men you never saw"*: Bancroft Papers, box 17, file 223.

126 *Gisevius slipped*: Bancroft, *Autobiography of a Spy*, 189.

CHAPTER 21: "I TREMBLED WITH EMOTION"

129 *Bazna's big break came when*: Richard Wires, *The Cicero Spy Affair: German Access to British Secrets in World War II* (Westport, CT: Praeger, 1999), 29–35.

129 *"I trembled with emotion"*: Delattre, *A Spy at the Heart of the Third Reich*, 133–34.

130 *"too good to be true"*: Ludwig Carl Moyzisch, *Operation Cicero* (London: Wingate, 1950), 99.

130 *When Donovan read Dulles's report*: Wires, *The Cicero Spy Affair*, 131.

130 *Ambassador Papen knew more*: Ibid., 130.

131 *"run riot all over Switzerland"*: Philby, *My Silent War*, 107.

131 *"They request that special congratulations"*: Srodes, *Allen Dulles*, 296.

132 *"Our rifling of the German Foreign Office safes"*: Dulles, *The Secret Surrender*, 25. Also see Nigel West, "Fritz Kolbe and Allen Dulles: Masterspies?" review of *Betraying Hitler: The Story of Fritz Kolbe* by Lucas Delattre, *International Journal of Intelligence and Counterintelligence* 19, no. 4 (2006): 760. West argues that part of the reason the British were cool toward Kolbe was that they

feared he could unwittingly jeopardize their famed code-breaking operation ULTRA.

132 *the Save Germany Group was quietly killed*: NACP, RG 226, microfilm, roll 52, frames 593–602.

132 *He described Russia as "mistress of the Continent"*: "Britain's Place in New Europe, Russia's Great Power, Striking Forecast by Smuts," *Sydney Morning Herald*, December 4, 1943.

133 *"It is possibly difficult for you"*: NACP, RG 226, entry 190c A1, box 2, file 23.

133 *"dominating force in determining"*: NACP, RG 226, entry 190c A1, box 2, file 24.

CHAPTER 22: "I DO NOT UNDERSTAND WHAT OUR POLICY IS"

134 *Berlin's Tiergarten, once a private hunting ground*: Erik Larson, *In the Garden of Beasts: Love, Terror, and an American Family in Hitler's Berlin* (New York: Crown, 2011), 49.

135 *In May, Gisevius and Waetjen met with Dulles to offer a bold gambit*: Dulles to Donovan and others, telegram, May 13, 1944, in Petersen, *From Hitler's Doorstep*, 288.

136 *"would abide by our agreements"*: Ibid., 289.

136 *"I do not understand"*: Dulles to OSS headquarters, telegram, January 17, 1944, in Petersen, *From Hitler's Doorstep*, 207.

136 *"the only real question today"*: Dulles to Washington, radiotelephone message, February 19, 1944, in Petersen, *From Hitler's Doorstep*, 225.

136 *"long after calmer judgment"*: Cordell Hull, *The Memoirs of Cordell Hull*, vol. 2, part 1 (Whitefish, MT: Kessinger, 2010), 1570.

137 *The ability to cooperate*: Armstrong, *Unconditional Surrender*, 87–89.

137 *At Italy's request*: Raymond G. O'Connor, *Diplomacy for Victory: FDR and Unconditional Surrender* (New York: W. W. Norton, 1971), 59.

137 *"Frankly I do not like the idea of conversation"*: Armstrong, *Unconditional Surrender*, 87.

137 *our only caution is to ensure*: OSS to Dulles, telegram, April 26, 1943, GCMF, Srodes Collection.

138 *"I do not predict"*: Dulles to Washington, radiotelephone message, July 13, 1944, in Petersen, *From Hitler's Doorstep*, 333.

138 *Meeting with a German informant*: Bundesarchiv, signature R 58/441.

CHAPTER 23: "THE SOVIET MAINTAINS A STEADY FLOW INTO THE REICH OF CONSTRUCTIVE IDEAS"

139 *On April 10, 1944, Kolbe stepped off*: Accounts of when Kolbe arrived in Bern in April differ slightly. See German Foreign Ministry Archives, PAAA, Nachlass Fritz Kolbe, Band 11, Dok 11, p. 38. Also see Delattre, *A Spy at the Heart of the Third Reich*, 161.

140 *Only after offering*: German Foreign Ministry Archives, PAAA, Nachlass Fritz Kolbe, Band 11, Dok 11, p. 38.

140 *"valuable Easter eggs"*: Von Hassell, MacRae, and Ameskamp, *Alliance of Enemies*, 199.

140 *"too old"*: Delattre, *A Spy at the Heart of the Third Reich*, 159.

140 *The Americans, he hoped, would provide*: German Foreign Ministry Archives, PAAA, Nachlass Fritz Kolbe, Band 11, Dok 11, p. 39a.

140 *"political status"*: Dulles, *Great True Spy Stories*, 29. Dulles is vague about when Kolbe first introduced his plan to raise a militia. Here he describes the conversation as taking place in late 1943 or early 1944. German Foreign Ministry records indicate the conversation took place during or after Kolbe's April visit.

141 *"The Soviet [Union] maintains"*: Dulles to OSS headquarters, telegram, April 21, 1944, in Petersen, *From Hitler's Doorstep*, 272.

141 *About the time of Kolbe's visit*: Delzell, *Mussolini's Enemies*, 336–37.

141 *"This unilateral action"*: Hull, *Memoirs of Cordell Hull*, 1556.

142 *"Finally, he agreed to stay on the job"*: Dulles, *Great True Spy Stories*, 29.

142 *Dr. Sauerbruch likewise traveled*: German Foreign Ministry Archives, PAAA, Nachlass Fritz Kolbe, Band 11, Dok 11, p. 33.

142 *Kolbe was so pleased*: Ibid., 34.

142 *The BBC, he proposed*: Quibble, "Alias George Wood."

143 *The message, as understood by Kolbe*: Ibid.

144 *the Germans had concentrated*: Telegram, May 13, 1944, in Petersen, *From Hitler's Doorstep*, 289.

144 *The attack was seen throughout Germany as made "on orders from Moscow"*: Petersen, *From Hitler's Doorstep*, 300–301.

CHAPTER 24: "AREN'T THEY READY TO ACT YET?"

145 *Gisevius chattered nervously*: Bancroft Papers, box 14, file 195.

146 *There had been an "indiscretion"*: Gisevius, *To the Bitter End*, 491.

146 *"They claim the assassination"*: Bancroft, *Autobiography of a Spy*, 208–9.

147 *"put a jinx"*: Ibid., 202.

147 *"It was necessary to return to Germany"*: Gisevius, *To the Bitter End*, 494.

147 *"For years I had hoped"*: Ibid., 492.

148 *"Undoubtedly this Stauffenberg"*: Ibid., 508.

149 *"hopeless 'Westerner'"*: Ibid., 509.

149 *"Perhaps our nerves were overstrained"*: Ibid., 511.

149 *"There is a possibility"*: Dulles to F. L. Mayer (Carib) and Whitney H. Shepardson (Jackpot), telegram, July 12, 1944, in Petersen, *From Hitler's Doorstep*, 330.

CHAPTER 25: THE WOLF'S LAIR

150 *Stauffenberg asked the pilot*: Manvell, Fraenkel, and Moorhouse, *The Men Who Tried to Kill Hitler*, 101.

151 *a cross between a monastery*: Ibid., 102.

151 *Nearby was an equally stout*: Pierre Galante, *Operation Valkyrie: The German Generals' Plot against Hitler* (New York: Cooper Square Press, 2002), 1–4.

152 *"A presidential announcement"*: Dulles to Washington, telegram, July 15, 1944, in Petersen, *From Hitler's Doorstep*, 335.

152 *Stauffenberg had tried twice before*: Manvell and Fraenkel, *The July Plot*, 93–95.

153 *Rather than employing*: Manvell, Fraenkel, and Moorhouse, *The Men Who Tried to Kill Hitler*, 101.

153 *He didn't place the other*: Fest, *Plotting Hitler's Death*, 257.

153 *Hitler was seated*: William L. Shirer and Ron Rosenbaum, *The Rise and Fall of the Third Reich: A History of Nazi Germany* (New York: Simon & Schuster, 2011), 1051.

154 *Bending over to set it up again*: Galante, *Operation Valkyrie*, 9.

154 *At 1:15, the Heinkel took off*: Ibid., 11.

155 *"I realized fully"*: Gisevius, *To the Bitter End*, 538.

155 *"something strange had happened"*: Manvell, Fraenkel, and Moorhouse, *The Men Who Tried to Kill Hitler*, 112.

156 *Not until Stauffenberg landed*: Shirer and Rosenbaum, *The Rise and Fall of the Third Reich*, 1057–58.

156 *General Fromm, however*: Ibid., 1059.

156 *Gisevius exchanged looks of "utter consternation"*: Gisevius, *To the Bitter End*, 542.

156 *The conspirators then seized Fromm*: Shirer and Rosenbaum, *The Rise and Fall of the Third Reich*, 1060.

156 *"A number of things"*: Gisevius, *To the Bitter End*, 548.

157 *He begged Stauffenberg to let him form an "officer's troop"*: Ibid., 552.

157 *"Down one street I saw"*: Ibid., 561.

157 *Remer dispatched patrols*: Shirer and Rosenbaum, *The Rise and Fall of the Third Reich*, 1063.

158 *"I am riding"*: Gisevius, *To the Bitter End*, 566.

159 *"There has been an attack"*: Wiskemann, *The Europe I Saw*, 189.

159 *That evening, Bancroft*: Bancroft, *Autobiography of a Spy*, 205.

CHAPTER 26: "COMMUNISM IS NOT WHAT GERMANY NEEDS"

161 *Tempting though the treat*: German Foreign Ministry Archives, PAAA, Nachlass Fritz Kolbe, Band 11, Dok 11, p. 43.

161 *"Sauerbruch thinks that we are lost"*: Delattre, *A Spy at the Heart of the Third Reich*, 181.

162 *The Charité Hospital, where many of his friends worked*: German Foreign Ministry Archives, PAAA, Nachlass Fritz Kolbe, Band 11, Dok 11, p. 44.

162 *One friend, Dr. Adolphe Jung*: Quibble, "Alias George Wood."

162 *"I was often very uneasy"*: Delattre, *A Spy at the Heart of the Third Reich*, 191.

163 *the anti-German activities of Hungarian prime minster Miklós Kállay*: German Foreign Ministry Archives, PAAA, Nachlass Fritz Kolbe, Band 11, Dok 11, p. 45a.

163 *The Soviets seemingly had little*: Koch, "The Spectre of a Separate Peace in the East," 539.

164 *The clerk closed Kolbe's bag*: Delattre, *A Spy at the Heart of the Third Reich*, 191–92.

CHAPTER 27: "I NEVER SAW THEM SO COMPLETELY DOWNTRODDEN"

165 *Crossing the barriers, Dulles was escorted*: Grose, *Gentleman Spy*, 204.

165 *"I never saw them so completely downtrodden"*: Wilhelm Hoegner, *Der Schwierige Aussenseiter; Erinnerungen eines Abgeordneten, Emigranten, und Ministerpräsidenten* (Munich: Isar Verlag, 1959), 172.

CHAPTER 28: REUNION WITH DONOVAN

167 *Donovan pulled him aside*: Waller, *Wild Bill Donovan*, 270.

168 *"a salient"*: Ibid., 268–69.

168 *"intensity and unshakable conviction"*: Casey, *The Secret War against Hitler*, 145.

169 *The OSS would at its peak*: Anthony Cave Brown, *The Secret War Report of the OSS* (New York: Berkeley, 1976), 18.

169 *was working about one hundred chief agents*: Ibid., 318.

169 *"merely the passive acceptance of intelligence"*: Donovan to Dulles, telegram, July 26, 1944, GCMF, Srodes Collection.

170 *"one of the real unsung heroines"*: Elizabeth P. McIntosh, *Undercover Girl* (New York: Macmillan, 1947), 248–51.

170 *They believed the punitive peace treaty*: Eleanor Lansing Dulles, *Eleanor Lansing Dulles, Chances of a Lifetime: A Memoir* (Englewood Cliffs, NJ: Prentice-Hall, 1980), 181–82.

170 *The end of the war, he wrote*: Dulles to Donovan, memo, October 7, 1944, NACP, RG 228, microfilm roll 81.

CHAPTER 29: LIGHT HAD GONE OUT

172 *"Zealous individuals who are ignorant"*: NACP, RG 226, entry 134, file 1214 3/3.

173 *The Sixth Army was hungry*: Brown, *The Secret War Report of the OSS*, 332.

173 *"There is vastly more"*: Grose, *Gentleman Spy*, 210.

173 *Was there anything the OSS could do*: Jürgen Heideking and Christoph Mauch, eds., *American Intelligence and the German Resistance to Hitler: A Documentary History*, with Marc Frey (Boulder, CO: Westview Press, 1996), 360–61.

173 *"Much of the sparkle and charm"*: Grose, *Gentleman Spy*, 209.

173 *"Dulles was most affable"*: Fritz Molden, *Exploding Star: A Young Austrian against Hitler* (New York: Morrow, 1979), 178.

174 *Over the next two days*: Ibid., 195.

174 *Visiting POW camps in Belgium and England*: Dulles, *The Secret Surrender*, 39–41.

175 *"Washington was now pretty well convinced"*: Ibid.

CHAPTER 30: "I FELT THAT THE WALLS OF THE CELLAR
WERE ABOUT TO COLLAPSE AROUND ME"

176   *He destroyed the ticket*: Gisevius, *To the Bitter End*, 567–68.

177   *"I felt that the walls of the cellar"*: Ibid., 576.

178   *"I implore you"*: Ibid., 585.

178   *"sheer torment"*: Gisevius, *To the Bitter End*, 585.

178   *Hassell left the meeting*: Von Hassell, *Ulrich von Hassell Diaries*, 359.

179   *Possibly tuning in to foreign radio broadcasts*: Von Hassell, MacRae, and Ameskamp, *Alliance of Enemies*, 249–50.

179   *Many of the people*: Bancroft, *Autobiography of a Spy*, 237.

180   *"Everyone has the moral right"*: Gisevius, *To the Bitter End*, 590.

180   *By the middle of January*: Ibid., 592.

180   *In November, the chief of the Berlin security police*: Bundesarchiv, NS 6/15.

181   *While the Nazis ramped up their investigation into the attack*: Von Hassell, MacRae, and Ameskamp, *Alliance of Enemies*, 233–34.

182   *Yet more time was lost*: Nigel West, *MI6: British Secret Intelligence Service Operations, 1909–1945* (New York: Random House, 1983), 224.

182   *Unable to use normal postal service*: Ibid., 115, 224.

183   *"I felt as if my pilgrimage"*: Gisevius, *To the Bitter End*, 598.

CHAPTER 31: "AN IMPLACABLE ENEMY OF BOLSHEVISM"

185   *Propaganda Minister Goebbels suggested*: Roger Manvell and Heinrich Fraenkel, *Heinrich Himmler* (New York: Putnam, 1965), 220.

186   *Between the summer of 1944 and early 1945*: Ibid., 198.

186   *"showed himself to be not only a man of high intelligence"*: Wilhelm Höttl, *The Secret Front: Nazi Political Espionage, 1938–1945* (New York: Enigma Books, 2003), 285.

187   *Höttl seemed to think*: Waller, *The Unseen War in Europe*, 368–97.

187   *Schellenberg suggested that the German army*: Dulles, telegram, April 5, 1945, in Petersen, *From Hitler's Doorstep*, 490.

187   *"I told Masson"*: Ibid.

CHAPTER 32: "A COMMON DESIRE TO KNOW
WHAT THE GERMANS WERE PLANNING"

189 *Major Max Waibel*: Dulles, *The Secret Surrender*, 67–68.

189 *"a strong bond both of friendship"*: Ibid., 68.

189 *the tendency of "north Italy to go communist"*: Memo, October 7, 1944, NACP, RG 228, microfilm roll 81.

190 *Convinced that a meeting wasn't worth his time*: Dulles, *The Secret Surrender*, 73.

191 *"dialectical pyrotechnics"*: Eugen Dollmann, *Call Me Coward* (London: William Kimber, 1956), 178.

191 *"Dollmann hardly filled the bill"*: Grose, *Gentleman Spy*, 231.

191 *Dulles had given him the means*: Dulles, *The Secret Surrender*, 76–77.

192 *Parri had been moved*: AWD Papers, series 1, correspondence, box 17, folder 18.

192 *"I listened with no enthusiasm"*: Dollmann, *Call Me Coward*, 180.

192 *"Sooner or later"*: Dulles, *The Secret Surrender*, 87.

CHAPTER 33: "GERO, ARE YOU STANDING OR SITTING?"

193 *"Gero, are you standing or sitting?"*: Dulles, *The Secret Surrender*, 89.

194 *"How did he do it?"*: Ibid., 90.

194 *"I shall never forget"*: Ibid., 94.

194 *"rather bleak building"*: Ibid., 90.

194 *Wolff's troops had committed*: Bradley F. Smith and Elena Agarossi, *Operation Sunrise: The Secret Surrender* (New York: Basic Books, 1979), 190. Also see "Gestorben, Karl Wolff, 84," *Der Spiegel*, September 23, 1984.

195 *There was a list of references*: Dulles, *The Secret Surrender*, 93.

195 *"After all, I reasoned"*: Ibid., 87–88.

195 *"in the event they should become"*: OSS Coordinator of Information to Dulles, telegram, February 27, 1945, CGMF, Srodes Collection.

196 *he and his group were forced to leave*: Max Waibel, *1945—Kapitulation in Norditalien—Operation Sunrise: Originalbericht des Vermittlers Max Waibel* (Basel: Novalis Schaffhausen, 2002), 54.

196 *"SS generals were not accustomed to waiting"*: Dulles, *The Secret Surrender*, 96.

196 *"as being a man of strong personality"*: AWD Papers, series 1, Correspondence, box 27, folder 3.

196   *"He always struck me as a leather-faced Puritan archangel"*: Ray Moseley, *Mussolini: The Last 600 Days of Il Duce* (Boulder, CO: First Taylor Trade Publishing, 2004), 180.

197   *Wolff explained that he had sabotaged*: Ibid.

197   *Exactly what Wolff sought in the meeting is still hard to fully determine*: Smith and Agarossi, *Operation Sunrise*, 70-71.

197   *Of one million German troops*: Waller, *The Unseen War in Europe*, 381.

197   *Wolff might be able to persuade Kesselring*: Dulles, *The Secret Surrender*, 97.

198   *His men, he told Schulze-Gaevernitz*: Ibid., 98.

198   *During the winter of 1944–45*: Ernest F. Fisher Jr., *Cassino to the Alps* (Washington, DC: Center of Military History, 1977), 412.

199   *German army manuals on the subject*: Rodney G. Minott, *The Fortress That Never Was: The Myth of Hitler's Bavarian Stronghold* (New York: Holt, Rinehart and Winston, 1964), 12.

199   *everything from sausages, flour, and sugar*: London to OSS Washington, transmission, March 27, 1945, CIA archives.

199   *Caves complete with air-conditioning*: Harry Vosser, "Hitler's Hideaway," *New York Times*, November 12, 1944.

199   *American generals feared*: Minott, *The Fortress That Never Was*, 19.

199   *"If the German was permitted to establish"*: Dwight D. Eisenhower, *Crusade in Europe* (Garden City, NY: Doubleday, 1948), 397.

200   *So in January, Goebbels created a special unit*: Minott, *The Fortress That Never Was*, 25.

200   *"The information we get here locally seems to tend"*: Dulles to Washington, telegram, January 22, 1945, in Petersen, *From Hitler's Doorstep*, 433.

200   *Whatever his motivation*: The ease with which the Nazis orchestrated the redoubt myth embarrassed American generals. As General Bradley put it after the war, the redoubt idea had grown "into so exaggerated a scheme that I am astonished we could have believed it so innocently as we did. But while it persisted, this legend of the redoubt was too ominous a threat to be ignored and in consequence it shaped our tactical thinking during the closing weeks of the war." Omar N. Bradley, *A Soldier's Story* (New York: Holt, 1951), 431.

CHAPTER 34: "I CAN SEE HOW MUCH YOU AND ALLEN CARE FOR EACH OTHER"

201 *Stepping onto the deck of the* Joam Bele: AWD Papers, box 18, folder 11.

202 *"My apartment is all ready"*: Ibid.

203 *The next day, she smoldered*: Grose, *Gentleman Spy*, 223.

203 *One morning not long after her arrival*: Hersh, *The Old Boys*, 148.

203 *"If I could only make out what Allen's goal is"*: Bancroft, *Autobiography of a Spy*, 244.

204 *"a bomb" waiting to explode*: Lorie Charlesworth and Michael Salter, "Ensuring the After-Life of the Ciano Diaries: Allen Dulles' Provision of Nuremberg Trial Evidence," *Intelligence and National Security* 21, no. 4 (August 2006): 574.

204 *"I was never able to discover"*: Ibid., 571.

204 *"I'll be glad if I've done something"*: Ray Moseley, *Mussolini's Shadow: The Double Life of Count Galeazzo Ciano* (New Haven, CT: Yale University Press, 2000), 248.

205 *Barnes possessed what Dulles considered*: Charlesworth and Salter, "Ensuring the After-Life of the Ciano Diaries," 583.

206 *Many of their photographs were so blurry*: There are several accounts for this. I used ibid., 585.

206 *"relentless in her disdain of pretense"*: Bancroft, *Autobiography of a Spy*, 242.

206 *"I think that's because you"*: Ibid., 244.

206 *Dulles knew there was nothing*: Ibid.

207 *"I want you to know I can see"*: Ibid.

CHAPTER 35: "I WAS PUZZLED ABOUT WHAT THE SOVIETS WOULD DO WITH THIS INFORMATION"

208 *American major general Lyman L. Lemnitzer*: Dulles, *The Secret Surrender*, 110–11.

210 *"It would have been a simple matter"*: Ibid., 109.

210 *True to form, Churchill remarked*: Robert Dallek, *Franklin D. Roosevelt and American Foreign Policy, 1932–1945* (New York: Oxford University Press, 1979), 508.

210 *When the United States suggested*: William D. Leahy and Harry S. Truman, *I Was There: The Personal Story of the Chief of Staff to Presidents Roosevelt and*

Truman, Based on His Notes and Diaries Made at the Time (New York: Whittlesey House, 1950), 329.

211 *"even more intolerable demands"*: Smith and Agarossi, *Operation Sunrise*, 87.

212 *The best the Americans could offer*: Leahy and Truman, *I Was There*, 331.

212 *"utterly unexpected and incomprehensible"*: Ibid.

212 *"The arrogant language of Molotov's letter"*: Ibid.

213 *"It has always amazed me"*: Dulles, *The Secret Surrender*, 113.

213 *Somewhere out on the lake was Clover*: Grose, *Gentleman Spy*, 237.

213 *Spotting the man walking down the road*: Ibid., 115.

214 *"I must say that I could not help wondering"*: Ibid., 117–18.

214 *He described Wolff as having "three chins and fat fingers"*: Smith and Agarossi, *Operation Sunrise*, 96–98.

CHAPTER 36: "I MAY BE CRAZY"

216 *"You must be crazy"*: Grose, *Gentleman Spy*, 232.

217 *Donovan had authorized Dulles to advance him $1,000*: Donovan to Dulles, telegram, January 24, 1945, GCMF, Srodes Collection.

217 *Mrs. Gisevius launched into*: Bancroft, *Autobiography of a Spy*, 238.

218 *"Well, then frankly I don't think"*: Ibid., 240.

219 *"I have seldom seen"*: Ibid., 261.

219 *Bancroft briefly spoke with one*: Ibid., 262.

220 *Bancroft's feeling of gloom would intensify*: Ibid., 263.

220 *In late April, she and Clover*: Bancroft Papers, box 14, file 198.

221 *a German soldier noticed*: Bancroft, *Autobiography of a Spy*, 249.

CHAPTER 37: "I CANNOT AVOID A FEELING OF BITTER RESENTMENT TOWARD YOUR INFORMERS"

222 *"because of objection on the part of Mr. Molotov"*: Leahy and Truman, *I Was There*, 333.

223 *Roosevelt "had failed to erase any of the fatigue from his face"*: Doris Kearns Goodwin, *No Ordinary Time: Franklin and Eleanor Roosevelt: The Home Front in World War II* (New York: Simon & Schuster, 1995), 598.

223 *"This circumstance is irritating to the Soviet command"*: Leahy and Truman, *I Was There*, 333.

223 *On April 3, Stalin asserted*: Ibid., 334.

223   *"It would be one of the great tragedies of history"*: Michael R. Beschloss, *The Conquerors: Roosevelt, Truman, and the Destruction of Hitler's Germany, 1941–1945* (New York: Simon & Schuster, 2002), 206.

224   *On April 4, General Deane in Moscow wrote*: Smith and Agarossi, *Operation Sunrise*, 122–23.

224   *Roosevelt's chief of staff, Admiral William Leahy*: Ibid., 124.

CHAPTER 38: "THIS IS THE MOST TERRIBLE NEWS I'VE EVER HAD"

226   *"I beg of you, where is 110?"*: Dulles, *The Secret Surrender*, 152.

227   *"The OSS is the most fantastic"*: Sterling Hayden, *Wanderer* (New York: Knopf, 1963), 329–30.

227   *he arranged on April 4 for Isadore Lubin*: Waller, *Wild Bill Donovan*, 303–13.

228   *"This is the most terrible news"*: Ibid., 319.

228   *Zimmer had promised Dulles that Wolff would soon return*: Smith and Agarossi, *Operation Sunrise*, 115.

228   *"Confronted with this determination"*: Albert Kesselring, *The Memoirs of Field-Marshal Kesselring*, 2nd ed. (London: William Kimber, 1954), 281–82.

229   *"wanted us to try everything"*: Dulles, *The Secret Surrender*, 146.

229   *and motored to the Hotel Adlon*: John Toland, *The Last 100 Days: The Tumultuous and Controversial Story of the Final Days of World War II in Europe* (New York: Modern Library, 2003), 478. There is some disagreement about the exact dates on which Wolff traveled to Berlin. I used those offered by Dulles in *The Secret Surrender*, 170.

231   *Shortly before 4:00 a.m.*: Kershaw, *Hitler*, 776.

231   *"Good! Please wait until the briefing is over"*: Toland, *The Last 100 Days*, 479.

231   *His mouth dripped*: Dulles, *The Secret Surrender*, 174.

231   *"Kaltenbrunner and Himmler have informed me"*: Toland, *The Last 100 Days*, 479. The following dialogue between Hitler and Wolff continues on page 480.

233   *"My Führer, isn't it clear which side"*: Dulles, *The Secret Surrender*, 177.

233   *"Fly back, and give my regards to Vietinghoff"*: Ibid., 178.

233   *"Before we come to an agreement with the Americans"*: Ibid.

CHAPTER 39: "IN VIEW OF COMPLICATIONS
WHICH HAVE ARISEN WITH RUSSIANS"

234 *Moscow, he wrote, wanted to "get [its] hands on Trieste":* Ibid., 162.

234 *The Soviets had placed a higher priority:* Petersen, *From Hitler's Doorstep,* 502.

235 *So complicated was the region:* Smith and Agarossi, *Operation Sunrise,* 172.

235 *That would allow either Soviet troops:* Dulles, *The Secret Surrender,* 147.

235 *"The actual status can be determined":* Smith and Agarossi, *Operation Sunrise,* 176.

235 *"especially in view of complications":* Dulles, *The Secret Surrender,* 162.

236 *"Very possibly our Joint Chiefs":* Ibid., 163.

236 *The three now wanted to see Dulles:* Ibid., 165.

236 *The Combined Joint Chiefs would never have:* Ibid. See also Toland, *The Last 100 Days,* 482.

238 *"I realized, of course":* Dulles, *The Secret Surrender,* 186.

CHAPTER 40: AN OVERLOADED MERCEDES-BENZ

239 *The final months of the war had been miserable:* German Foreign Ministry Archives, PAAA, Nachlass Fritz Kolbe, Band 11, Dok 11, p. 53.

240 *The four were so tightly crammed:* Delattre, *A Spy at the Heart of the Third Reich,* 202–3.

240 *they would have to be pulled:* Ibid., 203–5.

241 *On April 3, 1945, he arrived in Bern:* German Foreign Ministry Archives, PAAA, Nachlass Fritz Kolbe, Band 11, Dok 11, p. 59.

CHAPTER 41: "I WILL NEVER FORGET WHAT YOU HAVE DONE FOR ME"

243 *The Italian leading the shooting party:* Waibel, *1945—Kapitulation in Norditalien,* 131.

244 *"a Mexican tavern":* Dulles, *The Secret Surrender,* 191.

244 *"I will never forget":* Ibid., 192.

245 *There he set up a transmitter:* Ibid., 143–44, 199.

245 *Things were only marginally better:* Smith and Agarossi, *Operation Sunrise,* 147–50.

245 *With the help of Dulles, the two immediately departed:* Dulles, *The Secret Surrender,* 212–13.

246 *That same day, shortly after lunch*: Kershaw, *Hitler*, 828.

247 *Hitler lifted a Walther pistol*: There are several different accounts of the details of Hitler's suicide. See Kershaw, *Hitler*, 827, for the account I drew most heavily from.

247 *"Thus, around two in the morning"*: Dulles, *The Secret Surrender*, 235.

248 *"A cease-fire now will give"*: Ibid., 236.

248 *"With a tremendous sigh of relief"*: Ibid., 220.

CHAPTER 42: "COUNTLESS THOUSANDS OF PARENTS WOULD BLESS YOU"

249 *known somewhat romantically*: Jonathan Zimmerman, *Small Wonder: The Little Red Schoolhouse in History and Memory* (New Haven, CT: Yale University Press, 2009), 118.

249 *"Countless thousands of parents"*: Magruder to Dulles, telegram, May 3, 1945, GCMF, Srodes Collection.

249 *The race for Trieste had ended in a dead heat*: Smith and Agarossi, *Operation Sunrise*, 181–82.

250 *In the early hours of the morning of May 7*: Eisenhower, *Crusade in Europe*, 426. Also see Walter Bedell Smith, *Eisenhower's Six Great Decisions: Europe, 1944–1945* (New York: Longmans, Green, 1956), 206.

250 *"We'll clean up together"*: Grose, *Gentleman Spy*, 247.

251 *"His relationship to Foster"*: Bancroft, *Autobiography of a Spy*, 139.

251 *Shortly after Roosevelt's death*: Waller, *Wild Bill Donovan*, 335.

251 *A meeting on May 14*: Ibid., 322.

251 *Donovan delivered more disappointing news*: Smith, *OSS*, 234.

252 *the villa was known among the Americans*: Helms, *A Look over My Shoulder*, 56.

253 *"particularly vile Spanish brandy"*: Ibid.

253 *"I never wanted to hear the words* intelligence work *again"*: Bancroft, *Autobiography of a Spy*, 264.

253 *"Tiny" did travel to Germany for a time*: Swiss National Archives, Bern, report on Gisevius, E/27/10005—10024, 4.

253 *"I think in a sense I was lucky"*: Hot and Cold Wars of Allen Dulles, 1962, DVD, National Archives, 2010.

254 *"How the hell can you expect"*: Mosley, *Dulles*, 225.

254 *"There were so many, often conflicting, demands"*: Helms, *A Look over My Shoulder*, 61.

CHAPTER 43: THE CROWN JEWELS

255 *"middle-aged men Dulles hoped"*: Ibid., 55.

255 *At the same time, many had a hard time*: Von Hassell, MacRae, and Ames-kamp, *Alliance of Enemies*, 270–71.

256 *One of those aided*: Von Schlabrendorff, *The Secret War against Hitler*, 324, 336, 337.

256 *He had, for instance, agreed*: Delattre, *A Spy at the Heart of the Third Reich*, 209–11.

257 *"person of reference"*: Ibid., 211–16.

258 *Walking down a street*: Helmut Nordmeyer, *Hurra, wir leben noch: Frankfurt a. M. nach 1945: Fotografien, 1945–1948* (Gudensberg-Gleichen: Wartberg, 2000).

258 *In July, less than 10 percent*: John H. Backer, *Priming the German Economy: American Occupational Policies, 1945–1948* (Durham, NC: Duke University Press, 1971), 34.

258 *"moved like ghosts"*: Ibid., 33–34.

259 *"hunger was to be seen everywhere"*: John Dietrich, *The Morgenthau Plan: Soviet Influence on American Postwar Policy* (New York: Algora Publishing, 2003), 113.

259 *"It is all a very depressing sight"*: Walter Isaacson and Evan Thomas, *The Wise Men: Six Friends and the World They Made: Acheson, Bohlen, Harriman, Kennan, Lovett, McCloy* (New York: Simon & Schuster, 1986), 305.

259 *In the summer of 1945*: Dietrich, *The Morgenthau Plan*, 110.

259 *"We should not be disturbed at"*: Grose, *Gentleman Spy*, 260–61.

260 *The result apparently met Dulles's standards*: Hoegner, *Der schwierige Aussenseiter*, 165.

260 *"been more than nominal participants in its activities"*: Harold Zink, *The United States in Germany, 1944–1955* (Princeton, NJ: Van Nostrand, 1957), 156.

261 *By early July, a US Forces European Theater directive*: John Gimbel, *The American Occupation of Germany: Politics and the Military, 1945–1949* (Stanford, CA: Stanford University Press, 1968), 101.

261 *Derisively known among army officers*: Professor Vladimir Petrov, *Money and Conquest: Allied Occupation Currencies in World War II* (Baltimore: Johns Hopkins University Press, 1967), 228–29.

261 *By September 1945, they had rounded up 9,500 employees*: Richard D. Mc-Kenzie, oral history interview with Bernard Bernstein, 1975, Harry S. Truman Presidential Library and Museum.

261 *One celebrated target was Hermann Abs*: Thomas M. Bower, *The Pledge Betrayed: America and Britain and the Denazification of Postwar Germany* (Garden City, NY: Doubleday, 1982), 11–13.

261 *"The Americans wanted to get"*: Ibid., 12.

262 *By the end of the war, about eight million Germans*: Frederick Taylor, *Exorcising Hitler: The Occupation and Denazification of Germany* (New York: Bloomsbury Press, 2013), 227.

262 *"We have already found out that you can't run railroads"*: Allen Dulles, "That Was Then: Allen W. Dulles on the Occupation of Germany," *Foreign Affairs*, November–December 2003.

CHAPTER 44: "IT WAS THREE ALLIES AND ONE ENEMY"

264 *OSS men were quitting in droves*: Weiner, *Legacy of Ashes*, 13.

264 *Several of Dulles's men, attempting to arrest*: Mosley, *Dulles*, 228.

264 *Reports circulated that the Soviets had erected loudspeakers*: Clarence G. Lasby, *Project Paperclip: German Scientists and the Cold War* (New York: Atheneum, 1971), 70.

264 *"It was three Allies and one enemy"*: Srodes, *Allen Dulles*, 368–69.

265 *Operations as mundane as monitoring*: Weiner, *Legacy of Ashes*, 11.

265 *"It had been apparent for some weeks"*: Helms, *A Look over My Shoulder*, 63.

CHAPTER 45: "MOST OF MY TIME IS SPENT RELIVING THOSE EXCITING DAYS"

266 *"I must admit that these days I find it hard to concentrate"*: Grose, *Gentleman Spy*, 257.

267 *"entailing disastrous consequences"*: Ibid., 260.

267 *When Bancroft declined Dulles's offer*: Bancroft, *Autobiography of a Spy*, 264–70.

268 *"We have our Führer to thank for this!"*: Ibid., 265.

269 *"Eva had a fine literary style"*: Ibid., 270.

270 *"It was a fight for human rights"*: The Nuremberg Trial Proceedings, vol. 12, April 26, 1946, The Avalon Project, Lillian Goldman Law Library, Yale Law School, 277.

POSTSCRIPT

272 *"From Stettin in the Baltic"*: David McCullough, *Truman* (New York: Simon & Schuster, 1993), 489.

272 *Only through resolute action*: Ibid.

272 *The Soviet "policy of Communist world domination"*: Lucius Du Bignon Clay, *Decision in Germany* (Westport, CT: Greenwood, 1950), 123.

272 *The new party, the Socialist Unity Party*: Carolyn Woods Eisenberg, *Drawing the Line: The American Decision to Divide Germany, 1944–1949* (Cambridge, UK: Cambridge University Press, 1998), 212–16.

273 *"It was an early indication of Soviet effort"*: Clay, *Decision in Germany*, 134.

273 *Known as the "Long Telegram"*: George F. Kennan, *Memoirs, 1925–1950* (New York: Pantheon, 1983), 294, 547. Also see Randall B. Woods and Howard Jones, *Dawning of the Cold War: The United States' Quest for Order* (Chicago: Ivan R. Dee, 1994), 106.

273 *Evidence that appeared to support such an assessment*: Ibid., 94–95.

273 *"I'm tired of babysitting the Soviets"*: Robert L. Messer, *The End of an Alliance: James F. Byrnes, Roosevelt, Truman, and the Origins of the Cold War* (Chapel Hill: University of North Carolina Press, 1982), 158.

274 *A half-mile radius of destruction*: Allen Dulles, "Goodbye Berlin," *Collier's*, May 11, 1946, 80.

274 *"war hysteria"*: Michael Wala, *The Council on Foreign Relations and American Foreign Policy in the Early Cold War* (Providence, RI: Berghahn Books, 1994), 95.

274 *Dulles also began to develop new ideas*: Grose, *Gentleman Spy*, 265.

THE CHARACTERS

280 *"Wolff began to see the light in 1943"*: Dulles, *The Secret Surrender*, 254.

Illustration Credits

1. Department of Rare Books and Special Collections, Allen W. Dulles Papers, Public Policy Collection, Princeton University Library.
2. Schlesinger Library, Radcliffe Institute, Harvard University.
3. National Archives at College Park, Maryland.
4. Department of Rare Books and Special Collections, Allen W. Dulles Papers, Public Policy Collection, Princeton University Library.
5. Schlesinger Library, Radcliffe Institute, Harvard University.
6. Department of Rare Books and Special Collections, Allen W. Dulles Papers, Public Policy Collection, Princeton University Library.
7. Schlesinger Library, Radcliffe Institute, Harvard University.
8. Schlesinger Library, Radcliffe Institute, Harvard University.
9. German Federal Archives.
10. German Federal Archives.
11. German Federal Archives.
12. Martin and Güdrun Fritsch Collection, Berlin.
13. German Federal Archives.
14. German Federal Archives.
15. Department of Rare Books and Special Collections, Allen W. Dulles Papers, Public Policy Collection, Princeton University Library.
16. Schlesinger Library, Radcliffe Institute, Harvard University.
17. Department of Rare Books and Special Collections, Allen W. Dulles Papers, Public Policy Collection, Princeton University Library.
18. Schlesinger Library, Radcliffe Institute, Harvard University.

Index

About the Author

SCOTT MILLER is a former correspondent for *The Wall Street Journal*. His first book, *The President and the Assassin: McKinley, Terror, and Empire at the Dawn of the American Century*, was a *Newsweek* "must-read" summer selection. Mr. Miller holds a master's degree in international relations from the University of Cambridge and spent nearly two decades in Asia and Europe, reporting from more than twenty-five countries. He lives in Seattle with his wife and two daughters.